Racism and Discrimination in the Sporting World

Racism and Discrimination in the Sporting World

Edited by Eileen M. Angelini

Universitas Press
Montreal

Universitas Press
Montreal

www.universitaspress.com

First published in March 2019

Library and Archives Canada Cataloguing in Publication

Title: Racism and discrimination in the sporting world / edited by Eileen M. Angelini.
Names: Angelini, Eileen M., editor.
Identifiers: Canadiana 20190053488 | ISBN 9781988963068 (softcover)
Subjects: LCSH: Discrimination in sports. | LCSH: Racism in sports.
Classification: LCC GV706.32 .R33 2019 | DDC 796.089—dc23

TABLE OF CONTENTS

Eileen M. Angelini
Preface
vii

Alan E. Sexton
Idol Thoughts
xiii

Eileen M. Angelini
1946 Montreal: Home to Two of the World's Greatest
Sports Heroes
1

Richard Pioreck
From "No Joy in Mudville" to "I'm a Yankee Doodle Dandy":
Casey at the Bat and Irish Assimilation
15

Tatiana Prorokova
Black Men in White Sports: Film and Racial Politics in
1930s-40s' America
27

Jayson Baker
Bloodsport: Black Athletes, White Spectators, and the
United States Racial Imagination
39

Travis D. Boyce and *Stephanie M. Burchett*
Lynching and Spectacle: The Burning and Desecration of
Colin Kaepernick's Jersey
60

Michael J. Durfee
The Devil and Len Bias: How Politicians, Players and
Pushers Made the 1986 Crack Scare
and the Modern War On Drugs
85

Raúl Fernández-Calienes
Women and the Business of Dragon Boat Sport: Overcoming
Obstacles and Reaching for Success
112

Farieda Kahn
Ethnicity, Culture, Religion and Sport: Sectarianism
as an Obstacle to the Development of Sport in Cape Town,
South Africa during the First Half of the Twentieth Century
128

Gibson Ncube
Caster Semenya: Running Against Gender and
'Dysconscious' Racial Discrimination
149

Notes on Contributors
165

Preface

Eileen M. Angelini

In today's day and age of social media in a global economy where individuals come into contact with one another at a rapid pace, we all must work harder to understand and respect one another's point of view that may be directly influenced by an individual's native language, culture, and history. The sporting world is one such realm in which racism and discrimination take place that is often based in differences. The aim of this volume is to explore what it is about culture and society that creates an environment in which an athlete is able to excel or fail in his/her respective sport as well as which factors, such as racism, discrimination, financial advantage or hardship, propel or hinder an athlete's achievements. This volume also seeks to explore how the world of sports is often a microcosm of the real world and the many ways in which it uniquely reflects cultural and societal issues.

In "1946 Montreal: Home to Two of the World's Greatest Sports Heroes," Eileen M. Angelini shows how Montreal in 1946 was home to two of the world's greatest sports heroes: Maurice Richard of the Montreal Canadiens, the French-Canadian hockey team known affectionately as "les Habs" (for "les Habitants," the native inhabitants); and Jackie Robinson of the Montreal Royals, a minor league farm team of the Brooklyn Dodgers. Yet there was a common bond between Richard and Robinson that was much more significant than their talents in their respective sports: French-Canadian culture and society served as a support system to deal with and serve as a haven from linguistic, religious and racial discrimination. In Richard's case, he was a French-Canadian catholic in a city that was in direct conflict with the powerful English-Canadian protestant minority. In addition, the Catholic Church maintained tight control over the French Canadians. Therefore, although French Canadians had the population majority, their positions of power were quite limited. Throughout his career and most especially in 1955, when the people of Montreal rioted in huge masses to protest Richard's unfair suspension, Richard wore the bitter battles and hardships of his people on his shoulders every time he took to the ice both in Montreal as well as in the five other NHL cities (Boston, New York, Detroit, Chicago, and most especially, Toronto). In Robinson's case, he would be the one to break the "official" color barrier in Major League Baseball (MLB) but only after having suffered much torment and ridicule when playing games in the United States, particularly in ball parks south of the Mason and Dixon line, or while attending the Dodgers' spring training camp in Daytona Beach, Florida. This paper therefore explores how French-Canadian culture and society created the environment that propelled Richard and Robinson to excel at their respective sports. Specifically, by drawing on the example of Richard and Robinson, educators are able to expose their students to the cultural comparison between U.S. society, where historically racial discrimination was on the basis of the color of one's skin, and that of Canadian society, where racial discrimination was too often based on one's language. In making these cultural comparisons, one is able to understand why Quebecois society was so welcoming to Robinson.

In Richard Pioreck's "From 'No Joy in Mudville' to 'I'm a Yankee Doodle Dandy': *Casey at the Bat* and Irish Assimilation," he demonstrates that "Casey at the Bat" provides an opportunity to examine Irish-American assimilation, the Irish-American professionalism transformed the amateur game, innovations to the game by Irish-American ballplayers, and social and cultural opportunities for Irish-Americans. Pioreck explains how Ernest Thayer modeled the Mighty Casey on Mike "King" Kelly. Kelly was the first national baseball star who personified the sentiments behind the poem. "Casey at the Bat" is among the first pieces of American literature to capture the essence and meaning of baseball for Americans. Casey's great failure became a triumph for the thousands of Irish in America because only one of us could wring pity and pathos from all of us. The Irish-American could be said to have arrived with this strikeout in the clutch for as every American knows, "It's not how many times you get knocked down; it's how many times you get back up." This respect back up defines the star baseball player. Curiously, this quote is attributed to George Armstrong Custer, whom Mike Kelly passed in popularity in the bars of Boston as the lithographed image placed above the bar. DeWolfe Hopper's recitation of "Casey at the Bat" at Wallack's Theater in New York City in 1888 placed it on the cultural map. Kelly also took to the stage to recite "Casey at the Bat," and *The Sporting News* printed the poem substituting "Kelly" for "Casey." From 1888 to 1932, "Casey at the Bat" offered many insights into the Irish-American assimilation into the culture. Casey and Kelly were polar opposite manifestations of the Irish character popularized by Dion Boucicault in the 1850's as the stage Irishman. "Casey at the Bat" perhaps stands as the ultimate piece of Americana of its period. When Radio City Music Hall opened on December 27, 1932, Hopper performed his "Casey at the Bat."

Tatiana Prorokova explains in "Black Men in White Sports: Film and Racial Politics in the 1930s-40s' America," how after slavery was abolished in 1865, the life of African-Americans did not improve much, and their civil rights were not acknowledged for the next hundred years. Whereas there were obviously many smart and talented people among the ex-slaves, their skin color did not allow them to get a decent job and earn sufficient amount of money. In turn, white society overtly demonstrated that it was not ready to give blacks the same rights as whites had. There are many films that explicitly show the injustice that African-Americans faced in their professional life in the twentieth century, including the sporting world. This chapter focuses on Stephen Hopkins' *Race* (2016) and Brian Helgeland's *42* (2013) to reveal the discrimination that black athletes experienced in the 1930s-40s. Both films tell true stories of two outstanding sportsmen – Jesse Owens and Jackie Robinson – who had to compete not only for a better result but also – due to their skin color – for the recognition of their success among white Americans. Both films accurately render the atmosphere of the 1930s-40s America, when blacks were considered the lowest class, and could not even use the same bathroom facilities as whites did; yet the two examples also demonstrate what kind of hardships such sport legends as Owens and Robinson had to overcome on the field that, indeed, frequently turned into a war zone. While the films portray the racist America of the 1930s-40s, they both seem to argue that sport also managed to unite people of different races and thus helped fight racism and change attitudes of some of the whites at least for the time of a sportsman's performance. Displaying the hard lives of the sport "stars," the films seem to suggest that if such important African-American athletes as Owens and Robinson were not respected, then "ordinary" African-Americans had absolutely no chance for equality. Additionally, this article examines the attempt of *Race* to contrast and compare American racism and German Nazism, as the film narrates the story of Owens at the 1936 Berlin Olympic Games.

Jayson Baker's "Bloodsport: Black Athletes, White Spectators, and the United States Racial Imagination" deploys an interdisciplinary scholarly method to open up conversations about sports spectatorship and present-day racial thinking in U.S. culture through an analysis of Marco Ramirez' play, *The Royale*. Performance analysis reads stagecraft through *mise en scène* and engages the play's script to closely examine themes of black-on-black athletic violence as white spectacle, and ways the pleasure of viewing re-trenches racial hierarchies. These analytical approaches borrow the work of Black Studies and whiteness scholars to intervene textual and performance analyses. Theoretical interventions and close reading takes shape from the perspective of the white writer. The essay incorporates the writer's experiences as a parent of an African-American child and faculty chaperone attending the Lincoln Center production of *The Royale* with white students and colleagues. Keywords are sports spectatorship, racism and sports, Marco Ramirez, Rachel Chavkin, *The Royale*, boxing, whiteness, Black Studies, inter-racial parenting, race and memoir writing.

Travis D. Boyce and Stephanie M. Burchett's "Reproducing 'Lynching and Spectacle': Colin Kaepernick, the Burning and Desecration of Black Athletes' Jerseys, and the Creation of a Digital Hate Archive" takes an unique look at the ongoing debate surrounding events of Colin Kaepernick's protest actions. Prior to the start of the September 1, 2016 preseason National Football League (NFL) game, San Francisco 49ers quarterback Colin Kaepernick sat during the playing of the national anthem. He was protesting racial discrimination and police brutality against people of color. Subsequently, Kaepernick's peaceful protest was met with death threats coupled with hostile and racially charged videos, of fans burning his jersey. These videos feature mostly white men and at times women and children, who proclaim their disgust with Kaepernick while playing "The Star-Spangled Banner." Burning the jersey of professional sports players is not a new trend, but the number of videos posted to YouTube, as a response to Kaepernick is unprecedented. These videos have similar rhetoric and visual characteristics to lynching photographs created in the late nineteenth and early twentieth centuries. In their article, they first discuss the historical significance of lynching photographs. Second, they discuss African American athletes taking unpopular political positions. Sports in the United States hold cultural, social, and economic importance, therefore, it is critical that an academic narrative explain how the burning of Kaepernick's jersey shares the rhetoric with this nation's troubled racial history. The discussion demonstrates how the YouTube videos publically evoke the same emotion of fear and rhetoric found in the archive of photographs of lynching victims.

Michael J. Durfee's "The Devil and Len Bias: How Politicians, Players and Pushers Made the 1986 Crack Scare and the Modern War On Drugs" investigates how Len Bias' death became a political platform for the War on Drugs. At 8:50 a.m. on June 19, 1986, basketball talent Len Bias was pronounced dead at Leland Memorial Hospital in Maryland from cocaine-related cardiac arrest. An unlikely poster boy for the War on Drugs, Len Bias became more influential in death than he was in life. Bias's death proved timely for the broader agenda of politicians from both parties who spearheaded the call for a national mobilization against "crack" cocaine, as well as the drug's dealers and users. The agenda was clear: a unified, dramatized, forceful attack to be made upon popular opinions and attitudes regarding drug use had been issued on no uncertain terms. Instrumental to popular perceptions regarding the dangers of crack became the tragedy, and unique political opportunity, surrounding the death of Len Bias. Facing the prospect of a crucial midterm election in November, Democrats and Republicans both searched for an emotionally charged issue to galvanize electoral support. Bias's death generated the proverbial "juice" to the War on Drugs, providing a compelling storyline for campaign sound bites. By invoking Bias's death as a cautionary tale, politicians effectively conjured a powerful fear-based discourse regarding the threat of pervasive drug abuse in America. How did the War on Drugs become an acceptable opportunity to gain more votes in the eyes of Democrats? How had both parties reached a place where conservatives had begun to dictate the rules of play? Uniformly, scholars have ignored the work done by the Len Bias opportunity in this instance. An examination of the months following the Bias tragedy reveals the cultural mechanics of this seismic shift. Using Congressional records, national print media, and archival research in television news, this work examines the making of a national moral panic, a crisis surrounding drugs and urban space, as well as subsequent legislation which further decimated urban environments.

Raúl Fernández-Calienes' "Women and the Business of Dragon Boat Sport: Overcoming Obstacles and Reaching for Success" is a portrayal of women in the sport of Dragon Boat racing via an interview with the only woman owner of a dragon boat event production company in the United States: Penny Behling, of Dynamic Dragon Boat Racing. Women are a central part of the sport of Dragon Boating. Female dragon boaters participate at every level, from athletes to team captains and coaches, to event organizers, to company owners. With illustrations from her own experience producing almost thirty festivals per year and races all across the country, the article presents her perspectives on subtle and not-so-subtle barriers and obstacles as well as strategies for success and fulfillment. The article spans the period from her early days struggling to break into the industry to her widespread recognition for producing the 2010 U.S. Dragon Boat Club Crew National Championships – one of the official qualifying events for the World Championships – and to her groundbreaking work successfully raising millions of dollars for charity.

Farieda Kahn's "Ethnicity, Culture, Religion and Sport: Sectarianism as an Obstacle to the Development of Sport in Cape Town, South Africa During the First Half of the Twentieth Century" centers on South Africa's history of formal competitive sport, a history which dates back to the late nineteenth century when the first sports clubs – among them, cricket, rugby, football, tennis – were established. Given South Africa's colonial history of informal or de facto social segregation based on race, its sports history inevitably reflects the impact of the contemporary political environment on sport, resulting in the development of racially exclusive sports clubs and segregated public recreation and sporting facilities. From the late nineteenth century onwards – a period when legislated racial segregation was in its infancy – the hierarchical and rigidly stratified nature of society was often unquestioningly accepted by Black communities themselves, who then proceeded to voluntarily implement segregation based on culture, ethnicity or religion, within their own communities. Thus, in the early decades of the twentieth century, Coloreds separated themselves from Africans; Christians from Muslims; and Muslims separated themselves into those of Indian descent and those of Indonesian descent. In the sporting world, this took the form of separate sports clubs at community level and, aided by the authorities' provision of ethnically separate sports facilities, the exclusion of those perceived as outsiders from the use of those facilities. Through an exploration of the impact of de facto and de jure social segregation measures and sectarianism on the development of sport among Black communities in Cape Town during the first half of the twentieth century, this chapter contributes to an understanding of this historical legacy and the ways in which South African sport has been stunted by that legacy up to the present day.

Rounding out the collection is Gibson Ncube's "Caster Semenya: Running Against Gender and 'Dysconscious' Racial Discrimination." Since 2009, South African athlete Caster Semenya has been the subject of inordinate media scrutiny. This attention has mainly centered on her gender identity. Her body naturally produces more testosterone than the average woman. Scientific studies have found no direct relationship between high levels of testosterone in women and increased performance. Although she has undergone diverse sex-verification tests which cleared her to compete as a woman, her femininity has nonetheless perpetually been questioned and contested. This policing of Semenya's femininity and body begs the question as to what constitutes femininity and being a woman. Drawing on Judith Butler's postulations on gender construction, this chapter argues that in the face of prejudice and discrimination, Semenya challenges socially imposed gender categorizations and contends that the discrimination that Semenya has faced is certainly not new to strong black female athletes across the world. Venus and Serena Williams, for example, have perennially had their bodies denigrated as well as compared to the ideals of traditional-looking femininity. Terms such as "manly" and "savage" have been used to describe the Williams sisters, often overlooking their athletic abilities. Such othering of strong female black bodies is embedded in "dysconscious racism" in which these bodies are deemed too masculine or strong to be feminine. The chapter concludes that the "querying" of Semenya speaks to a form of dehumanization of the female black body and the policing of Semenya is inevitably laced with an untoward triad of racist, misogynistic and transphobic discrimination.

Idol Thoughts©

If intellect is being used as a measuring scale
Giving you the power to decide if those around you pass or fail
And if they fail you sometimes mock them and laugh
It seems to me that intellect's become your golden calf

After all intellect is simply just one gift from above
If misused it can surely obstruct the greatest gift, God's love
The one that should be passed on to those who have the need
After all it's our responsibility to plant the sacred seed

Then we can watch it bring forth the blessed fruit
That we all need to guide us in our divine pursuit
When we focus on our differences instead of how we're alike
 It's the lack of love, not intellect that's the lethal strike

Divisiveness is not the path to what we all need
When we choose to follow it you know who takes the lead
It's the goals we have in common that lead to progress
Love will always eliminate the need to pass any test

Alan E. Sexton

1946 Montreal:
Home to Two of the World's Greatest
Sports Heroes

EILEEN M. ANGELINI

Montreal in 1946 was home to two of the world's greatest sports heroes: Maurice Richard of the Montreal Canadiens, the French-Canadian hockey team[1] known affectionately as "les Habs" (for "les Habitants," the native inhabitants); and Jackie Robinson of the Montreal Royals, a minor league farm team of the Brooklyn Dodgers. Yet there was a common bond between Richard and Robinson that was much more significant than their talents in their respective sports: French-Canadian culture and society served as a support system to deal with and as a haven from linguistic, religious and racial discrimination. Richard was a French-Canadian catholic in a city that was in direct conflict with the powerful English-Canadian protestant minority. In addition, the Catholic Church maintained tight control over the French Canadians. Therefore, although French Canadians had the population majority, their positions of power were quite limited. Throughout his career and most especially in 1955, when the people of Montreal rioted in huge masses to protest Richard's unfair suspension, Richard wore the bitter battles and hardships of his people on his shoulders every time he took to the ice both in Montreal as well as in the five other NHL cities (Boston, New York, Detroit, Chicago, and most especially, Toronto). In Robinson's case, he would be the one to break the "official" color barrier in Major League Baseball (MLB) but only after having suffered much torment and ridicule when playing games in the United States, particularly in ball parks south of the Mason and Dixon line, or while attending the Dodgers' spring training camp in Daytona Beach, Florida.

This paper therefore explores how French-Canadian culture and society created the environment that propelled Richard and Robinson to excel at their respective sports. Specifically, by drawing on the example of Richard and Robinson, educators are able to expose their students to the cultural comparison between U.S. society, where historically racial discrimination was on the basis of the color of one's skin, and that of Canadian society, where racial discrimination was too often based on one's language. In making these cultural comparisons, one is able to understand why Quebecois society was so welcoming to Robinson.

Due to multiple injuries at the start of his professional career in 1942, Richard was initially thought to be too fragile to play professional hockey—so fragile, in fact, that the Canadiens' management even hoped to trade him to another team but failed in its efforts as no other team wanted him. Moreover, while most players avoided conscription as it could easily curtail the length and quality of one's playing career, he was even rejected in his quest to serve in the Canadian military at the outset of World War II because his ankle, femur, and wrist injuries had not healed properly.[2] However, Richard's injury-prone start to his professional career would not be derailed by his desire to help his team win, a team that desperately needed a hero to not only increase ticket sales so that the Montreal Canadiens organization would not fold but more importantly, to represent its oppressed people. By 1946, Richard proved himself as a much-feared force to be reckoned with in the National Hockey League (NHL), having been the first player in the history of the NHL to score 50 goals in 50 games during the regular season (1944-1945, the season in which the Canadiens only lost eight games out of the fifty-game season). In addition, Richard was awarded the Hart Memorial Trophy for the 1946-1947 season, in which the Montreal Canadiens won the Stanley Cup. The Hart Memorial Trophy is the oldest and most prestigious individual hockey award and is awarded annually to the player who is deemed to be the most valuable to his team. During his 1944-1960 legendary career, Richard won eight Stanley Cup Championships in three different decades, with five of them being in a row (1944; 1946; 1953; 1956; 1957; 1958; 1959; and, 1960), and as such, Richard's career became the foundation for future dominating success by the Canadiens, a true hockey dynasty. It is thus no small wonder then that the Hockey Hall of Fame waved the mandatory three-year waiting period to induct Richard into the Hall one year after his retirement. Poetic justice was rightly served for Richard for all the derogatory and disparaging insults he received at the start of his professional career, least of which was when Toronto Maple Leafs owner Major Conn Smythe, well-known for his bigotry towards French Canadians, offered $25,000 cash for Richard's contract when Smythe return home at the end of World War II.

Equally impressive was Robinson's year with the Montreal Royals: at age 27, he led his team to its first-ever Little World Series title over the Kentucky Colonels with a .349 batting average (so outstanding a batting average as to win Robinson the International League batting title—he was the first Montreal Royal to achieve), 65 Runs Batted In (RBIs) and 40 stolen bases. The Montreal Royals had such a dominating season in 1946 (they won 100 games, the first minor league team ever to do so, and won their pennant race by 18.5 games) that the team is still considered to be one of the best minor leagues teams of all time.[3] Robinson's year with the Montreal Royals would prove to be the stepping-stone for success in his ten-year Hall of Fame career with the Brooklyn Dodgers, a career in which he helped to lead the Dodgers to their first World Series title in 1955 as well as their World Series runner-up status in 1947, 1949, 1952, 1953, and 1956. Like Richard, Robinson was not initially considered to be one of the best athletes: he played shortstop for the Negro League's Kansas City Monarchs but scouts reporting to Branch Rickey, the Brooklyn Dodgers executive who was at the head of the movement to integrate Major League Baseball (MLB), stressed that Robinson's throwing arm was not strong enough to play shortstop in the Major Leagues. In fact, in an effort to prove his athletic abilities during his 1946 season with the Montreal Royals when he played second base, Robinson sat out multiple games due to injuries brought on by his trying so hard. But he was a quick learner and in his transition from shortstop to second base, Robinson had the best fielding percentage. When he went on to play a solid first base for the Brooklyn Dodgers, Robinson also became highly respected for his offensive ability to get on base consistently and to make things happen. Yet no better praise can be given for Robinson's year with the Montreal Royals than that by Clay Hopper, team manager who had initially begged Rickey to put Robinson on another Dodgers team. Chris Lamb elucidates on the transformation of Hopper's attitude after his request to Rickey was denied:

> "Please don't do this to me," Hopper reportedly told Rickey. "I'm white and I've lived in Mississippi all my life. If you're going to do this, you're going to force me to move my family and home out of Mississippi."
>
> Rickey refused.
>
> Hopper remained the team's manager, and, according to Robinson, put aside his racist attitudes and treated the ballplayer fairly well during the season. . . . By overcoming his own sense of bigotry, Hopper became redeemed. But more than that, he represented how countless others—ballplayers, mangers, spectators, and even those who previously given little thought to baseball were transformed by Jackie Robinson.
>
> As the 1946 regular season progressed, Hopper was more and more enthusiastic in his praise of Robinson, who later said he was always treated fairly by the manager. When the season ended and the Royals won the league championship, Hopper warmly shook Robinson's hand. "You're a great ballplayer and fine gentleman," Hopper told Robinson. "It's been wonderful having you on the team.

Hopper recommended Robinson for promotion to the Brooklyn Dodgers the following year.[4]

Yet there was a common bond between Richard and Robinson that was much more significant than their talents in their respective sports: French-Canadian culture and society served as a support system to deal with and as a haven from racial discrimination. To have a fuller appreciation of how essential a role French-Canadian culture and society played in the lives and careers of Richard and Robinson as well as their lasting legacies, it is meaningful to consider briefly how racial and ethnic prejudice and discrimination have been traditionally viewed in Canada. Canadian sociologist Vic Satzewich explains:

> The ease with which racism is now invoked to label and describe a whole range of individuals, events, ideas or social institutions is, in many ways, a positive development. Historically, many Canadians have been reluctant to admit that they, their ideas and their behaviours have contributed to the social marginalization, denigration and inferiorization of others based on the negative evaluation of "race" difference. Furthermore, one of our most enduring national myths is that there is less racism here than in the United States. A close examination of the historical record (Bolaria and Li, 1988), and a recent comparative study (Reitz and Breton, 1994), suggests that Canadians do not have anything to be smug about. Racism was an important part of the process of state formation in this country [Canada] (Ng, 1988) and the dichotomy between a supposedly multicultural Canada and an American melting pot appears to be significantly overdrawn.[5]

Also of note is the study conducted by Jeffrey G. Reitz and Raymond Breton that compared prejudice and discrimination in Canada and the United States by examining overt racism and negative racial stereotypes, anti-Semitism, social distance, employment discrimination, and collective and government action against discrimination. Reitz and Breton, who define prejudice as a question of "attitudes" and discrimination as one of "behavior"[6] concluded that despite historical differences, "Canadians and Americans are roughly similar in their attitudes and behavior toward racial minorities."[7] However, the key distinction to be made and that is often overlooked by many Americans is that discrimination does not always begin with the color of one's skin or what one looks like.

In Richard's case, he was a French-Canadian catholic in a city that was in direct conflict with the powerful English-Canadian protestant minority. In addition, the Catholic Church maintained tight control over the French Canadians. Therefore, although French Canadians had the population majority, their positions of power were quite limited.

To comprehend fully these sharp divisions felt so deeply by French-Canadians, one must have an appreciation for what daily life in Montreal was like prior to Quebec's *Révolution Tranquille*/Quiet Revolution. On June 22, 1960 Jean Lesage was sworn in as Premier of Quebec, the event generally viewed as the starting point of Quebec's *Révolution Tranquille*/ Quiet Revolution. In December of 2010, Herb Kauderer sat down with Paul-André and Rolande Fournier, two Quebecers, born in 1944 and 1945 respectively, as well as Isabelle Fournier, a certified interpreter,[8] to try to understand the differences in everyday life wrought by the revolution.[9] The interview targeted everyday experiences and how they changed with the revolution, uncovering views long hidden by language and oppression. The interview was done with the goal of bringing these views and experiences across a half century and into the Anglo-American world. Although Paul-André Fournier would have been only two years old in 1946 when both Richard and Robinson were at the start of their careers in 1946 Montreal, his perspective is particularly illustrative on the time period as a whole:

> Si tu allais magasiner à Montréal par exemple, dans un magasin important, si tu cherchais quelque chose dans le magasin, si tu t'adressais à un employé il parlait seulement anglais. Si tu voulais avoir une information, tu allais voir le balayeur. Il te donnait l'information parce qu'il était français (French-speaking and not a person from France).[10]

> When you went to Montreal, if you were going to a big store, and you were looking for something, you would not ask an employee, you would ask the guy who was pushing the broom because he was the one speaking French.[11]

While providing simultaneous interpretation of Paul-André's comments to Kauderer, Isabelle Fournier further clarified the situation:

> That tells you how much the big jobs were for English-speaking people, and the French-speaking people could get only some lower jobs. That's an important distinction.[12]

Paul-André's recollections of the time period are striking because there is an unmistakable similarity between the unfair social treatment of Quebec's Francophones and that of African Americans in the United States. It is thus not difficult to understand the social pressure that both Richard and Robinson endured throughout their professional playing careers. Specifically in Richard's case, throughout his career and most especially in 1955, when the people of Montreal rioted in huge masses to protest Richard's unfair suspension, Richard wore the bitter battles and hardships of his people on his shoulders every time he took to the ice both in Montreal as well as in the five other NHL cities (Boston, New York, Detroit, Chicago, and most especially, Toronto). Charles Binamé's 2005 feature-length film, *Maurice Richard*,[13] adeptly portrays Quebecois society from 1930 to 1960 with a particular emphasis on the political situation between the French and the English Canadians. Essential to note in this cinematic account of Richard's life and hockey career, are the scenes in which he seeks the assistance of a journalist to ghostwrite articles for him on the unfair treatment that French-Canadian players experienced in the NHL. It was exactly these ghostwritten articles that served as one of the main reasons for engendering then NHL President Clarence S. Campbell's[14] fervent frustration with Richard.

In Robinson's case, he would be the one to break the "official" color barrier in the MLB[15] but only after having suffered much torment and ridicule when playing games in the United States, particularly in ball parks south of the Mason and Dixon line, or while attending the Dodgers' spring training camp in Daytona Beach, Florida. And this was all after having endured a humiliating tryout with the Boston Red Sox in 1945.[16] Robinson, however, was able to find a public forum for the racial discrimination faced by African Americans prior to his breaking of the MLB color barrier in a much more direct fashion than that of Richard. In 1950, he was able to star in his own life story in the movie directed by Alfred E. Green and co-starring Ruby Dee and Minor Watson. In a compelling and symbolic change of events, at the end of Green's film, Robinson is shown speaking in front of United States Congress so as to promote the protection of the American way of life, most likely from the dangers of Communism. Unfortunately, neither Green's beloved classic film nor Brian Helgeland's hugely popular 2013 film on Robinson, *42* (for the number that Robinson wore throughout his career with the Brooklyn Dodgers system and which was universally retired by the MLB in 1997[17]), depict Robinson's experience of living among French-Canadians in Montreal and how the experience there gave Robinson the courage to continue with his dream of helping to win the battle of integrating baseball.

When Brooklyn Dodgers executive Rickey chose Montreal as the city in which to start the experiment of integrating MLB, he chose it for a reason. Although Montreal, as every major city does, had its own social tensions, its tensions were linguistic and religious. At that time, discrimination was not based on the color of one's skin as it was so predominantly in the United States. However, it is essential to note that the Robinsons lived in a French-Canadian neighborhood. Thus, they lived among people who understood repression first-hand. Moreover, so beloved was Robinson to his Montreal fans that Chris Iorfida reported: "It's been documented that the Montreal fans would pay close attention to any ear-to-the-ground or press reports of racism or mistreatment Robinson and the Royals received when playing on the road. Fans of the Royals would voice their displeasure when that city's team visited

Delorimier Stadium."[18] Robinson himself had nothing but the most positive of comments to make about the city of Montreal and his fans there: "Had it not been for the fact that we broke in in Montreal, I doubt seriously we could have made the grade so rapidly," Robinson said in a 1964 CBC interview. "The fans there were just fantastic and my wife and I have nothing but the greatest memories."[19] When remembering the racial taunting he faced at the Royals' 1946 training camp in Florida as well as how he and his wife regained their sense of dignity in Montreal and had their faith in humanity restored, Robinson stated in a 1972 interview with Bill Mann: "I experienced no racism here. None. That was a huge relief for my wife and I. The French-Canadian people welcomed us with open arms."[20]

In February 2011, the United States government officially recognized Robinson's home in Montreal's Villeray district. Robinson's widow Rachel explained so eloquently to *the Canadian Press* that home life in Montreal was extremely important because of the stressful and difficult road trips her husband had to make to the United States: "You can't make [enough] of the house because it's where the experiment started and the experiment went on to be a national success, so it led to something."[21] She further elucidates on the warm welcome she received from their French-Canadian landlady who spoke English: "She received me so pleasantly. Then she poured tea for me and agreed to rent the apartment to me furnished and she insisted I use her things – like her linens and her china. It was an extraordinary welcome to Canada."[22] More comforting still is the knowledge that Jackie and Rachel Robinson developed fond attachments with their Montreal neighbors. In the April 4, 2013 Canadian Baseball Network Podcast Special, "Paradise – Jackie Robinson in Canada," Kevin Glew, author of the blog Cooperstowners in Canada, explained to Peter Bean, host of the Canadian Baseball Network's Podcast Specials, that in 1946 Rachel Robinson was pregnant with her first child and neighbors were highly protective of her, most especially the children who lived in the upstairs apartment of their duplex, and that Jackie Robinson reveled in the fact that he could walk freely down the streets, have fun interactions with the French-Canadian children, and eat where he wanted. Touchingly so, Robinson was as popular with fans in Montreal as a Montreal Canadiens hockey player.[23]

While in Montreal, the Robinsons formed a life-long friendship with the famous Montreal sportswriter Sam Maltin and his wife Belle. When the Montreal Royals won the 1946 Little World Series, it was Maltin who coined the famous phrase that described the scene when Robinson was being chased outside Delorimier Stadium by his adoring fans: "It was probably the only day in history that a black man ran from a white mob with love instead of lynching on its mind."[24] In a May 30, 2013 telephone interview with Jean-Pierre Roi, one of Robinson's Montreal Royals teammates, I heard firsthand the deep fondness that his teammate had for him. Just one month shy of his 93rd birthday, Roi vividly recalled how the people of Montreal loved Robinson as a player and as man. With deep emotion that was palpably audible in his voice, Roi added that Robinson was so highly respected for his playing abilities and how he handled himself in the face of insults and bad treatment that everyone wanted Robinson to succeed with his dream of helping the people of his race while at the same time being respectful of others.[25]

Yet, while it is clearly evident that Montreal was a haven for Robinson and his wife from the racial discrimination that they faced in the United States, what deserves further exploration is the discriminatory environment in which Richard played hockey. While the 1955 Richard Riots protesting Richard's unfair suspension by NHL President Campbell have been well documented as well as the way other NHL teams would encourage their players to goad Richard into a fight so as to land him in the penalty box and as a key result, keep him from scoring, much less attention is attributed to the day-to-day struggles that Richard faced. Prior to the Richard Riots, one would think that if French Canadians had the majority population backed by their strong Catholic faith, one would naturally deduce that the French Canadians had control of Montreal. Yet this was not the case, as Charles Foran explains so carefully the misperception of the French Canadians:

> If they didn't – and truth was, the city was ruled by a small autocracy and run by Church dictates and Anglo and French money equally – it was only because French Canadians weren't yet aware of their own size. Told they were a "small people," a helpless minority cast adrift by history in a vast sea of North American difference, they denied what their own eyes and ears reported. They had also been taught that ultimate reward for the faithful lay not in this life, but in the life everlasting. Catholicism preached philosophical quietude, a convenient forbearance for those wishing to remain in political and economic charge.[26]

Foran further elucidates the impact of the Catholic Church upon 1930s Quebec when describing the effects of *la revanche des berceaux/* revenge of the cradles:

> The Richards [Maurice's parents, himself, and his siblings], regulars at mass at nearby Saint Joseph's, did not need to consciously heed the Church's la revanche des berceaux ("revenge of the cradles") policy intended to counter the dilution of "pure" Quebec by the arrival of foreigners. Neither did they have to listen closely to the priest's message, louder now that times were especially tough, about the decadence of cities and how the "real" Quebec lay in the very towns and countryside many had fled for Montreal and its jobs. These instructions and allegiance were transmitted as naturally as prayers learned

first in school, then at church, then kneeling by the bed each evening. In 1936 Maurice Duplessis was elected premier. As the leading exponent of the populist social conservatism that would so profoundly shape Quebec over the next three decades, he believed that secret forces hostile to the "small people" had too long controlled the province, and had even brought on the global financial crisis. Fiercely anti-Communist and sympathetic to fascism, the premier envisioned a French Canada for *les habitants* – knowing their place, and happy with it.[27]

It was thus that the 1955 Richard Riots truly proved to be the straw that broke the proverbial camel's back in terms of how the French Canadians would no longer tolerate oppression. Indeed, the Richard Riots exemplified a long-brewing pot of frustration and were the stepping stone for the *Révolution Tranquille*/Quiet Revolution that would lead the Québécois away from *la grande noirceur*/the Great Darkness of the Maurice Duplessis era to the more enlightened era of a modern, secular society led by René Lévesque, leader of the separatist Parti Québécois. In 1975, while being interviewed for the news program *The Fifth Estate*, Richard commented: "The fans were a hundred percent behind me because I was French Canadian, and I scored lots of goals,"[28] severely understating his "canonization during the 1940s and '50s as 'Saint Maurice,' avenger of the injustices suffered by those same France Canadians."[29]

On the ice, Richard was a much-feared opponent and never backed down from a fight. In sharp contrast, Rickey specifically chose Robinson for the fact that Robinson exhibited the strength of character to not fight back. In his secret plan to integrate MLB, Rickey had extensive research conducted on Robinson and happily discovered that, along with having successfully played four different college sports (football, basketball, baseball, and track and field) with white players, Robinson was a man of solid character: he did not smoke, drink alcohol, or party. As an added bonus, both Rickey and Robinson were Methodist and thus shared the same belief system. It thus came as no surprise that Robinson agreed in a signed contract to the difficult task to not to retaliate if he was provoked on or off the field. Iorfida sheds further light on Robinson's temperament:

> What's not well known is that Dodgers owner Branch Rickey also signed an African-American pitcher, Johnny Wright, with the intention that he would play for Montreal in the 1946 season. But in his autobiography *I Never Had It Made*, released just weeks after his death from a heart attack in 1972, Robinson said Wright just didn't have the temperament for the challenge. "He couldn't withstand the pressure of taking insult after insult without being able to retaliate," Robinson wrote of Wright, who played a few games for Montreal before returning to the Negro Leagues.[30]

Off the ice, Richard was humble, shy, and quiet: even after his retirement, Richard lived in a very modest home near his childhood home in the north end of Montreal, drove an equally modest car, ate in the neighborhood family restaurants, and went to the same barber that he had frequented his entire life. After their retirements from their respective sports, both Richard and Robinson[31] would endure frustration with "life after sports" but both had reached iconic status in the record books as well as most especially in the hearts of their adoring fans.[32] In short, both Richard and Robinson continue to serve as inspiration for future generations of athletes.

In conclusion, did Richard and Robinson ever meet in person in the great city of Montreal? While some say that Richard attended the April 18, 1946 Opening Day game between the Montreal Royals and the Jersey City Giants, there are no documented photos of these two great athletes together[33] on this historic day when Robinson hit a three-run home run and three singles as well as stole two bases to lead the Royals to a dominating 14-1 victory over the Giants.[34] Wondering about the mutual respect and admiration that these two humble men must have had for one another, I was most fortunate that Roi was able to provide me with some first-hand insight. He explained that in addition to Richard coming to the April 18, 1946 Opening Day game, he knew of many times that the two great athletes spoke with one another and that Richard greatly admired Robinson. Moreover, he recounted that Richard was a very good baseball player and played in an amateur baseball league in Montreal.

Indeed, Montreal proved to be a very special city to both Richard and Robinson as they were equally special to their legions of Montreal fans. Both have statues that have been erected in their honor: Richard's statue, created by Marc André J. Fortier, is located at La Place du Centenaire (Centennial Plaza), outside of Le Centre Bell. It was inaugurated on December 4, 2008, the 100th anniversary of the Montreal Canadiens. Along with Richard's statue are ones dedicated to Howie Morenz, Jean Béliveau, and Guy LaFleur as well as 20,000 bricks personalized by Canadiens fans, a plaque for each of the twenty-four Stanley Cup Championships won by the Canadiens, a small monument for each player who had had his number retired by the Canadiens, and bricks celebrating the 100 most memorable moments in the history of the Canadiens.[35] Robinson's statue, by sculptor Jules Lasalle and which tenderly depicts Robinson with two youngsters, is in front of the Olympic Stadium.[36] How truly fitting it is that the quote on Robinson's statue speaks to his love of the city of Montreal: "I don't care if I ever get to the majors, I told myself this is the city for me, this is paradise …"[37]

Notes

[1] In his article "The Formation of Class, Ethnic, and National Identities: The Case of the Richard Riot of 1955," David Di Felice provides the background of how the Canadiens came to be a French-Canadian team and a symbol of French Quebec: "The founding of the Montreal Canadiens in 1909 and the formation of the National Hockey Association (N.H.A.) in 1910 were a reflection of the changing status of sport in Canadian popular culture. The Canadiens were the first professional sports organization in Quebec to provide working-class Francophones with a team to follow and familiar athletes they admired. . . .The history of the Montreal Canadiens began on December 4, 1909 with the initial financing of the team by two northern Ontario Anglophone mining moguls, J. Ambrose O'Brien and T.C. Hare. These multi-millionaires provided funding for the creation of a professional hockey team in Montreal on the condition that '. . . the team be transferred to French-speaking ownership from Montreal as soon as possible. . .' and then an all French-Canadian hockey team be organized. From its inception, the Canadiens' founders orchestrated the creation of a hockey club that had an irrefutable French-Canadian design that worked to garnish the ethnic image of the team and reinforce its association with the local populace. By initially establishing itself as a 'French-Canadian' organization, the Montreal Canadiens laid the foundation upon which a genuine connection with its Francophone fan base could be developed in the years to follow. Even though the Canadiens would not see French ownership until 1921, French Canadians were nonetheless found throughout other team positions." [*Putting It On Ice, Volume I: Hockey and Cultural Identities*. Colin D. Howell, ed. Halifax, NS: Saint Mary's University Gorsebrook Research Institute, 2001: 85-86.]

[2] In 1944, Richard tried a second time to enlist in the Canadian military, this time as a machinist. However, as he did not finish high school and therefore lacked a high school diploma nor did he yet have his technical trade certificate, he was yet again denied entry into the military.

[3] Kevin Glew, author of the blog Cooperstowners in Canada, suggests during the Canadian Baseball Network's Episode 5 Podcast, "Paradise – Jackie Robinson in Canada" on April 14, 2013, with host Peter Bean, that Brooklyn Dodgers executive Rickey may have stacked the 1946 Montreal Royals team so as to take pressure off of Robinson. http://www.canadianbaseballnetwork.com/featured/17262/.

[4] Lamb, Chris. "How Clay Hopper's Attitude Was Transformed by Jackie Robinson." Online. http://arts.nationalpost.com/2013/04/09/how-clay-hoppers-attitude-was-transformed-by-jackie-robinson/

[5] Satzewich, Vic, ed. "Introduction." In *Racism and Social Inequality in Canada*. Toronto: Thompson Educational Publishing, Inc., 1998: 11.

[6] Reitz, Jeffrey G. and Raymond Breton. "Prejudice and Discrimination in Canada and the United States: A Comparison." In Satzewich, Vic, ed. *Racism and Social Inequality in Canada*. Toronto: Thompson Educational Publishing, Inc., 1998: 47.

[7] Ibid., 63.

[8] Provenance: The source interview was conducted on October 11, 2010, in Kauderer's kitchen at 19 Scott Street, Lancaster, New York, over coffee and tea. The interviewees were Paul-André Fournier (Kauderer's father-in-law) and Rolande Fournier (Kauderer's mother-in-law). Kauderer's wife, Isabelle Fournier, served as interpreter. Isabelle has a B.A. and an M.A. in Translation, and is accredited as a translator by notable accrediting agencies and governments,

including the provincial governments of Québec and Ontario, and the Canadian Federal government. The interview was conducted in French, accompanied by simultaneous interpretation in both directions by Isabelle. On December 30, 2013, at his home in Québec, an English version of the edited transcript was presented to Paul-André for his approval. With Rolande present, he reviewed and approved the text.

[9] Having served as the Panel Moderator for "Communication and Identity in North America" – Crossing Borders 2014, A Multi-Disciplinary Student Conference on the United States, Canada and Border Issues, University at Buffalo – The State University of New York (SUNY)'s Center for Tomorrow, Amherst, NY: March 13-14, 2014, I had the distinct pleasure of working with Herb Kauderer, ABD in Canadian Studies and an Associate Professor of English at Hilbert College (MFA from Goddard College, Plainfield, VT). Kauderer graciously shared the audio files of his interview with Paul-André and Rolande Fournier after I heard him deliver the presentation, "Fifty Years After the Quiet Revolution: An Anglo-American Tries to Understand," so that I could include a first-hand perspective of pre-revolution Montreal in this paper.

[10] Throughout the entire interview, Paul-André and Rolande Fournier referred to French-speaking people as "français," and not as francophone, as well as to the English-speaking people as "anglais," and not as Anglophone. Given their age, this is a clear cultural indicator of the time period in which they grew up.

[11] Written transcription of audio files of the Paul-André and Rolande Fournier interview are my own.

[12] Ibid.

[13] Binamé's film stars Roy Dupuis in the title role. Dupuis had previously played Richard in two popular Canadian television series.

[14] Campbell, third president of the NHL, was its president from 1946 to 1977. One might ponder if it was coincidence or fate that Campbell began his career as NHL president in the same year that Richard had become the marquee player of the Montreal Canadiens.

[15] There is some reported evidence of light-skinned black players in the 1880s. Furthermore, at the beginning of the twentieth century, some teams had players of African-American origins that were described as "Mexican," "Cuban," or "Indian."

[16] For a detailed discussion of Robinson's disastrous 1945 tryout with the Boston Red Sox, see: Bryant, Howard. *Shut Out: A Story of Race and Baseball in Boston*. New York and London: Routledge, 2002.

[17] Active MLB players were allowed to continue wearing the number 42 but no new players were allowed to wear it. The highly regarded Marino Rivera of the New York Yankees was the last remaining active player to wear number 42 and when he retired at the end of the 2013 season, no other player would wear it. The fact that Rivera was so respected in both the American and National Leagues, increased the honor paid to Robinson.

[18] Iorfida, Chris. "Jackie Robinson's Momentous Year in Montreal." Online. http://www.cbc.ca/sports/baseball/mlb/story/2013/04/15/.

[19] Ibid.

[20] Mann, Bill. "My Interview with Jackie Robinson." *USA Today*. Online. 10 April 2013.

[21] "Robinson's Apartment in Montreal to be Marked with Plaque: Jackie and Rachel Lived on de Gaspe for the 1946 Season." *The Canadian Press*, 27 February 2011. Accessed on-line via the CBC Digital Archives at *www.cbc.ca/archives/*.

[22] Ibid.

[23] Canadian Baseball Network's Episode 5 Podcast, "Paradise – Jackie Robinson in Canada" on April 14, 2013. http://www.canadianbaseballnetwork. com/featured/17262/.

[24] "Robinson's Apartment in Montreal to be Marked with Plaque: Jackie and Rachel Lived on de Gaspe for the 1946 Season." *The Canadian Press*, 27 February 2011. Accessed on-line via the CBC Digital Archives at *www.cbc.ca/ archives/*.

[25] I am deeply grateful to Colin Howell, Director of the Centre for the Study of Sport and Health at Saint Mary's University who recommended that I speak with Jean-Pierre Roi and to Scott Crawford, Director of Operations at the Canadian Baseball Hall of Fame who put me in touch with Roi.

[26] Foran, Charles. *Maurice Richard*. Part of the Extraordinary Canadians Series edited by John Ralston Saul. Toronto, ON: Penguin Group (Canada), 2011: 21-22.

[27] Ibid, 30-31.

[28] Ibid, 2.

[29] Ibid.

[30] Iorfida, Chris. "Jackie Robinson's Momentous Year in Montreal." Online. http://www.cbc.ca/sports/baseball/mlb/story/2013/04/15/.

[31] A concise wealth of information on Robinson's post-playing career is available from the Library of Congress Mercian Memory Collection. Among the many details, one learns that "Robinson used his national celebrity and commitment to equal rights to fuel many efforts to help African Americans achieve full citizenship through the 'ballot and the buck.' For example:
1963: began annual "Afternoon of Jazz" concerts, with Rachel Robinson; first year's proceeds sent to Southern Christian Leadership Conference (of which Martin Luther King was president) to support civil rights work and voter registration drives in the South.
1964: helped found and served as board chairman for the Freedom National Bank, a minority-owned commercial bank based in Harlem, New York.
1964: became one of six national directors for Nelson Rockefeller's Republican presidential campaign, and later worked as special assistant for community affairs when Rockefeller was re-elected governor of New York in 1966.
1970: formed the Jackie Robinson Construction Company to build low and moderate-income housing." http://memory.loc.gov/ammem/collections/robinson/ jr1957.html.

[32] When Richard died in May 2000, he was given a provincial state funeral, the first time an athlete had been honored in such a manner. It is estimated that approximately 115,000 people of many generations paid their respects while his body lay in state at Le Centre Bell. For the remainder of the 2000 MLB season, the Montreal Expos wore Richard's number 9, in black, on their right sleeves, to honor the revered athlete.

[33] An extensive search through the on-line source http://paperofrecord.com (the purpose of which is to create the world's largest searchable archive of historical newspapers) conducted in May 2013 produced no results of a photograph of Richard and Robinson together. It is thus that I contacted Paul-André Linteau, Professor of History at the Université du Québec à Montreal, who has published several highly respected histories on the city of Montreal about the possible existence of such a photograph. Not knowing of such a photograph, Linteau then put me in touch with Mario Robert, Chef de la Section des archives, Division de la gestion des documents et des archives et de l'accès à l'information, Direction du greffe, Ville de Montréal, who unfortunately informed me that he as well did

not know of the existence of a photograph of the two great athletes together. Nonetheless, Robert did refer me to other online archives, such as the Bibliothèque et Archives Canada and Bibliothèque et Archives nationales du Québec. Still having no luck at finding a photograph of Richard and Robinson together, I further searched through the Ville de Montréal Archives Service as well as CBC Radio-Canada Archives and have not discovered the desired photograph of Richard and Robinson together or even of Richard in attendance at the April 18, 1946 Opening Day game between the Montreal Royals and the Jersey City Giants.

[34] "1946: Jackie Robinson debuts with Montreal Royals." Online. http://www. cbc.ca/archives/on-this-day/jackie-robinson-debuts-with-montreal-royals.html/.

[35] For further information on the Richard statue, see: http://www.flickr.com/photos/wallyg/3823559700/.

[36] For beautiful color photographs of the Robinson statue, see: http://www.dcmemorials.com/index_indiv0008318.htm.

[37] As discussed by Peter Bean, host of the Canadian Baseball Network's Podcast Specials, and Kevin Glew, author of the blog Cooperstowners in Canada, during the Canadian Baseball Network's Episode 5 Podcast, "Paradise – Jackie Robinson in Canada" on April 14, 2013. http://www.canadianbaseballnetwork. com/featured/17262/.

Bibliography

Bryant, Howard. *Shut Out: A Story of Race and Baseball in Boston*. New York and London: Routledge, 2002.

The Canadian Press, 27 February 2011. Accessed on-line via the CBC Digital Archives at *www.cbc.ca/archives/*.

http://www.dcmemorials.com/index_indiv0008318.htm.

Di Felice, David. "The Formation of Class, Ethnic, and National Identities: The Case of the Richard Riot of 1955." *Putting It On Ice, Volume I: Hockey and Cultural Identities*. Colin D. Howell, ed. Halifax, NS: Saint Mary's University Gorsebrook Research Institute, 2001: 85-86.

http://www.flickr.com/photos/wallyg/3823559700/.

Foran, Charles. *Maurice Richard*. Part of the Extraordinary Canadians Series edited by John Ralston Saul. Toronto, ON: Penguin Group (Canada), 2011.

Glew, Kevin. Canadian Baseball Network's Episode 5 Podcast, "Paradise – Jackie Robinson in Canada" on April 14, 2013. http://www. canadianbaseballnetwork.com/featured/17262/.

Iorfida, Chris. "Jackie Robinson's Momentous Year in Montreal." Online. http://www.cbc.ca/sports/baseball/mlb/story/2013/04/15/.

Lamb, Chris. "How Clay Hopper's Attitude was Transformed by Jackie Robinson." Online.
http://arts.nationalpost.com/2013/04/09/how-clay-hoppers-attitude-was-transformed-by-jackie-robinson/.

Mann, Bill. "My Interview with Jackie Robinson." *USA Today*. Online. 10 April 2013.

"1946: Jackie Robinson debuts with Montreal Royals." Online. http://www.cbc. ca/archives/on-this-day/jackie-robinson-debuts-with-montreal-royals. html/.

Reitz, Jeffrey G. and Raymond Breton. "Prejudice and Discrimination in Canada and the United States: A Comparison." In Satzewich, Vic, ed. *Racism and Social Inequality in Canada*. Toronto: Thompson Educational Publishing, Inc., 1998: 47-68.

Satzewich, Vic. "Introduction." *Racism and Social Inequality in Canada*. Ed. Vic Satzewich. Toronto: Thompson Educational Publishing, Inc., 1998: 11-24.

From "No Joy in Mudville" to "I'm a Yankee Doodle Dandy": *Casey at the Bat* and Irish Assimilation

RICHARD PIORECK

In the bottom of the ninth inning at Citi Field in New York City on May 28, 2013, less than a week before the 125th anniversary of the publication of Ernest Thayer's *Casey at the Bat*, the Mets David Wright, an Irish-American, singled off the Yankees Mariano Rivera. As Daniel Murphy, another Irish-American, slid home with the tying run, Mets broadcaster Keith Hernandez chirped, "Oh, there is joy in Mudville," alluding to one of the earliest Irish-American heroes.[1]

When the Irish first began immigrating to the United States at the time of the potato famine, they were not embraced by the nativist Americans as most of them were English and the enmity between the English and the Irish dated from the early 1500s. The Irish were vilified for their laziness, shiftlessness, drunkenness, and packs of children that they did not care for, who became a scourge of street urchins on society. Indeed, the Irish were the first group of immigrants to be so libeled. Also, for their Popish allegiance, Irish men seeking work encountered N.I.N.A. (No Irish Need Apply) signs in newspaper ads, shops and workplaces.

The Mighty Casey, the earliest incarnation of an Irish-American hero, much like Paul Bunyan, is an icon of American confidence, fortitude and belief that no task is too big or difficult to be undertaken. Considering how it marks a significant cultural milestone in the Irish's acceptance in America, *Casey at the Bat* is relevant in overcoming the barriers to the Irish being viewed as pariahs and the discrimination fostered by it. That Casey becomes a hero is interesting considering that the Irish were persona non-grata fewer than 50 years before. In the 1840s when the Irish diaspora scattered the Irish to North America, the West Indies and Australia, "some scientists believed the Irish were, like Africans, more closely related to apes than to other Europeans, and in some cases in the U.S., Irish immigrants were classified as Blacks, not Whites."[2] In the rural south, the Irish worked clearing the land with slaves, but the Irish were sent ahead of the slaves in the swamps because "If a slave dies, you lose a piece of property. If an Irishman dies, you can get another one."[3] Irish workers later competed with free African-Americans for skilled labor as bakers, blacksmiths, carpenters and bricklayers, suffering discrimination similar to the racial discrimination endured by blacks, for anti-immigrant and anti-Catholic bias.[4]

Service in the Union Army during the Civil War provided the Irish with a modicum of respect, yet the real indication of acceptance and assimilation of the Irish comes through boxing and baseball. Boxing and baseball were areas where the Irish excelled. John L. Sullivan was the last American bare-knuckled champion and the first American modern heavyweight champion, while the equally pugnacious Irish-American baseball players molded the respectable gentleman's club game into the American national pastime.

Baseball had been part of American culture for years before the first professional leagues were formed. The Irish have always loved games of strength and skill and baseball became the perfect outlet for these old-world traits to be transferred to their new American culture. The rise of the significance of the Irish on baseball mirrors the strides the Irish made in American society and culture. As shown in the writings of James T. Farrell, Nelson Algren and Peter Finley Dunne, among the Irish in Chicago, boys considered prowess in baseball a necessity to becoming an American. The Irish engaged in many sports requiring skill and dexterity as well as a demonstration of strength and endurance.

When *The San Francisco Examiner* published *Casey at the Bat* 130 years ago on June 3, 1888, the long climb to assimilation and respectability began. Two and a half months later on August 14, Thayer's birthday,[5] De Wolf Hopper, a leading comic actor of the day, and a lifelong baseball enthusiast and New York Giants fan, inserted Thayer's then-unknown *Casey at the Bat* into a performance of *Prince Methusalem* at Wallack's Theater on Broadway in order to entertain members of the Chicago White Sox and New York Giants attending the performance.[6] Hopper recited the poem to a great ovation. Hopper says that he saw Buck Ewing's mustache nervously twitch as the audience, after a moment of silence, roared its approval at the anticlimactic denouement, shouting with glee at the poem and Hopper's performance. The crowd demanded several encores, and Hopper happily complied.[7] And with that, the Mighty Casey became the first baseball literary hero and icon. Hopper almost singlehandedly made Casey an American literary and cultural icon. His recitations of *Casey at the Bat* placed it on the cultural map. Hopper notes that he recited the poem more than 10,000 times and appeared in the first film adaptation of the poem in 1916.[8] *Casey at the Bat* became such an example of the American spirit that Hopper was asked to perform it on Radio City Music Hall's inaugural program on December 27, 1932, 44 years after premiering the poem at Wallack's Theater.[9]

The journey for the Irish from persona non grata to Yankee Doodle Dandy was arduous yet rather quick for assimilation considering the sentiment expressed by Thayer in 1888. Hopper came to fame in Harrigan and Hart's plays about urban life that often featured baseball as a subject, particularly in regards to showing the Irish affinity for the game during the late 1870s.[10] These plays did much to remove the stereotyped "stage Irishman" popularized in the 1850s by the jointly claimed Irish and American theater artist Dion Boucicault. The stage Irishman in green top hat, morning coat knickers, and a corn cob pipe was not unlike the African American Uncle Tom character. Both characters served as the butt of jokes for true Americans. The empowered, non-stereotyped Irish characters Hopper successfully portrayed in Harrigan and Hart's popular plays about urban life included realistic Irish characters, helping to pave the way for the acceptance of the Irish in society.

Looking at the early professional era, baseball gained national recognition in 1876, largely with nativist American players, but by 1888 when *Casey at the Bat* was published, Irish ballplayers were presented as the heroes in the poem. In this relatively short time, Irish players dominated professional rosters perhaps because the Irish took their baseball play seriously rather than as a social gathering for those members of men's clubs. Many of the innovations that changed the staid gentlemen's club game into the American national pastime were introduced by Irish-American ballplayers. Mike "King" Kelly's singular popularity in particular also helped move baseball from being a gentleman's club activity to being the national pastime. When he played right field, Kelly would use his considerable charm to banter with the fans. This went over well not only at home, but on the road as well. This pleasant rapport made Kelly a fan favorite not only in Chicago, but throughout the league. Kelly loved entertaining fans with his trick plays even though his talents were such that he didn't need to resort to tricks. Kelly's favorite trick was scoring from second, while he "somehow forgot to go by way of third, slighting the bag entirely by 15 feet, thereby saving much valuable time and distance."[11] Fans at home and on the road loved this brazen play in the years when only one umpire officiated at major league games. Kelly pulled one over on the authorities with this trick play and the crowd appreciated his cleverness in thwarting them.

While these innovations were not coordinated to change the game, nevertheless they did. Once overhand delivery was acceptable and the pitcher no longer had to pitch the ball as requested by the batter, Candy Cummings, an Irish-American, was credited with developing the curve ball.[12] This pitcher's weapon helped move baseball from the gentleman's game, where everyone was given an opportunity to hit the ball, to a more skilled game. Coupled with this pitching innovation was the practice shared by many catchers, but credited to another Irish-American in 1886, Connie Mack, of crouching behind the plate to receive the pitch rather than standing five to ten feet behind home plate.[13] This innovation increased the excitement because the catcher's crouching behind the plate brought the umpire that much closer to the action, improving ball and strike calls, heightening the competition between pitcher and batter, and providing close plays at the plate, making scoring not as leisurely as in the gentleman's game. Mack changed the tactics and strategy of how baseball was played. Yet Mack's influence on the game's demeanor also helped the Irish assimilate. Red Smith said of Mack, "Connie entered the game when it was a game for roughnecks. He saw it become respectable . . ."[14] Kelly claimed to be the first catcher to use finger signals to get the pitcher to throw the pitch Kelly wanted.

During this period, Mike Kelly introduced the catcher's mitt, mask and chest protector, as well as the hook slide to evade being tagged out.[15] In this same period, Roger Connor popularized the pop-up slide, which allowed him to advance on a fielding error mental lapse.[16] In 1907, Roger Bresnahan, one of the many Irish-American ballplayers John McGraw brought to the New York Giants, completed the catcher's equipment by adding shin guards as well as supplemental padding that served as a shock absorber to the catcher's mask in 1908.[17] All these innovations to the catcher's position changed baseball to the game it is today, while at the same time created acceptance for the Irish in the game and in American society.

Mike "King" Kelly has long been acknowledged by many as Thayer's model for the Mighty Casey. While Kelly makes an attractive model for Casey, his contemporary, Roger Connor comes closer to embodying Casey's traits. Mighty Casey implies someone larger than his contemporaries, like Goliath or Henry VIII. Connor stood 6'3" compared to King Kelly's 5'10", and at 230 pounds Connor outweighed Kelly by 60 pounds.[18] Even today social psychologists maintain that by mere physical presence, men at least 6'2" command respect. With most of his average contemporaries at 5'8", Connor's size awed many just as Casey would have. Some believe Connor's size and home run prowess inspired the New York Gothams to be christened the New York Giants. Connor's presence and demeanor helped change the public's perception of the Irish. They were no longer universally condemned as irresponsible drunks who beat their wives and neglected their children; Connor projected a picture of the sober, responsible family man who was no longer the exception, but the rule.

While the home run was a rarity in the 19th-century dead-ball era, Connor was one of the few sluggers of the day. *Casey at the Bat* implies that Casey is a home run hitter who can win the day for Mudville,

there was Jimmy safe at second and Flynn a-hugging third.

Then from 5,000 throats and more there rose a lusty yell;
it rumbled through the valley, it rattled in the dell;
it knocked upon the mountain and recoiled upon the flat,
for Casey, mighty Casey, was advancing to the bat.[19]

Connor hit 39 home runs through 1887, the year before *Casey at the Bat* was published, and although King Kelly had 43 home runs through 1887, his career began two years earlier than Connor's. Connor's 138 career home runs was the record until Babe Ruth passed it in 1922.

The dramatic climax of *Casey at the Bat* is Casey's striking out to end the game, which reflects the incredulity of that action by Connor, who struck out only 455 times in 18 seasons, and hit the first walk-off grand slam.[20]

> Oh, somewhere in this favored land the sun is shining bright;
> . . . but there is no joy in Mudville – mighty Casey has struck out."[21]

Connor like Kelly was the son of Irish immigrants. He was among a number of Irish-Americans on the Giants. Many of Connor's teammates fit the description of the roughnecks that were pre-dominant in baseball. Connor was reticent, a gentleman on and off the field, respectful of his wife, Angeline, for the 47 years they were married. His demeanor helped make the game respectable. Although forgotten until Hank Aaron broke Ruth's career home run record in 1974, Connor was, in that hoary 19th-century phrase, a credit to his race.[22]

King Kelly on the other hand embodied every negative stereotype about the Irish at the time. He enjoyed drinking hard liquor, sometimes playing games hung over, and he was popular with the ladies, much like that expected of a matinee idol. Like Hopper, Kelly also took to the vaudeville stage to recite *Casey at the Bat*. *The Sporting News* printed the poem substituting "Kelly" for "Casey," further perpetuating the myth that Mike "King" Kelly was Thayer's inspiration for the Mighty Casey. Kelly was the first national baseball star who personified the sentiments behind the poem in the public's imagination.[23]

Famous for his exploits on the field, his style of play was commemorated in the popular song, "Slide, Kelly, Slide." Kelly was no longer a baseball star, but a celebrity known to fans and non-fans. The sheet music for "Slide, Kelly, Slide" sold millions of copies. When records were produced in the 1890s, "Slide, Kelly, Slide" became America's first hit record.[24] Before "Slide, Kelly, Slide" was popular, Kelly played vaudeville, and the year *Casey at the Bat* was published, Kelly produced the first baseball autobiography, *Play Ball: Stories from the Ball Field*.[25] Kelly's off-field success demonstrated how far the Irish had come since N.I.N.A and the contempt nativist Americans had held them.

Casey at the Bat's popularity rests on iconography that fixes the poem in American culture. While *Casey at the Bat* sprung from baseball, today the poem is bigger than baseball, part of the cultural fabric known to just about every American whether a baseball fan or not. When placing *Casey at the Bat* as a cultural icon, be mindful of the subtitle, "A Ballad of the Republic." *Casey at the Bat* is a folk tale, a romance for those drawn to Casey and even to those who have only a nodding acquaintance with the poem. So besides the questions often asked – who is Casey? And where is Mudville? – the larger question is, "What does *Casey at the Bat* mean to Americans?"

Novelist Reed Farrel Coleman remarked, "*Casey at the Bat* floods me with memories about the poem and about the age at which I first heard it. *Casey at the Bat* evokes images of old time baseball, of burly mustached men in dirty, loose-fitting uniforms and strange caps. Men who chewed tobacco and spat juice and who used chipped and pitted bats the size of tree limbs. *Casey at the Bat* captures the essential nature of baseball, of how it is a game of dashed hopes and failure."[26] This image rests on the photographs of the early stars of the game who were 40% Irish.

> And now the pitcher holds the ball, and now he lets it go,
> and now the air is shattered by the force of Casey's blow.[27]

Bernard Malamud pays tribute to *Casey at the Bat* in *The Natural* where Roy Hobbs strikes out the Whammer on a sequence of three pitches similar to those thrown to Casey. One meaning found in *Casey at the Bat,* which Malamud features, is "pride goeth before a fall." This fits with the Celtic, very Catholic, black and white take on morality.

As does the view that the poem cautions that heroes should lead a life of humility and not make a show of false humility so as to avoid being humbled as Casey was. Why? America likes her heroes humble and grateful for their success. Heroes should not behave as if success and adulation are their due. On the other hand, many see the message of *Casey at the Bat* as overcoming adversity by picking yourself up and trying again, something the Irish were painfully aware of in their struggle with the potato famine and in immigrating to the United States, beginning a new life in a hostile culture.

Casey's great failure became a triumph for the thousands of Irish in America because one could wring pity and pathos from everyone. The Irish-American could be said to have arrived with this strikeout in the clutch, for as every American knows, "It's not how many times you get knocked down; it's how many times you get back up." This respect accorded those who get back up defines the star baseball player. Curiously, this quote is attributed to George Armstrong Custer, who Kelly passed in popularity in the bars of Boston as the favorite lithograph image placed above bars in Boston.

In New York, Coogan's Bluff, a cliff overlooking the Polo Grounds along the Hudson on the Upper West Side was owned by an Irish businessman, who allowed his countrymen to congregate there to watch the ballgame they could not afford to attend. Crowds gathered to watch the New York Giants with its cast of Irish-American ballplayers led by John McGraw. These gatherings showed the beginning of Irish acceptance in the midst of the heavily Irish Upper West Side neighborhood near the Polo Grounds which was given the derogatory sobriquet Murphyville.

Much of what I learned of baseball history, and in particular New York baseball history, rich with the stories of Irish-American ballplayers, I learned watching the inaugural seasons of the New York Mets with my grandfather, Richard McDonough. Born and raised in Manhattan, my grandfather was a 12-year-old New York Giants fan when McGraw's Giants won their first World Series. As announcers Ralph Kiner, Lindsay Nelson and Bob Murphy told stories about Casey Stengel, my grandfather told me of others who had played for McGraw's Giants. I learned of the feats of Mack and of John J. McGraw. Stengel had learned managing well from McGraw, McGraw was the genius who made baseball indispensable to scores of Irish-American boys like my grandfather. While Kiner, Nelson and Murphy extolled Casey Stengel's longevity and genius, my grandfather explained McGraw's baseball acumen as the font of Stengel's genius. My grandfather held up McGraw as an example of how someone without advantages, but with drive and determination, was able to harness his skills and be a success.

McGraw's skill and cunning added to the strategy and tactics of the game. McGraw is credited with introducing the Baltimore chop, the hit-and-run, and the pinch-hitter; he coined the term for Mike Donlin because he can hit in a pinch, and the relief pitcher used to stop a rally.[28]

What of the poem *Casey at the Bat* itself? What is its literary value? I discovered *Casey at the Bat* watching television with my grandfather. We saw Jackie Gleason's dramatic reading as Reginald Van Gleason II à la Hopper. When my grandfather laughed and told me *Casey at the Bat* was an old poem about an Irish baseball hero, I wondered why we did not read poems like it in school. Hopper called *Casey at the Bat* "the only great American comic poem."[29] While Thayer was not of the Irish, whose passion infused the new spirit of play in baseball, making it no longer a gentlemen's club sport, the poem exudes the attitudes of the fan and the professional player. A close reading of the poem allows us to conclude that *Casey at the Bat* is not great poetry, but it is a great poem. It lacks density, but wears its heart on its sleeve. *Casey at the Bat* carries the 19th century's emotional charge for the United States as Tennyson's *Charge of the Light Brigade* did for Great Britain. And as the subtitle proclaims, "A Ballad of the Republic, Sung in the Year 1888," the form is a short narrative poem that offers an emotionally stirring and memorable folk ballad that is historically and culturally important.

One last point to highlight is that of the Irish-American vaudeville star George M. Cohan, the Yankee Doodle Dandy star and his association with baseball. Cohan was one of the most popular entertainers of his time, and a fierce baseball fan, which shows how far the Irish had come as far as assimilation, including the significance of baseball as a means of assimilation. Unlike Hopper, the great vaudevillian Cohan had nothing to do with *Casey at the Bat*. But Cohan had at least two less-than-sterling associations with the game. In 1919, travelling in New York circles that overlapped those in which Arnold Rothstein travelled (Rothstein had been a partner in a Manhattan pool hall with McGraw), Cohan got inside information on the World Series and bet heavily on Cincinnati.[30] Unfortunately, Cohan chose not to reveal the fix, or nullify his bets, and cleaned up when many of his friends took gambling losses on the 1919 Series.[31]

Ironically, Ring Lardner, whose faith in baseball was shaken by the 1919 World Series, wrote a short story entitled, "Hurry Kane," about a pitcher who conspires to throw games for gamblers. Cohan approached Lardner about adapting the story for the stage. Thus, they collaborated on *Elmer the Great*, which was neither a critical nor a financial success, although the movie version with Joe E. Brown did better. Cohan may have understood sentiment and melodrama, but he did not understand baseball in the manner of *Casey at the Bat* as Lardner did. One problem with the play was that Cohan did not understand Lardner's humor and kept changing the jokes for melodramatic plot twists that were based on his understanding of the vaudeville audience. This led Lardner to observe, "It's a double thrill collaborating on a play with Mr. Cohan because you can attend the performance and then go home and read your own script and that gives you two complete shows in one evening."[32] Cohan, like baseball, began as a gentleman, but as his popularity grew, the gentleman trappings were more honored in the breech.

What does a close reading of *Casey at the Bat* reveal about the American spirit and the Irish influence on American culture?

> And then when Cooney died at first, and Barrows did the same,
> a sickly silence fell upon the patrons of the game.
>
> A straggling few got up to go in deep despair. The rest
> clung to that hope which springs eternal in the human breast;[33]

The poem's tone is hopeful for the future even in the face of defeat. This embodies the American spirit. Given an opportunity, a person might succeed. And yet, if a person fails, another opportunity is sure to present itself.

> Then from 5,000 throats and more there rose a lusty yell;
> it rumbled through the valley, it rattled in the dell;
> it knocked upon the mountain and recoiled upon the flat,[34]

Lose a fortune today, make a new fortune tomorrow. In baseball terms, anyone can go from last to first, move from the outhouse to the penthouse.

There was ease in Casey's manner as he stepped into his place;
there was pride in Casey's bearing and a smile on Casey's face.
And when, responding to the cheers, he lightly doffed his hat,
and now the air is shattered by the force of Casey's blow.[35]

Here it shows how a true man knows how to behave in the face of
the pressure of adversity.

Oh, somewhere in this favored land the sun is shining bright;
the band is playing somewhere, and somewhere hearts are
light.[36]

This sentiment demonstrates the indomitable American spirit
whether in triumph or tragedy. *Casey at the Bat* does not need to be
explained for anyone to comprehend it. Americans understand baseball
because of what baseball means to Americans. This is because those who
grasp the game of baseball understand American hearts and minds. The
hearts and minds of America accepted the Irish in large part due to the
exploits of these men who played a boys' game.

Oh, somewhere in this favored land the sun is shining bright;[37]

And there is joy in Mudville – and Murphyville, and everywhere
in America where the Irish have ascended to the top of the social heap.
Mighty Casey has prevailed.

Notes

[1] Hernandez, Keith. NY Met Game Broadcast. *SNY.* 28 May 2013.

[2] Sharp, Gwen. "Negative Stereotypes of the Irish." https://the societypages. org/socioimages/2008/10/06. Accessed 17 Jan 2017.

[3] Mulraney, Frances. "Black Irish Identities: The Complex Relationship Between Irish and Africa Americans." www.Irish Central.com. Accessed 17 Jan 2017.

[4] Jamison, S. Lee. "How Green Was My Surname; Via Ireland, a Chapter in the Story of Black America." www.New York Times, March 17, 2003. Accessed 17 Jan 2017.

[5] Pioreck, Richard. "Struck Out and Never Retired." *Memories and Dreams.* Summer 2013, pp. 8-9.

[6] Fields, Arnold & Fields, Marc. *From the Bowery to Broadway.* Oxford University Press, 1993, 160.

[7] Pioreck, Richard. "Struck Out and Never Retired." *Memories and Dreams.* Summer 2013, pp. 8-9.

[8] Slide, Anthony. The *Encyclopedia of Vaudeville.* Greenwood Press, 1994, 249.

[9] Jackson, Kenneth T. editor. *The Encyclopedia of New York City.* Yale University Press, 1991, 975.

[10] Slide, Anthony. The *Encyclopedia of Vaudeville.* Greenwood Press, 1994, 249.

[11] Appel, Marty. *Slide, Kelly, Slide.* Lanhan, 1999, 41-48.

[12] "William Arthur "Candy" Cummings." Baseball Hall of Fame. http://baseballhall.org/hof/mack-connie. Accessed 2 Feb 2017, 1.

[13] "Connie Mack." Baseball Hall of Fame. http://baseballhall.org/hof/mack-connie. Accessed 2 Feb 2017, 5.

[14] ibid.

[15] Gordon, Peter M. "King Kelly." www.Society for American Baseball Research. Accessed 2 Feb 2017, 2.

[16] Lamb, Bill. "Roger Connor." www.Society for American Baseball Research. Accessed 2 Feb 2017, 3.

[17] Thomas, Joan M. "Roger Bresnahan." www.Society for American Baseball Research. Accessed 2 Feb 2017, 1.

[18] "Mike "King" Kelly," and "Roger Connor." http://www.basebalreference.com/players/k/kellyki01.shtml. Accessed 2 Feb 2017.

[19] Thayer, Ernest. *Casey at the Bat. San Francisco Examiner,* 1888.

[20] Lamb, Bill. "Roger Connor." www.Society for American Baseball Research. Accessed 2 Feb 2017, 2-3.

[21] Thayer, Ernest. *Casey at the Bat. San Francisco Examiner,* 1888.

[22] Lamb, Bill. "Roger Connor." www.Society for American Baseball Research. Accessed 2 Feb 2017, 2-3.

[23] Appel, Marty. *Slide, Kelly, Slide.* Lanhan, 1999, 128.

[24] Gordon, Peter M. "King Kelly." www.Society for American Baseball Research. Accessed 2 Feb 2017, 3.

[25] ibid., 4.

[26] Coleman, Reed Farrel. "Re: *Casey at the Bat.*" Received by Richard Pioreck, 26 Mar. 2013.

[27] Thayer, Ernest. *Casey at the Bat. San Francisco Examiner,* 1888.

[28] Jensen, Don. "John McGraw." www.Society for American Baseball Research. Accessed 16 Feb 2017, pp. 1-2.

[29] Slide, Anthony. The *Encyclopedia of Vaudeville.* Greenwood Press, 1994, 249.

[30] Jensen, Don. "John McGraw." www.Society for American Baseball Research. Accessed 16 Feb 2017, 2.

[31] Asinof, Eliot. *Eight Men Out.* Holt, Rinehart & Winston, 1963, 156.

[32] Pioreck, Richard. "The Other Worlds of Ring Lardner." *Art, Glitter and Glitz,* edited by Arthur Gewirtz and James J. Kolb. Praegar Press, 2004, 172.

[33] Thayer, Ernest. *Casey at the Bat. San Francisco Examiner,* 1888.

[34] ibid.

[35] ibid.

[36] ibid.

[37] ibid.

Works Cited

Appel, Marty. *Slide, Kelly, Slide.* Lanhan, 1999.

Asinof, Eliot. *Eight Men Out.* Holt, Rinehart & Winston, 1963.

Coleman, Reed Farrel. "Re: *Casey at the Bat.* Received by Richard Pioreck, 26 Mar 2013.

"Roger Connor." http://www.baseball-reference.com/players/c/connoro01.shtml.
Accessed 2 Feb 2017.

"William Arthur "Candy" Cummings." http://baseballhall.org/hof/mack-connie. Accessed 2 Feb 2017.

Fields, Arnold & Fields, Marc. *From the Bowery to Broadway.* Oxford University Press, 1993.

Gordon, Peter M. "King Kelly." www.Society for American Baseball Research. Accessed 2 Feb 2017.

Hernandez, Keith. NY Met Game Broadcast. *SNY.* New York, 28 May 2013.

Jamison, S. Lee. "How Green Was My Surname; Via Ireland, a Chapter in the Story of Black America." www.New York Times, March 17, 2003. Accessed 17 Jan 2017.

Jensen, Don. "John McGraw." www.Society for American Baseball Research. Accessed 16 Feb 2017.

"Mike "King" Kelly," and "Roger Connor."
http://www.basebalreference.com/players/k/kellyki01.shtml. Accessed 2 Feb 2017.

Lamb, Bill. "Roger Connor." www.Society for American Baseball Research. Accessed 2 Feb 2017.

"Connie Mack." http://baseballhall.org/hof/mack-connie. Accessed 2 Feb 2017.

Mulraney, Frances. "Black Irish Identities: The Complex Relationship Between Irish and African Americans." www.Irish Central.com. Accessed 17 Jan 2017.

Pioreck, Richard. "The Other Worlds of Ring Lardner." *Art, Glitter and Glitz,* edited by Arthur Gewirtz and James J. Kolb. Praegar Press, 2004.

Pioreck, Richard. "Struck Out and Never Retired." *Memories and Dreams.* Summer 2013.

Sharp, Gwen. "Negative Stereotypes of the Irish." https://the societypages.org/socioimages/2008/10/06. Accessed 17 Jan 2017.

Slide, Anthony. The *Encyclopedia of Vaudeville.* Greenwood Press, 1994.

Thayer, Ernest. *Casey at the Bat.* San Francisco Examiner, 1888.

Thomas, Joan M. "Roger Bresnahan." www.Society for American Baseball Research. Accessed 2 Feb 2017.

Black Men in White Sports: Film and Racial Politics in 1930s-40s' America

Tatiana Prorokova

There are many films that explicitly show the injustice that African Americans faced in their professional life in the twentieth century, including the sporting world. This chapter focuses on Stephen Hopkins' *Race* (2016) and Brian Helgeland's *42* (2013) to reveal the discrimination that black athletes experienced in the 1930s-40s. Both films tell true stories of outstanding sportsmen – Jesse Owens and Jackie Robinson – who had to compete not only for a better result but also – due to their skin color – for the recognition of their success among white Americans. Both films accurately render the atmosphere of the 1930s-40s America, when blacks were considered the lowest class, and could not even use the same bathroom facilities as whites did; yet the two examples also demonstrate what kind of hardships such sport legends as Owens and Robinson had to overcome on the field that, indeed, frequently turned into a war zone. While the films portray the racist America of the 1930s-40s, they both seem to argue that sport also managed to unite people of different races and thus helped fight racism and change attitudes of some of the whites at least for the time of a sportsman's performance. Displaying the hard lives of the sport "stars," the films seem to suggest that if such important African-American athletes as Owens and Robinson were not respected, then "ordinary" African Americans had absolutely no chance for equality. Additionally, this article examines the attempt of *Race* to contrast and compare American racism and German Nazism, as the film narrates the story of Owens at the 1936 Berlin Olympic Games.

"A life is not important except in its impact on other lives."
-Jackie Robinson, *I Never Had It Made*

Sport and Racism in the U.S.

The problem of racism in the United States has already generated a wide scholarly response. Racism as an ideology has impregnated American society and evidently continues to corrupt it today. While it would be wrong to talk about "degrees" of racism, it is apparent that racism was particularly strong during the times of slavery and until African Americans received their civil rights.[1] The racial discrimination manifested itself on social, political, cultural, and economic levels. Even after slavery had been abolished, African Americans continued to experience inequality. Just like in any other racist society, racism in America was a phenomenon that helped explain inequality as "a God-given part of nature."[2] With time, the racial discrimination has dangerously and solidly permeated throughout the American society. Indeed, even after the abolition of slavery, African Americans could not be proper members of American society as they were literally excluded from the country's social, cultural, and political spheres, thus not being able, for example, to receive a good education, build a career, vote, and, crucially to this analysis, compete with whites in sports.

Scholars have already noted that "[w]ithin sports history research in the USA, race plays a prominent role, exceeding almost any other area of focus."[3] The evident reason for that is the initial division between athletes according to their skin color: competitions majorly included white sportsmen, while blacks were strictly excluded from any "white" sporting events and were allowed or forced or relegated themselves to organize their own competitions and compete among each other. During colonialism, blacks could take part in various sports "on plantations or in larger cities."[4] However, until the 1860s, only few sports records set by blacks were acknowledged. During the last decades of the nineteenth century and at the beginning of the twentieth century, blacks were only allowed to compete with their own teams and within their own leagues; the exception perhaps being only the few particularly promising black sportsmen who came into sport through university competitions.[5] Later, during the 1920s-30s, more black sportsmen started to emerge; however, they were frequently viewed as a potential menace by and to white athletes, who were largely influenced by the findings of racist scientists. According to those findings, blacks were performing so well due to their racial belonging that stipulated their physical strength and endurance. Nevertheless, the appearance of the so-called "globalizing sporting culture" made black sportsmen "visible" to white athletes and audiences as competitions moved to the international level. Among the first most prominent black sportsmen of the end of the nineteenth century were boxers Peter Jackson and George Dixon. Later, in the 1930s, track-and-field athlete Jesse Owens' fantastic performance at the 1936 Summer Olympics drew the attention of the whole world. The triumphal achievements of those athletes were the beginning of the end (or at least of a significant reduction) of racial discrimination in sport.[6] Finally, the inclusion of the African-American baseball player Jackie Robinson in the Brooklyn Dodgers in 1947 is recognized as "the official entry of [an African American] into professional baseball,"[7] which destroyed the system of "separate sporting organizations" in the United States.[8]

Black Men in White Sports

While the significant shifts in the complex relationship between sport and race were roughly taking place during the 1880s-1950s, the 1930s-40s deserve a special investigation. Without undermining the importance of the events that took place during prior decades, this article contends that the 1930s-40s were a crucial time in the sporting history of the United States for two principal reasons. First of all, the two decades were indelibly marked by the complex political events that were happening throughout the world, unavoidably affecting U.S. domestic problems. While in the U.S. racism was a burning issue, in Europe the Nazi ideology was vigorously promoted by Adolf Hitler. The inevitable involvement of the United States in World War II, primarily explained by the country's eagerness to fight against the Nazi regime and thus free the oppressed, is particularly interesting when realizing that millions of people were socially, politically, and economically oppressed in the U.S. during that time. Second, the 1930s-40s are famous for the emergence of two African-American athletes – real stars of that time – Jesse Owens and Jackie Robinson. The significance of those men to the history of the world sport and of American sport in particular is immeasurable. It is not surprising that the performances of the two athletes are discussed even today. Their autobiographies are considered some of the most influential books in the sporting world. The courage of the two sportsmen, their will to win, and desire to represent their race as contributing Americans[9] are impressive even today, which is arguably proved by the recent releases of two films – Stephen Hopkins' *Race* (2016) and Brian Helgeland's *42* (2013) – that tell the stories of Owens and Robinson respectively.

While providing historical backgrounds of the sporting achievements of Owens and Robinson, this article primarily focuses on the cinematic portrayals of the athletes' success. The reason for that is not only the lack of scholarly analysis of those depictions, but also the medium and the nature of those representations. There are numerous examples of cinematic portrayals of African Americans in film. Yet scholars contend that the representation of black athletes is particularly controversial. On the one hand, such portrayals display African Americans as "active and successful, achieving goals and receiving popular acclaim,"[10] which eventually "offers role models to young black people."[11] On the other hand, such images "still serve to reproduce stereotypes that underpin racism" (e.g., "the myth of natural superiority")[12] and they also "offer false hope"[13] because "sporting success can only provide an escape from poverty for a very small minority."[14] This chapter, therefore, investigates to what extent *Race* and *42* can be characterized as "stereotypical" films about black athletes, considering that they narrate the stories of real athletes, who, significantly, became sports heroes. This article also examines the complicated relationship between sport and race in the 1930s-40s through the cinematic portrayals of the U.S., racial politics, sport, and black athletes of that time.

Fighting against Racism and Nazism: Jesse Owens' Success at the 1936 Summer Olympics in Stephen Hopkins' *Race* (2016)

Jesse Owens is one of the very few famous black athletes of the 1930s. His contribution to sport is considerable; yet his contribution to the eradication of racial segregation in sport is even more so. These are the two issues that Stephen Hopkins' recent film *Race* (2016) examines. *Race* zeroes in on arguably the most significant years of Owens' life as an athlete, namely from his time in college, when he impresses his coach with outstanding results, to his fantastic performance at the 1936 Berlin Summer Olympics, held in Nazi Germany. The strength of the film as a biographical – if not a historical – narrative consists not only in the accurate portrayal of Owens' struggle to success on the field but also in the acute representation of the tense 1930s, saturated with the ideology of racism in the U.S. and Nazism in Germany. Thus, while concentrating on the story of Owens, the film's main purpose is to comment on the problem of racial hatred that apparently even such prominent people of that time as Owens could not escape.

Owens is known as "the most remarkable athlete of his time."[15] The media literally made him a celebrity, which was simply unique considering that he was a black athlete,[16] calling him "'the bounding Buckeye bullet,' 'phenomenal,' 'the great Buckeye blizzard,' 'Mercury in motion,' 'a perfect symphony in racing rhythm' with 'torpedo-like speed,' the 'streaking spearhead of speed' who 'combined the speed of an express train with the grace of a faun'"[17] as well as a "perfect piece of running machinery" and the "Cleveland comet."[18] All the praising epithets aside, it was not easy for Owens to build a career in racist America; and this is what *Race* extensively comments on. There are multiple short but significant moments in the film that never allow the audience to forget about racial segregation in the U.S. in the 1930s. For example, when Owens (portrayed by Stephan James) gets on the bus and accidentally pushes a white woman with his suitcase, she indignantly tells her friend that "that colored pushed [her]."[19] Or when Owens and his African American friend want to use a shower after training, white sportsmen allow them to do that only after they, i.e., the white men, have taken a shower first. In addition, when Owens talks to a white coach – Larry Snyder (portrayed by Jason Sudeikis), he always looks down, afraid to look into the man's eyes. The same attitude is noticeable on the field, where white athletes harass Owens verbally, joking that he is "just back from the jungle."[20] However, coach Snyder understands that regardless of the place where Owens will have to perform, i.e., in the U.S. or in Germany at the Olympics, the black man will always face racial prejudices. Therefore, Snyder tells Owens not to pay attention to the racist assaults but concentrate instead on his job as a sportsman.

While Owens seems to be able to subtract himself from the racism on the field - although, of course, with significant efforts, and the psychological pressure from those assaults noticeable throughout the film - the situation changes for the athlete once he finds out that the African American community does not support his choice to go and perform at the Olympics. While Owens considers the Games a great opportunity to prove to everyone that a black man can also achieve success, his African American friends disapprove of where the Games will be held, clearly hinting at the political subtext of the 1936 Olympics. Being aware of the national discrimination that is at the heart of Hitler's politics, the black community laments: "How can you justify taking part in Germany when there is so much discrimination here at home?"[21] There was, in truth, a great deal of controversy concerning Owens' participation in the 1936 Olympic Games. Those who were against Hitler's regime urged that no black athlete should compete because that would mean that the U.S. was shutting its eyes to the actions of the Nazis or even supported the oppression in Europe. In reality, Owens said: "If there is racial discrimination against minorities in Germany, then we must withdraw from the Olympics."[22] However, it is known that the withdrawal was never meant seriously due to the "financial - and psychological - investment" in the preparation to as well as the participation in the Games.[23]

Race explicitly shows that African American athletes were not welcome in Nazi Germany. Those who supported black sportsmen were considered opponents of the regime. Right before Owens is ready to appear on the field, the viewer witnesses the athlete and his coach looking at the agitated audience. The camera, however, films the two men against the light, which makes them appear as two black figures. The film thus not only underlines, if not intensifies, the racial belonging of the African American athlete, making him appear fully black, but it also symbolically equates his white coach to an African American - arguably for his support of Owens. While accentuating the discrimination that was promoted by the Nazis, the film does not necessarily shift the focus from American racism but rather intends to intensify it. Without a doubt, the participation of the African American athlete in the 1936 Berlin Olympic Games made many think that "the United States made a statement to the world, and specifically to Hitler, about the nature of democracy and equality";[24] yet it is clear that it was hypocritical. How could the country that was discriminating against the large African American population teach another country about freedom and democracy? Roy Wilkins, one of the representatives of the National Association for the Advancement of Colored People (NAACP), lamented:

For black Americans, there was an unmistakable irony behind the headlines: a country that denied democracy to millions of its citizens in the South was suddenly rousing itself to defend democracy thousands of miles away across the Atlantic; a country that placidly countenanced lynch ropes and faggots for Negroes was suddenly expressing horror over the persecution of minorities in Europe; a country that abominated Nazis still winked at the Ku Klux Klan and the white master race ideology of Southern Democrats. The truth was that a black person could not escape the stain of race anywhere in America.[25]

The film's contrast of racism and Nazism in the two countries is, therefore, crucial as it implicitly suggests that the spread of the Nazi ideology and the soon-to-begin Second World War aptly distracted one's attention from American racism to an even "bigger" threat, Nazism.

Yet unlike most Americans in the 1930s-40s, *Race* does not forget the problem of racial discrimination in the U.S. Having won four gold medals at the 1936 Summer Olympics,[26] Owens is shown proudly standing on a pedestal, while the American anthem is playing. Ironically, while Owens trained hard to perform at the Games and represent the United States, the country itself does not recognize him as an equal member of society. Yet at the Olympics, Owens undoubtedly managed to prove to the whole world that a black person can achieve high results, too, thus giving hope for future success and equality to all representatives of the African American community. The words of the real Owens aptly corroborate this argument: "I am proud that I am an American. . . . Maybe more people will now realize that the Negro is trying to do his full part as an American citizen."[27]

Recognition of Owens' achievements, however, did not come in the 1930s-40s. The film skillfully comments on this poignant issue towards the end, when Owens attends a dinner held in his honor. At the entrance to the dinner, Owens and his wife are stopped by a butler and asked to use the service entrance. As Owens and his wife walk to the service entrance, the film adds: "The White House never publicly acknowledged Owens, or his success in the 1936 Olympics."[28]

Like the majority of other films about sport, *Race* attempts to make a statement that "politics has no place in sport,"[29] particularly by centering on such a grandiose sporting event as the Olympic Games and eventually presenting images of a fair competition, friendship, and equality on the field, which underlines the power of sport to, at least temporarily, eliminate multiple problems, including racial inequality. At the same time, the film quite overtly suggests that in the 1930s-40s, politics did intervene in sports and although Owens was allowed to perform as part of the American team, neither he as an athlete nor his sporting achievements were recognized by the country. Race was the key issue in the 1930s-40s, including in the sporting world. The ambiguity of the film's title also seems to suggest that: while for Owens a "race" was part of a competition, his belonging to a specific human "race" made it particularly hard for him to participate in and win various contests, ultimately advancing his career in sport. Although Owens' success was evident, his skin color, like a veil, made it invisible to the majority of people, and the only manifestations of public acknowledgement were, according to the film, such rare moments as when a white boy in an elevator awkwardly asked for the athlete's autograph. *Race* concludes with the inscription – "In 1990, Jesse was awarded a congressional gold medal in posthumous recognition for being 'An Olympic hero and an American hero every day of his life'"[30] – that once again draws the audience's attention to the fact that in the 1930s American society could never accept Owens as a sporting hero due to its racist views.

"A Black Man in White Baseball":[31] The Story of Jackie Robinson in Brian Helgeland's 42 (2013)

Another important figure in American sport in the 1940s America was Jackie Robinson. At the age of twenty-six, Robinson joined the Negro Leagues but soon was noticed by the Brooklyn Dodgers[32] and eventually became the first African American to be an official member of a white baseball team. Robinson's story of success was as tough as Owens' and was recently reflected in Brian Helgeland's *42* (2013).

Although the film was criticized for its inability to "unearth the roots of Robinson's strength of character"[33] as well as for its tendency to "select the superficial and easy over the complex and, at times, unpleasant paradox of race, talent, and prejudice in post-war American sport,"[34] it still managed to capture the racist era of 1940s America and the place of black athletes in sport. Like *Race*, *42* also provides glimpses into racism that existed both on and off the field. Thus, the audience witnesses white baseball players (particularly those who are from the South) who refuse to play with or against the African American, the indignation of a white crowd that does not want to see a black person on the field, the crowd's refusal to applaud Robinson (portrayed by Chadwick Boseman) when he scores, and the judge who nullifies Robinson's scoring of a run. Finally, the film highlights the existence of public toilets available only for whites.

Yet the film's primary advantage is its exclusive commentary on the state of sport in post-war America. Indeed, while *Race* reveals the attitude of the U.S. to the problem of racism before the country conducted a military intervention in Europe, *42* illustrates the situation after Nazism had been defeated. In this respect, the film's contention is that even after having fought the war against oppression in Europe, some white Americans remained racially intolerant to African Americans. The film definitely acknowledges U.S.'s "victory over fascism in Germany" and the necessity of having "the victory over racism at home;"[35] yet such an intention only seems to be acknowledged but, in principle, it is never fulfilled. Just like in the 1930s, in the 1940s the black athletes had to continue to fight for the eradication of racist attitudes in sport. Therefore, it is unsurprising that 42 includes multiple scenes that depict the intolerance of whites, frequently manifested in Robinson being called a "nigger"[36] and his being told that he should go back to the "jungles."[37] Robinson's hard work as an African American player included not only his physical training but also his attempts to numb himself to the constant verbal assault that was spewed upon him.

The film also provides an interesting commentary on the reason for allowing the inclusion of an African American player in a white team, a purely financial one. Unlike *Race* that portrays the relationship between Owens and his coach as friendship, 42 displays the motive of an economic profit rather explicitly, when Brooklyn Dodgers general manager and part owner Branch Rickey (portrayed by Harrison Ford) explains his interest in making Robinson part of the team: "Dollars aren't black-and-white, they're green."[38] Introducing "a black man in white baseball,"[39] the manager of the team clearly does not aim at fighting racism on the field but is only interested in the team's victory. Despite that mercantile interest, it is, however, worth mentioning that Robinson is viewed as, first and foremost, a valuable baseball player, at least by the coach, Leo Durocher (portrayed by Christopher Meloni), who cannot bear any racism within his team: "I don't care if he is yellow, or black, or has stripes like a zebra! If Robinson can help us win, and everything I've seen says he can, then he is gonna play on this ball club! Like it! Lump it! Make your minds up to it! Because he's coming!"[40] Paradoxically, even Branch Rickey values Robinson as a player: desiring to get more money from the upcoming games, Rickey particularly counts on Robinson because he understands that Robinson is the best player on the team. Although it is worth mentioning that Rickey believed in it not because he thought Robinson was a *talented* player but because he was convinced that Robinson's *racial belonging* guaranteed the player's outstanding physical capabilities.[41]

Acknowledging the success of Robinson on the field and thus finishing the film on a positive note, 42 to a certain extent distorts history. Robinson's achievements in such a "white" sport as baseball, indeed, deserve attention; the fact that he managed to succeed already in the 1940s as an African-American is clearly a very rare case. The successful story of Robinson (although considering the racism that Robinson had to face, it is highly problematic to call this story "successful"), as represented in 42, of course, should not be applied to every African American in the 1940s. Furthermore, despite the fact that the film attempts to balance the racism aimed at Robinson, on the one hand, and his acceptance by a white team, by a white coach, and by white fans, on the other hand, it is clear that the life of Robinson or any other African American was full of racial prejudices. Robinson understood it very well and therefore continued to fight for racial equality after he stopped playing professional baseball. Elliott Abramson writes about the crucial facts from Robinson's life upon which 42 remains silent: "If I could have added material to the movie, I would have given some indication of the massive amount of civil rights and community work Robinson did after retiring from baseball. It is not frivolous to say that in some ways his real career was postbaseball. He marched with King; he played basketball with kids, white and black."[42] Jules Tygiel sums up the main qualities of Robinson:

> In Robinson, Rickey had uncovered not only an outstanding baseball player, but a figure of charisma and leadership. For blacks, Robinson became a symbol of pride and dignity; to whites, he represented a type of black man far removed from prevailing stereotypes, whom they could not help but respect. He would not fade into obscurity after retirement as most athletes do. Robinson remained an active advocate of civil rights causes and Afro-American interests.[43]

Just like Owens, Robinson was an example of success and justice to many African Americans. Robinson broke stereotypes and made a major contribution to the fight for equality and against racism, both in sport and in the United States in general. In 42, Rickey once shares with Robinson that he saw a boy imitating the actions of Robinson on the field – "a little white boy, pretending he is a black man."[44] Although this sounds rather shocking to both Rickey and Robinson, the actions of that boy prophesy the most significant change in the relationship between sport and racial politics that started to take place in post-war America, when the first African American player became part of Major League Baseball.

Conclusion

The abolition of slavery that took place in 1865 guaranteed physical freedom to the black people in the United States, yet it did not give them civil rights. The severe racism that African Americans faced after the abolition of slavery lasted for the next hundred years. During that time, the African American population was deprived of those basic rights that could help them be equal members of society. Inequality could be seen literally in every sphere – from politics to economy and beyond.

Being unable to receive the education they wanted from which to build a career of which they dreamt, African Americans also faced injustice in professional spheres, including sport.

Although there were talented sportsmen among African Americans, racial segregation that explicitly existed in U.S. sport did not allow black athletes to be part of the national team and become American sport legends. Only a few sportsmen drew attention of white fans at the end of the nineteenth and the beginning of the twentieth centuries. Politics were interwoven with sport during those years and the racist ideology did not allow talented black athletes to develop professionally. Yet with the successful performances of Owens and Robinson in the 1930s-40s, sport in the United States arguably started to experience a major transformation. And although the two African American athletes could not eradicate racism in sport as a whole and in the U.S. particularly, their will for victory undoubtedly made many whites look at blacks and see them, first and foremost, as human beings. It also became symbolic for millions of other African Americans to never give up in their fight for civil rights. The 1930s-40s were also a crucial time because the emergence and the ultimate defeat of the Nazi regime influenced a number of Americans in their attitude to and treatment of the oppressed. However, being opponents of Nazism, many white Americans still remained deeply racist towards the African American population. Yet the shift for the better started to take place in the 1930s-40s. One certainly cannot talk about equality as such; yet the examples of Owens and Robinson – both from real life and from *Race* and *42* – demonstrate that in the sporting world, racial equality began to root.

Notes

[1] The problem of racial and ethnic discrimination in sport in the United States concerns numerous racial and ethnic minorities, among which are Native Americans, Latin Americans, and African Americans. This chapter, however, focuses only on the latter.

[2] Pope, S.W. "Decentering 'Race' and (Re)presenting 'Black' Performance in Sport History: Basketball and Jazz in American Culture, 1920-1950." *Deconstructing Sport History: A Postmodern Analysis*, edited by Murray G. Phillips. State U of New York P, 2006. 151.

[3] Nauright, John, and David K. Wiggins. "Race." *Routledge Companion to Sports History*, edited by S.W. Pope and John Nauright. Routledge, 2010. 148.

[4] Ibid., 150.

[5] Ibid., 148-151.

[6] Ibid., 152-153.

[7] Thompson, Richard. *Race and Sport*. Oxford UP, 1964. 4.

[8] Nauright, John, and David K. Wiggins. "Race." *Routledge Companion to Sports History*, edited by S.W. Pope and John Nauright. Routledge, 2010. 157.

[9] Angelini, Eileen. "1946 Montreal: Home to Two of the World's Greatest Sports Heroes."

[10] Horne, John, Alan Tomlinson, Garry Whannel, and Kath Woodward. *Understanding Sport: A Socio-Cultural Analysis*. 2nd ed. Routledge, 2013. 95.

[11] Ibid.

[12] Ibid.

[13] Ibid.

[14] Ibid.

[15] Zirin, Dave. *A People's History of Sports in the United States: 250 Years of Politics, Protest, and Play*. The New P, 2008. 73.

[16] Ibid., 74.

[17] Qtd. in Caponi-Tabery, Gena. *Jump for Joy: Jazz, Basketball & Black Culture in 1930s America*. U of Massachusetts P, 2008. 39.

[18] Ibid., 45.

[19] *Race*. Directed by Stephen Hopkins, performances by Stephan James, Jason Sudeikis, Eli Goree, and Shanice Banton, Focus Features, 2016.

[20] Ibid.

[21] Ibid.

[22] Qtd. in Zirin, Dave. *A People's History of Sports in the United States: 250 Years of Politics, Protest, and Play*. The New P, 2008. 76.

[23] Zirin, Dave. *A People's History of Sports in the United States: 250 Years of Politics, Protest, and Play*. The New P, 2008. 76.

[24] Caponi-Tabery, Gena. *Jump for Joy: Jazz, Basketball & Black Culture in 1930s America*. U of Massachusetts P, 2008. 35.

[25] Qtd. in Caponi-Tabery, Gena. *Jump for Joy: Jazz, Basketball & Black Culture in 1930s America*. U of Massachusetts P, 2008. 35-36.

[26] Zirin, Dave. *A People's History of Sports in the United States: 250 Years of Politics, Protest, and Play*. The New P, 2008. 74.

[27] Qtd. in Caponi-Tabery, Gena. *Jump for Joy: Jazz, Basketball & Black Culture in 1930s America*. U of Massachusetts P, 2008. 44.

[28] *Race*. Directed by Stephen Hopkins, performances by Stephan James, Jason Sudeikis, Eli Goree, and Shanice Banton, Focus Features, 2016.

[29] Ibid.

[30] Ibid.

[31] *42*. Directed by Brian Helgeland, performances by Chadwick Boseman, Harrison Ford, Nicole Beharie, and Lucas Black, Warner Bros. Pictures, 2013.

[32] Zirin, Dave. *What's My Name, Fool? Sports and Resistance in the United States*. Haymarket Books, 2005. 42.

[33] Hardy, Nickolas. "*42: The Jackie Robinson Story*." Rev. of *42*, dir. Brian Helgeland. *Journal of Sport History*, 41.1, Spring 2014, 147. https://muse.jhu.edu/article/544526. Accessed 12 Feb. 2017.

[34] Ibid., 148.

[35] *42*. Directed by Brian Helgeland, performances by Chadwick Boseman, Harrison Ford, Nicole Beharie, and Lucas Black, Warner Bros. Pictures, 2013.

[36] Ibid.

[37] Ibid.

[38] Ibid.

[39] Ibid.

[40] Ibid.

[41] This is a pivotal issue that has already been widely discussed by multiple scholars. John Entine, for example, speculates that the dominance of black athletes in sport today raises two main questions: "Are race and genetics significant components of the stunning and undeniable dominance of black athletes? Or is the notion nothing but white voodoo designed to banish blacks to the modern plantation – the track, the basketball court, and the football field – while whites control the boardrooms?" (4) Such racist issues have also been raised in the 1930s, when the phenomenal achievements of black athletes at the 1936 Olympics were explained as follows: "The Negro excels in the events he does because he is closer to the primitive than the white man. It was not long ago that his ability to sprint and jump was a life-and-death matter to him in the jungle. His muscles are pliable, and his easy-going disposition is a valuable aid to the mental and physical relaxation that a runner and jumper must have" (Cromwell qtd. in Caponi-Tabery 49). The black British athlete Harry F.V. Edward commented on that theory: "For years it has been said that Negroes can sing and dance. From now on we will hear the platitude that all Negroes can run and jump" (qtd. in Caponi-Tabery 49).

[42] Abramson, Elliott. "*42: The Jackie Robinson Story* Written and Directed by Brian Helgeland." Rev. of *42*, dir. Brian Helgeland. *NINE: A Journal of Baseball History and Culture*, 22.1, Fall 2013, 179. https://muse.jhu.edu/article/538600. Accessed 12 Feb. 2017.

[43] Tygiel, Jules. "A Lone Negro in the Game: Jackie Robinson's Rookie Season." *Major Problems in American Sport History*, edited by Steven A Riess, Wadsworth Cengage Learning, 1997, 390.

[44] *42*. Directed by Brian Helgeland, performances by Chadwick Boseman, Harrison Ford, Nicole Beharie, and Lucas Black, Warner Bros. Pictures, 2013.

Bloodsport:
Black Athletes, White Spectators, and the United States Racial Imagination

Jayson Baker

Representations of the boxing arena in U.S. culture disclose conflicting attitudes and feelings regarding race relations, citizenship rights, and upward mobility. The boxing image in popular culture often frames contenders from poor and working-class black, Latino, emerging immigrant, and established white groups battling each other. Fictional and real depictions of boxing dramatize thinning and thickening racial borders that mirror and provoke shifts in the way the national culture thinks about race. Boxing rings illuminate the U.S. racial imagination by requiring singular winners and losers, rarely a draw. Losers are literally "knocked out," technically defeated, which usually means the contender is too bloodied to compete, or unanimously judged by a scorecard of body blows. If defeated, the contender frequently re-trains to re-assert his or her fitness for public recognition and the winner re-enters the ring to maintain his or her status. The winner achieves championship glory and the bout's purse, and with victory comes assumptions the champ can exceed hierarchies delimiting mobility based on race, class, ethnicity, and other forms of marginalized social positions. The champ's wealth and fame imaginatively enable a kind of social transcendence whereas defeat suggests more barriers yet to overcome. The dichotomous winner-loser outcome weaves into national narratives explaining politically disenfranchised, economically excluded, and culturally degraded groups eager to get bloodied in pursuit of full citizenship rights and privileges only possible through wealth and fame. Fights thereby situate audiences as sport spectators negotiating representations of groups historically and presently denied full citizenship rights agitating a rethinking of race and privilege.

Take *Rocky* (1976) as just one popular example of staged racial conflicts through images of a first-generation Italian-American and African-American Apollo Creed, who Rocky later befriends. The once rivals become buddies in *Rocky II* (1981) in which Apollo helps Rocky defeat Clubber Lang, a street thug played by Mr. T whose self-styled Mohawk punches up his character's villainy and harnesses centuries-old white fear. Racial borders thin in one respect, through Rocky and Creed's friendship, and thicken in another as Clubber and Rocky's verbal insults intensify and anticipate physical exchanges staged in the arena. The first two *Rocky* films manipulate racial borders in post-Civil Rights eras to describe white-black relations as enemy-friends. In *Rocky III* (1982), Sylvester Stallone distances Balboa's Italian heritage and absorbs the hero figure into a fuller image of whiteness. Rocky transforms from an ethnicized, working-class underdog into an image of American power "with ever-broadening pectoral muscles in global conflict."[1] With the assistance of Apollo Creed in *Rocky III*, the twosome confront Russian contender Ivan Drago whose blond-haired crew cut and blued-eyed whiteness vilifies the Soviet Union in a homogeneous image at the height of the Cold War. In *Creed* (2015), Stallone's latest film, Rocky becomes a father figure to Adonis Creed, Apollo's troubled son, and prepares him for a bout with Pretty Ricky Conlan, played by bi-racial English boxer Tony Bellew. *Creed* redraws racial differences through Balboa's white paternalistic benevolence willing to mentor Adonis because boxing is "in his blood." Stallone's paternalism suggests a posture where whites support a youthful up and comer whose time has finally come, as long as Adonis has the endorsement of the white establishment standing behind him. In present-day globalism, *Creed* illustrates domestic unities and international divisions conjoining and splintering racial lines. Sports culture "is a complex cultural form [operating] on many levels simultaneously, gaining new meanings as they are experienced and read within different historical, political, and social contexts".[2] This brief overview of the *Rocky* franchise illustrates how the boxing image iterates as cultural contexts change and thus "the ring" reports shifts in the way many imagine race.

Boxing-themed narratives mirror and shape racial attitudes regarding national citizenship and cultural belonging, a point made clear to me as a teacher-scholar of American Culture Studies and faculty chaperone for the Communication Department's trip to New York City. One of our excursions accompanied students to the Lincoln Center production of Marco Ramirez' play *The Royale*,[3] which loosely parallels the circumstances of Jack Johnson, the first African-American heavyweight contender demonized by white publics at the onset of the 20th century. Jack Johnson entered the white imagination when he rivaled Jim Jeffries for the heavyweight championship in 1910. Jeffries, the white champion, symbolized "the epitome of manhood, and hence of evolution" and was thought to earn an easy victory over Johnson.[4] Johnson, however, "thrashed" Jeffries setting off "waves of panic across white America" and all "theatrical replays of the bout were banned."[5] The events surrounding Jack Johnson's career and public life have since intermittently entered the public sphere: the documentary *Jack Johnson* (1970) directed by Jimmy Johnson became famously known for its musical score by the inter-racial jazz tandem of Miles Davis and John

McLaughlin. In 2004, *Unforgiveable Blackness: The Rise and Fall of Jack Johnson* (2004) features Ken Burns' directorial signature editing sepia tone and black and white photography, an aesthetic re-mediating the past for present audiences. Ramirez' play fictionalizes Jay "The Sport" Jackson's ascension to fame in pursuit of the world heavyweight title and championship purse in the early twentieth century. "The Sport" (Khris Davis) embodies the cultural contradictions of black-athletic achievement in a nation with traditions seeking to preserve racial hierarchies as part of Jim Crow-era disenfranchisement. As Jay eliminates fellow black competitors, he increasingly attracts hostility and violence from white audiences and communities.

My academic training assisted in locating the play's thematic exposition and close reading theatrical form, but I also experienced the play as a white father of an adopted African-American son. My partner is African-American too and thus our family's racial differences are stark. When not in my son's presence, many colleagues and acquaintances assume my daily life navigates the comfortable whiteness of suburbia with few multicultural encounters, and it does. In turn, my son is one of a few black boys present in his public sphere. One activity we frequently enjoy includes casual sport-play in the yard or at a nearby playground, and I coach his baseball and football teams. My son thrives on athletic performance and the attention he receives from our largely white community. As a parent, sensing *The Royale's* themes of black-athletic achievements and reactionary white publics against the backdrop of early-twentieth-century racism deeply moved me. Rachel Chavkin's direction dithers the line separating the theatrical audience from sports spectators. Fear swept over me as I observed the way *The Royale* describes racial hierarchies unmoored from the past, loosened from a temporality imagined as bygone, and now actively refracting and informing the present. The play directly counters feel-good assumptions written into popular culture by deploying inter-racial buddy performances showcasing a kind of sham equality – the stuff of Hollywood fiction like Rocky and Apollo or Rocky and Adonis, and the human-interest stories in sports entertainment news stressing inter-racial unities scrubbing clean racism past and present. Popular sport media tend to whitewash or elide real attitudes and feelings undergirding racism and discrimination in the United States.

The Royale entangles a racial past-presence and deliberately confuses temporal borders and histories. The opposition created through the play's black athletes and largely white spectators re-stages racial hierarchies articulated through the enjoyment of viewing. In a different racialized context and time, Frantz Fanon reminds us of "the black man's dimension of being-for-others . . . to exist absolutely for others . . . [and how years of degradation urge many to] position themselves in relation to the civilizing language: i.e., the metropolitan culture."[6] Manhattan's Lincoln Center transforms into a boxing arena resembling the way sports complexes fill with mostly white patrons gazing and looking at brown-skinned athletic performances. The work happening takes place on stage, in the arena, and on the field of play, while leisure classes gawk, cheer, or shout abusive, vitriolic slurs – some racially coded – others seemingly less so. Sport culture distributes viewpoints through which the black body performs for whites momentarily seated as comfortable classes "taking in" the bout – on the other side of the ropes, viewing from the other side of the performer-spectator border. The black athlete supplies, the white spectator demands: an economic model of contemporary sports culture. The black body in theatrical spaces and sports complexes thereby illuminates crises of citizenship and belonging.

Audiences of *The Royale* experience the contemporary national crises embedded in bleakly different perceptions of race, citizenship, and privilege. I label the current crisis the cultural logic of Obama-Trayvon, or how a transcendent figure like President Obama inspires white publics to deepen racial divisions and exact racial violence under various legal protections: property rights, gun rights, vague fears reversing perpetrator and victim roles, and so forth. Trayvon Martin, Eric Gardner, Michael Brown, Freddy Gray, Walter Scott, Tamir Rice, Tanisha Anderson, Sandra Bland, and many other victims of police and community brutality enter the national consciousness by way of the short-lived media segment. The murder of nine Christians at Emanuel African Methodist Episcopal Church harkens a kind of trans-historical violence evoking the Civil Rights era, which traces its roots to the Civil War and Abolitionist movements. Contemporary cultural attitudes about race relations illuminate through demonstrations celebrating the Confederate Flag under the pretext of preserving the "heritage" of slave states. Honoring the Confederacy throughout the Obama Presidency, whose very image signals a willingness to foreclose antebellum culture to the past, reports a desire to re-trench racial hierarchies in the present. *The Royale* intervenes the current context with its themes of "blacklash" or retribution motivated by perceptions that groups historically disenfranchised have somehow usurped lines of division. This boxing narrative resonates with the way many imagine Barack Obama's ascension to the nation's highest political office. Jay "The Sport" Jackson's athletic prowess breaches racial borders and circulates within white consciousness too. "The power of blackness," Toni Morrison writes in *Playing in the Dark*, animates the white imagination's "social fears."[7] Within the context of the play, racial borders must be re-instantiated triggering acts of violence by whites in black communities. By activating the past, *The Royale*'s plot tracing the aspirations of the first would-be black heavyweight champion of the world circulates in the imaginations of the theatrical crowd and intervenes contemporary attitudes about race shaping the national psyche.

Spectator theories usefully explain the subject-object dynamics activating the audience's imagination. Film scholar André Bazin explains how theater is based on a "reciprocal awareness of the presence of audience and actor, but only as it relates to the performance. The theater acts on us by virtue of our participation in a theatrical action across the footlights . . ."[8] For Bazin, audiences and actors vacillate across subject-object positions: spectator subjectivity actively reads movements and stagecraft informing and transforming thought. The actor, aware of his or her objectification, solicits the audience, returns the gaze and repositions spectators drawing them into the discourse happening onstage. Bazin limits the engagement to the performance and does not imagine how theater or sports arena encounters interact with thought outside the entertainment venue. The mostly white audience at the Lincoln Center carries subjective engagements to the Newhouse Theater stage where they grapple with racial hierarchies happening inside and outside the opulent Lincoln Center complex. When spectators imaginatively cross theatrical footlights, directors, playwrights, and performers evoke public thought and feeling harbored by many within a given society. The theater and theatergoers are not outside culture, and sports arenas and sports fans cannot be divorced from historical contexts surrounding the game. Black cast members in *The Royale* exploit these slippages between fictional and real worlds calling spectators out of their seated positions by pointing to events outside the boxing arena shaping Jay's prospects for a better life. Manthia Diawara determines a kind of double consciousness operates through an exchange of glances for spectators: in one instance, spectators are compelled to see the racist inscription written onto African-American representation highlighting white ways of looking at black bodies.[9] Looking is a form of empowerment with the looker garnering leverage in the exchange by holding the gaze and objectifying the person in view. The viewer enjoys levels of privilege by retaining his or her subjectivity and denying subjectivity of the performer. From this theoretical and theatrical perspective, viewers partially identify and accept downgraded social positions articulated through dominant white viewpoints. Yet in another instance, spectators resist objectification of the black body as a repetition of the history of degradation written for and seen by white audiences.[10] For *The Royale*'s white audiences, looking at black performances creates a double lens by adopting white viewpoints looking at black bodies and staging black opposition to this very mode of disempowerment.

The Royale articulates empowered and disempowered positions between black athlete-performers and white audience-spectators through *mise en scène* confining, restricting, and "boxing" in aspirations, and a lighting scheme emulating early photography's flashbulb whiteness piercing the set and audience shrouded in the blackened theater. Through the darkness, audiences gaze at the racial degradation and cultural limitations many African-Americans confront and contend. Max (John Lavalle), the only white cast member, plays roles as announcer and promoter, and signifies several white positions as sports journalists and the audience. Max handholds the audience through his onstage and off-stage announcements orienting the crowd onto "The Sport's" sculpted and stripped down black body. The play begins with a heavy punching bag hanging in the middle of the ring with a pin spot[11] whitening Max in the darkness. Max focuses the audiences' attention: "Ladies and gentlemen, the fight you've paid your hard-earned green for" keys spectators to Fish (McKinley Belcher III) "with a wingspan of a mighty black albatross."[12] Max promptly directs the arena again: "Ladies and gentlemen, the man you came for, the man who casts a shadow in the dark, Your Negro Heavyweight Champion, you know him, you love him, Jay 'The Sport' Jackson!"[13] Max racially codes the athletes to distinguish black performativity happening on stage from white subjective viewing positions ready to enjoy the bout. On-stage clapping (clap-clap-clap, clap-clap-clap, clap-clap-clap) performed by Jay, Fish, Max, and Wynton (Clark Peters), "The Sport's" manager and trainer, interrupt the introductions. The pronounced clapping rhythms enter and exit the stage piercing and fading from the room, and emulate short-lived sports fan applause. This temporary praise confuses pleasures of viewing as an expression of inclusion when spectating repeats power relations happening outside the ring. Max signals the audience's empowered position by racializing Jay as an object of their possession with the introductory idiom, "Your Negro Heavyweight Champion." The announcer then turns to animalize the up and coming Fish as a "mighty black albatross" threatening the crowd and their favorite surrogate charged with denying black-athletic achievement in the ring.

This pugilistic battle participates in national discourses exposing racial and ethnic attitudes drawing white-black divisions based in perceptions of "blood." Ramirez stresses the interplay between blood and sport in the opening scene when Jay competes with Fish. Audiences experience and interpret shouts of "blood" following and anticipating each body blow in the opening scene, and later when Jay's spars with Fish to prepare for the title fight with the white champion, Bixby. "Blood" therefore signposts each landed punch suggesting a racial betrayal when Jay pummels his much younger and slighter opponent. Announcing "blood" symbolizes a kind of kinship violation as Jay beats down a fellow black boxer *en route* to the world championship title. When Jay rises, Fish falls. Deborah Waire Post observes how early-twentieth-century racial viewpoints were largely a matter of "caste than class and that, unlike other caste systems, it is not cultural, but biological."[14] Opening scenes of Jay and Fish initiate the "blacklash" theme by way of a fight contained within blackness: if Jay wins it must come at the expense of Fish's aspirations. Ramirez's black-only ring divides performers from the largely white audience who are surrogates for an arena crowd. Blood functions to legitimize divisions, unities, and betrayals within and across race. This battle within black blood pronounces the zero-sum game thematic narrating ways Jay's upward social mobility in turn delimits Fish's opportunities to improve his circumstances. *The Royale* segregates athletes and audience members whose history of separation finds origins in biological arguments justifying black inferiority based on tainted strains of African blood. Henry Louis Gates Jr. explains how animalistic imagery signifies another way biological claims born in blood dehumanize the black body: "Blacks were most commonly represented on the [Great Chain of Being] either as the 'lowest' of the human races, or as first cousin to the ape."[15] Blood serves to rationalize divisions within the so-called human family, suggesting members of African-American communities are less than human and thus should not be accorded full citizenship rights. Bloodline inferiority establishes a legal architecture legitimizing the establishment of miscegeny and Jim Crow laws working to separate race in the public sphere, to include the establishment of various Negro leagues.

Athletes and audiences reproduce strictures limiting African-American social mobility happening outside the ring. Staging Jay and Fish as black-only rivals orients the objectified black body for whiteness that never directly enters the ring. The contenders address white absences by hailing the audience seated in theatrical darkness. *The Royale* hones its focus on intra-racial bouts with whiteness on the periphery; fights appear contained within blackness dramatize black-on-black violence as viewing pleasures for whites. Jay therefore focuses on tormenting Fish, "Hey kid, how many rounds you want?" Later ridiculing his opponent by calling him "Break-a-Sweat" to demean Fish's fitness as a black heavyweight contender.[16] In turn, Fish attempts to convince himself of his worth, "Don't Lock, Knees Bent."[17] Fear and intimidation diminishes Fish's self-willed confidence in this black-only bout. Functioning as a kind of white replacement, Jay receives the crowd's support and appears insurmountable by already occupying Fish's thoughts before the bout begins. The opening round draws exchanges between Jay and Fish with the young rival landing a few punches prompting Jay to return fire with a series of forceful combinations. "The Sport" lands lefts and rights drawing a rush of blood in Fish's mouth with Max following: "And ladies and gentleman, that's The Sport we know."[18] Racial lines retrench in *The Royale* by displacing whiteness to the auditorium seats where they support and are protected from violence they endorse.

Without a white representative contending in the ring, the Lincoln Center audience experiences a double consciousness when Chavkin externalizes thoughts and feelings of black bodies fighting each other. The spectator's subject position shifts momentarily to the objectified black body's point of view. Jay desires to beat up other blacks so he can finally get a title bout with the current white heavyweight champion, Bixby, whose recent retirement reports another form of white absence from the ring. A ghostly white specter haunts the arena and seeks to ensure black disenfranchisement. Fish's fear and uncertainty complicates white viewing positions by supplying a sympathetic though overmatched rival's perspective whose odds of winning seem impossible given Jay's swaggering brutishness. Audiences negotiate Jay and Fish's thoughts and body movements absorbing each other's punches, a tension underscored with Max reinforcing white vantage points. For Jay, Fish stands in the way of ultimate glory: to face the white champion and achieve victory enlarges his standing even as black-only champ – an advantaged though still occluded position. When the young upstart Fish tastes his own blood, the announcer again makes a point to align white audiences with the pugilist attacking his younger black counterpart: "that's 'The Sport' we know." The double entendre signals white spectator approval of Jay Jackson's boxing prowess. Though in another way, Max's narration reports the racial dynamics happening in arenas throughout the nation situating black bodies battling each other while whites view from seemingly inaccessible locations. These instances of white displacement thereby shape a double consciousness for spectators rooting for a black surrogate to deliver knock out blows restricting Fish's possibilities. "That's 'The Sport' we know" also powerfully suggests the spectacle of black-on-black sport violence restricted to the ring, stadium, or arena maintains unassailable white vantage points. The ring ironically restages racial hierarchies seemingly diminished by the crowd's approval of Jay beating up Fish.

Mise en scène in *The Royale* describes the social strictures happening inside and outside the arena too. The direction compresses the boxing ring cornering Jay and Fish to small portions of the set, with the audience reoriented as sports spectators in the darkness. Fish expresses another perspective to *The Royale*'s themes from the position of a young black boxer rivaling the established black-only champion. The dichotomous winner-take-all stakes endorsed by whites refract in black communities as well: there can only be one winner. Even in team sports "Most Valuable Player" awards illuminate individual accomplishments above team victories. Sports thereby become a kind of metaphor for individualized social power over the community in United States culture. There are only so many empowered social positions and thus Fish needs only to beat Jay to own "the sport," to improve his prospects beyond the arena, ostensibly the terrain policed by white audiences. Chavkin's direction splits the ring hampering the movements of the half-naked, black-on-black spectacle of violence and tightens the space in which the black fight occurs. Advantaged positions are suggested by further distancing whiteness to the margins, narrowing and foreclosing the bout to a restricted space on the mostly darkened stage. The initial round economizes the theme of black-on-black athletic violence as white spectacle at the expense of Fish. Jay and Fish bob and weave, jab and breathe, punches land, and the ensemble shouts "OOH!" Flits of pleasure blear through white flashes of light leaving Fish limp and exasperated at the end of the first round.

This blood sport narrative challenges audience and reader perception of race based in biological rationales enabling political, legal, cultural, and social divisions across whiteness and blackness. In *Against Race*, Paul Gilroy observes the way sport spectating "[fudges] the relationship between entertainment and politics, and [produces] the most potent and enduring of racial archetypes."[19] Sport stories deploy hero narratives embedding codes of individualism supporting cultural attitudes reducing large-scale social problems like racism into easily decipherable personal attributes and ambitions. Jay's ascension is a personal one whose ramifications if achieved resonate with the "overcoming all obstacles" ethos assigned to American heroism stories, yet his accomplishments threaten African-American communities throughout the United States. Jay's bravado, machismo, and enthusiasm for violence showcase a boastful persona weaving together attributes of an intently focused champ with a bloodthirsty villain white audiences fear. Yet, audiences may read Jay and Fish another way. Black studies scholar Manthia Diawara identifies how "the image of the disciplined and punished black man"[20] supplies pleasure for white audiences by making the black male "less threatening."[21] When Jay eviscerates Fish with blow after blow, the black-only champ's successes while accelerating his own chance for fame and fortune deny the fortunes of a member of his own racial group. Jay's story services two cultural narratives: one resembling heroism which usually accompanies wealth and recognition minimizing racism as a real stricture impeding black upward mobility; and two, Jay's willingness to work on the behalf of the white establishment seeking to ensure its empowered status within a racial hierarchy born in blood.

The rounds in *The Royale* connote the perpetual struggle for members of disenfranchised communities in continuous pursuit of athletic achievement to improve their economic prospects: an imagined end-around sidestepping the failed promises of political, legal, economic, and cultural equality. Yet with each victory or record-breaking milestone the financial empires of sport industry owners embolden. Max again announces, "Round Seven! And Jay 'The Sport' Jackson comes into the ring with newfound energy." Jay continues taunting Fish by once again hailing the audience, "Y'all came to see The Sport, huh? Y'all came to see The Sport?" Blow after blow land on Fish and he screams, "Ohmygod . . . Fists, Eyes, God, Blood." Jay delivers another combination and the ensemble returns, "Ooh!" Then Fish yells again, "Blood." The stagecraft follows Jay talking in the third person: "It's a shame what you 'bout to do, Jay. It's a damn shame…" Fish again, "Blood." The ensemble, "Ooh." Max concludes, "THE SPORT HAS DONE IT AGAIN!!! Laying his challenger out, flat on the canvas."[22] The interplay of Jay and Fish's internal monologues weave together the double consciousness entwining subject-object gazes. Jay speaks for himself and for audience members claiming the need to decidedly defeat his opponent to elevate his chances to fight

Bixby. "Y'all come to see the sport" aligns spectator perspectives with the black hero's ambition to knock out the black competitor standing in the way of Jay's better rivals. An eager crowd watches Jay victimize Fish in service to "The Sport." "Fists, Eyes, God, Blood" announces the racial betrayal when one black body exacts violence on another; Fish performs an oral scorecard accounting for each punch. Shouts of "blood" remind audiences of the racial borders demarking the ring from the audience's temporarily protected position. Fish's screams resituate spectators in support of the champ who seeks to knock out his contender to improve his chances at becoming world heavyweight champion.

With Fish out of contention, Chavkin directs the specter of whiteness to haunt the ring by way of Jay imagining winning a bout with Bixby. Confronting whiteness begins in Jay's imagination, a mental exercise of sorts. To embolden "The Sport's" chances, Wynton hires Fish as Jay's sparring partner in preparation for the world championship contest the black-only champion has long sought. The White Man's Worker's Union, Liberty's Guardians, and The Society for the Preservation of True American Culture have stymied Jay's boxing career through protest, back channel collusion, and Jim Crow-era legislation. The public groundswell energized and mobilized by a few special interest organizations alludes to contemporary conflicts across race and the many modes deployed to preserve and reinstate racial hierarchies. These social, cultural, and political organizations exist in *The Royale*'s theatrical world to entrench borders and restrict Jay to the black-only ring: the appearance of social borders thinning within the sport activates white fear of diminishing lines of division outside the arena. Like the real whiteness encircling and peering onto the stage, the empowered social institutions delimiting black achievement, athletic and otherwise, hauntingly surround the room but never appear in the ring. Max then presses Jay by asking him if boxing prowess is in his blood: "why is it the coloreds have taken to boxing?"[23] The question evokes the savage, violent, and bloodthirsty image characterizing black men that Henry Louis Gates, Jr. identifies as endemic to black representation in United States culture. Descendants of former slaves have the "natural" interest and ability to excel in sport violence, and have the taste for blood. So, Jay rebuts Max's association, "Oldest sport in the world, ain't it? Poorest at least."[24] Jackson's rebuff challenges Max's effort to align black-athletic achievements to biological arguments by pointing out how class similarities draw members of poor communities to the sport.

Yet Max pushes his argument suggesting an inherent bloodlust intrinsic to black experiences motivate participation in boxing; "do you think your people have a predilection for fighting?" Jay then slyly refutes Max: "I don't know about that. Looking out them first ten rows . . . I'd say your people have a predilection for watching?"[25] Max's retort registers as an offence by undermining Jay's success as only possible because of his biological inferiority. Bixby is a champ because of his skill while Jay achieves greatness because of his biological weakness. Jay recognizes the cultural contradictions of black-athletic achievement: the spectacle of brutality unique to the black body strikes the white imagination and drives their attendance at black boxing rings across the nation. Thus, Jay punches back too through his quip reassigning white interest in black-on-black sport violence as the economic motivation for black athletes. Blacks enter the ring, rival each other, and members from other disenfranchised communities for the purse put up by largely white-controlled sports industries. Without white attendances, black-only blood sports would not exist. Here again *The Royale* stresses how viewing and performing positions restage racial hierarchies redrawing social borders in the ring and in the main.

An inter-racial title bout with Bixby presents the chance for Jay to transcend borders within and beyond the ring. A black-only champion is contained, restricted by racial borders, hemmed off from full-fledged greatness – to be simply champion – no hyphen demarcating "black-only." There are no qualifiers when Jay is heavyweight champion of the world. In turn, whiteness feels at risk by the opportunity accorded blackness. Equality is perceived as a threat. The cultural, social, and economic advances of black communities consolidate in the image of the black athlete's achievement – Jay "The Sport" Jackson's superior boxing prowess therefore escapes the ring. At a press conference amplifying the racial tension the night before the championship event, Max quizzes Jay on his knowledge of violence happening outside the arena. "Are you aware that four different men were stopped at the door, and on their persons, four different firearms were confiscated. . . . Four white men, taken into custody, Sport. And it don't take much to speculate what their intentions might've been."[26] The mere prospect of a black champion in an integrated title bout ignites white mobs and gives license to threaten, intimidate, and kill members from communities perceived to usurp lines of racial division. In the boxing world of zero-sum game competitions, acknowledging the improved status of Jay Jackson as emblematic of his community must mean Bixby's potential defeat symbolizes downgraded whiteness in the bargain. The racial imagination happening within the theatrical world provokes white gangs to terrorize black communities in an effort to reverse attempts to weaken hierarchies securing white advantage.

The turning point in *The Royale* entangles intra-racial and inter-racial conflicts when Nina (Montego Glover) enters the champ's dressing room before her brother's bout with Bixby. As Jay prepares to battle Bixby, the contender's sister appears to convince Jay to stop the fight. Nina begins by informing "The Sport" of the pride the community back home feels given the champ's rise to national prominence and celebrity stature: an entire community now places its hopes on Jay to defeat Bixby as symbolic of an equal ability in the face of its unequal standing and limited resources. Nina pulls out and points to a picture of her children: "Came home with a busted lip last week. Said kids in the schoolyard didn't believe he was the nephew of Jay 'The Sport' Jackson. Said he showed 'em it runs in the blood."[27] Despite Jay's increased public recognition, members of his own family experience blacklash. Nina admonishes Jay's failure to recognize how his national fame affects black families around the nation who must fend off body blows in their community. Outside the ring, whiteness feels unencumbered by neighborhood borders and willfully terrorizes black communities. The siblings verbally spar highlighting ways Jay's success instigates white retaliatory desire: "In the middle of the title-fight championship nonsense, have you stopped to think, for one second – That you gon' up and get somebody killed?"[28] Jay: "Man said they can't sneak a toothpick into this fight. They got thirty-two checkpoints. Ain't nothing gonna happen."[29] Failing to recognize the real fear his personal story brings to bear on black publics, Nina singles out the many black communities now at risk as a result of Jay's perceived upward mobility. "Where's the checkpoints in Harlem, Jay? Where's the checkpoints in Oakland, New Orleans, Brownsville? 'Cause you know as well as I do what happens when you knock that bastard out."[30] Blacklashes erupt across different regions when sports spectators perceive the inter-racial title bout thins racial borders and provides ways for groups historically excluded from opportunities to improve their circumstances.

A sold-out crowd fills the auditorium on the night of the title bout. Max returns to amplify the winner-take-all stakes cast in blackness and present racial divisions under attack: "In these twenty feet, will decide once and for all the holder of the Title of Heavyweight Champion of either race from this day forward. So without further ado, I present your challenger . . . The Dark, Defiant Contender, The Big, Black Bringer of Retribution, The Negro Heavyweight Champion of the World . . . Jay 'The Sport' Jackson."[31] Earlier, Max assigns white interest in black athletes to the brutalism and savagery tainting black blood, but now attributes white attendance as spirited by resentment for Jay appearing in the ring. Desire for retribution operates in the spectator's imagination yet the announcer aligns these emotions to Jackson. Max's narration articulates ways the U.S. racial imagination reverses and reassigns the behavior of whites onto black communities. White groups fill the arena in fear Jay's success signals seismic shifts shaking the very foundation of deeply rooted racial hierarchies. Max again: "Out of retirement for one night and only one night. . . . Coming all the way from Massachusetts. . . . The one, the only, the Unrivaled Heavyweight Champion of the World..."[32] Ramirez stages Nina entering the ring at which point Chavkin directs a spotlight onto Jay's sister with Wynton calling out, "Fists up!"[33]

The Royale sets up audience expectations for an inter-racial title bout between Jay and Bixby only to restage the contest between Jay and

Nina – another iteration of black-on-black violence now happens within the familial bloodline. Bixby and whiteness never enter Chavkin's ring but remain in rapt attention on the peripheries of the arena. The climax and conclusion of this intra-racial bout: more white, bright, lights – the title bout – and the specters of Bixby's power replaced by Nina in the ring and the mostly white audience's bated breath. Enter Jay stripping out of his cream-colored suit displaying his black flesh against his sister's blood. The intra-racial knock-out blows performed by brother and sister circling the ring report the real inter-racial violence happening outside arenas in the 21st century present. The fight contained within the black family adds force to ways sports spectating realigns social power through viewing and performing positions. Replacing Bixby with Nina again pushes white viewpoints to the seats where white-spectator power no longer enjoys Jay and Fish's black bodies pummeling each other, but finds attentive displeasure in destroying black families. The siblings confront each other with Nina glaring at the Lincoln Center crowd for its complicity: "And, don't look at those faces. . . . Foamin' at the mouth, these people. . . . These animals."[34] Nina animalizes the crowd. The pin spot brightens Jay and Nina's athletic choreography softening "The Sport's" swagger and diminishing his optimism by acknowledging the fear he produces. Jay conceptualizes the way black communities across the United States absorb the body blows, bob and weave in an attempt to safeguard their members from white retribution.

Nina confronts the Newhouse Theater attendees interrupting the imagined barrier between spectators and performers. The champ's sister agitates passive engagements whereby viewing roles insulate audiences from any responsibility in this intra-racial drama in the ring, and inter-racial hostilities beyond the Lincoln Center. Nina transforms the audience and pulls the crowd out of the darkness re-appropriating spectators as actively taking part and encouraging racial violence as forms of pleasure. Audiences learn the championship bout with Nina standing in as the retired white champion promises levels of fame Jay would otherwise not achieve, yet the opportunity to improve his personal fortune are stacked against him with ninety percent of the bout's purse going to Bixby win or lose. The conditions in which Jay agrees to fight Bixby report another way sports spectatorship restricts the black-only champ's social and financial mobility despite appearances. Public attention illustrates easing racial barriers. "Make him earn that ninety percent," Fish bellows from ringside."[35] Nina retorts, "What happens if you get him on the floor? These people might just stand still – in shock – But they might move on you – Rip you apart, limb from limb, Eat you alive like locusts."[36] Nina's announcement highlights phony sports accolades as bogus racial tolerances disguising resentment and fear of black-athletic achievement.

Black-athletic success in arenas surrounded by largely white spectators misrecognizes applause for approval when in actuality cheers communicate racial anxiety for thinning racial borders. Max gives voice to the audience's frenzied enthusiasm: "The crowd is in-*sane* folks! Jay's circling Bixby like a Matador! Bixby's cornered like a bull. The energy in the room is *supernatural!*"[37] In a stunning series of lefts and rights, Max narrates Jay's success to stoke audience attention and clarify how publics imagine thinning racial dividing lines when black athletes win. Ramirez hyphenates "in-*sane*" to accentuate the ways in which sports spectating cultures acquire a hyperawareness of racial hierarchies and mark athletic victories indicators of an African-American citizenry loosening social strictures of the past. Max continues to promote Jay's imminent victory as upsetting racial strictures in United States culture signified by reversing the animalization frequently assigned to black representation onto Bixby. Jay is humanized and upraised as a matador while Bixby's esteem and stature downgrades to the status of a farm animal: the black handler whoops and beats the prized white bull in the public stockade. Max describes the "*supernatural*" crowd to once again provoke the audience to imagine the way biological arguments persistently justify the less-than-human status of African-American communities, which in turn provide the legal rationale to delimit citizenship rights. Jay's victory signals an historic reversal of the biological argument. When the black-only champ defeats Bixby, the basis for a social order imposed by natural law authorizing racial hierarchies gives way to the possibility of black equality. Here again zero-sum game heroics promote black social mobility only possible when whites are characterized or made to feel unequal.

"The Sport's" personal accomplishment ignites fear and produces "blacklashes" across the United States. "We did it," Fish shouts. "Not yet." Nina anticipates. To which Max soberly addresses the crowd of Jay's ascension to world heavyweight champion by pacing out, "Ladies and Gentlemen..."[38] Nina, in turn, reports the violence happening within black communities as whites seek to reverse perception that Jay's success indicates the promise of equality beyond the ring. Nina imagines, "There's a hand on a knife. . . . A man walks through the front door, smells the bourbon, sees the world changing around him."[39] Her vague story describes reactionary white publics seeking retribution in black communities for the successes of one of its own. "Blood," Fish adds and leaves the light. "You did it," whispers Wynton.

Turn on the houselights: a cheering Lincoln Center crowd on the edge of weeping and exhilaration. I too delivered from the blackened crowd and thrown into a whiteness that looks at itself under the evenly illuminating light. Rachel Chavkin's direction intermittently dismantles the Brechtian fourth wall transforming theater audiences into sports spectators participating in the pleasure of black-on-black sport violence; the play's zero-sum thematic couples black ascension with white desire to embolden divisions imagined to have been breached. Calling me out of the theater's darkness and into the role of participant-spectator thins the suspension of disbelief built around an early twentieth century stage set and costuming. I vacillated between play attendee and sport spectator sluicing through and returning behind Chavkin's theatrical borders: at once situated in my assigned seat and thrown into racialized theatrics. Seated with white colleagues whose generosity secured my low-cost ticket to the performance alongside all white students intensified my privileged subjective viewpoint. Thus students, like myself and colleagues, assembled part of the mostly white Lincoln Center audience who were likely members of comfortable classes spectating black actors dramatizing the effects brought to bear on black communities when one of its own manages to gain white admiration and anger. I was a privileged sport spectating member in nearly every way and reinforced as such through the play's direction.

A deceptive interplay happens across performer-viewer roles in the arena or theater: many imagine those who garner the spotlight enjoy empowered social positions given the fame or fortune ostensibly transferred to the performer by the mass attention received. Black athletes and the perceived social capital garnered by media attention and multi-million dollar contracts, many of which can be immediately terminated, become charged symbols of national acceptance or racial transcendence. The black sports hero suggests "the democratic spread of privilege, so the very entry of the black male body into a formerly segregated white field of sports [indicates] a signal social change."[40] The imagined community fictionalizes weakening racial, economic, and political divisions and broadcasts black sport achievement as evidence of a new political equality erasing all of the unpleasantness tied to the nation's history. When black athletes convey displeasure of any sort, express an opinion contesting viewpoints held by groups outside the field of play, or announce a concern for a social agenda or political cause, many spectator classes interpret these actions as a kind of violation or betrayal of the perceived privileges black athletes acquire in the exchange. Black athletes should be performing, not challenging perceptions of many audience members who stand as representative of the national community including, by viewing black bodies, groups historically occluded from full citizenship.

Perceptual differences of race and citizenship through sports spectatorship were punched up as an American Culture Scholar and father whose white maleness and terminal degree undoubtedly mark my enabled status at the Lincoln Center in April of 2016. I am reminded of Richard Dyer's prophetic expression theorizing responses to whites writing about whiteness: "Studies of dominance by the dominant should not deny the place of the writer in relation to what s/he is writing about it, but nor should they be the green light for self-recrimination or trying to get in on the act."[41] Critics aim various theoretical lenses at cultural productions to illuminate the way power operates within a given social system and rarely redress their own skin in the game. When we intervene, theorize, and interpret the creative work of others, we write from safe seemingly impenetrable positions. As I slowly sauntered through the quickly assembled and exiting crowd, I learned students and faculty would have the opportunity to meet the cast – another identifier of my privileged role outside the theater. My distracted and aloof gaze, the kneejerk displays of civil inattention, the go to look for exiting crowds, may have disguised my deep introspection. I kept thinking about my son and how I may be setting him up for perhaps the biggest betrayal of his life. Right now, the white community temporarily accepts my son because his boyish preteen frame un-threatens and my whiteness serves as a liaison for our community to access blackness. I acknowledge that many whites may feel more comfortable engaging my son when he's with me: asking for a high five, rubbing his afro, and even publicly kissing him because I am perceived as an ambassador or member of white communities. I may thereby enable members of the white community to bridge deeply entrenched racial divides many wish to see dismantled or fear to personally transgress without a chaperone present. These gestures of inclusion I suspect will dissipate as he gets older and no longer requires a parent handholding him through our immediate and distant social worlds. He will have to confront whiteness in and out of the ring on his own. Yet with my son's privileged, comfortable upbringing, and should his athletic interests develop into his teenage years, it seems possible the local community may turn on the bright lights and illuminate his black-athletic achievements.

Our larger mixed-race family plays a part too. We elevate my son's sports ego and bolster his competitiveness by showering praise from the various athletic peripheries we populate: neighborhood fields, front yards, for profit sports complexes, the town hockey rink. In part driven by the positive attention from familial and local crowds, it's difficult not to notice how my son aims to please spectating parents, grandparents, uncles, aunts, cousins, neighbors and friends. And these communities respond in kind. "You got yourself a real athlete there!" my cousin once yelled to me from across the lawn after exchanging a few kicks of a soccer ball to garner and hold my son's attention. My African-American brother-in-law bought, built, and delivered a basement basketball hoop and net. Recently at a neighborhood party, his white uncle threw a football with increased velocity and distance to a willful and ready-to-please nephew. My brother turned to me and said: "Dude, he's unbelievable. He'll catch anything." These spectacles of sports attention sprinted through my thoughts as I took pictures of students and faculty alongside the mostly black cast outside the Lincoln Center.

Part of the reason for my remoteness in the shadowy and chilly promenade, my inability to get into the picture with students and colleagues, had to do with thinking through the roles I play fostering my son's interest in black-athletic achievement. To ensure he did not get lured into New England Patriots fandom, my brother bought him an Alshon Jeffrey[42] jersey. As a preemptive measure to secure his non-citizenship status on the border of Red Sox Nation, near our home, I bought him a Derek Jeter[43] jersey. He dresses like a successful African-American sports celebrity and on occasion, plays the part. I recently put up a trophy shelf in his room to showcase his sports accomplishments. These seemingly innocent gestures are no longer considered innocuous overtures to me. I am extending my sports-viewing heritage onto my son, contributing to his enthusiasm and drive to demonstrate his sports prowess and knowledge for mostly whites praising him for it. To own "the sport" in competition with his friends and teammates shifts family and community attention, and momentarily garners some kind of fleeting social power in the bargain. I learned from *The Royale* that harnessing the attention of the audience duplicitously deceives viewer and performers alike. As his white father, I develop my son's willingness to perform his black body for the largely white communities he and I intersect.

So, I am a white father raising a black son in the cultural logic of Obama-Trayvon grappling with contradictions of black achievement, athletic and otherwise. I am frightened by the inconsistencies of the white imagination negotiating racial tolerances on the one hand and newer iterations of racial violence on the other. Nina's concern for her children and community shine the light onto black-athletic performance and white spectatorship. The perceived upraised social condition of black communities imagined in no small part by the two-term election of the first black president produces blacklashes all over the country: Jefferson, Houston, Baltimore, New York, Cleveland, Charleston, Oakland, and there are others. The U.S. racial imagination patted itself on the back in 2008. What is it doing now? Complaining about Colin Kaepernick's right to protest the national crisis and giving President Donald Trump a period to undo nearly every accomplishment of the Obama administration. Blacklashes everywhere. Right now my son experiences the praise of a community with his white dad as a kind of bridge for mostly white publics gazing at my son's achievements and abilities. *The Royale* lifted the curtain of my naivety and positioned my son under the pin spot. I know and fear our community must also harbor attitudes making blacklash possible here. His boyishness and not-yet-teen body poses little threat to white suburbia but there is no evidence our community climate rejects attitudes enabling racial retribution in this era. He dances, struts, and asserts his confidence on sports fields resembling a little Jay Jackson in the ring. And like "The Sport," the attention he garners in athletic contexts provisionally secures a social position always shape-shifting the U.S. racial imagination.

While I stood in the white shadows on the glistening marbled Lincoln Center promenade against the deep and darkening April evening sky waiting to meet the cast, I felt complicit in an impending familial betrayal. How might my role as father, coach, and playmate ill-prepare my son for white spectatorship inside and outside of the ring? Can I instruct white ways of viewing and thinking without building ceilings before dreams take flight? Or put another way, how do I avoid reproducing white stereotypes and still protect and enable my son to distill current iterations of the nation's racist logic on his own? Through a side door and out of costume, Khris Davis and McKinley Belcher III, Jay and Fish respectively, emerge dressed in hoodies looking like teenagers keeping warm in the early spring evening. Students and colleagues took selfies with the cast members, but I could not get myself to enter the image. I was too withdrawn in the imagination and thus wished to retain the spectator's posture outside of the theater. I wanted to keep looking and did not want to enter the private stage students and colleagues constructed. In this moment, the chiseled bodies of Jay and Fish cloaked in loose fitting sweatshirts looked more like the frames of Trayvon Martin and Michael Brown than high-performing actors playing athletes. During these reflective instances, images of my son began to speed through my imagination. His deep interest playing and watching sports reinforced and stoked by a largely white, comfortable suburban community marveling at his black-athletic ability: he can hit a baseball, throw and catch 20, 30, 40 yard spirals, and he's not afraid to blow up an advancing left or right wing headed toward the hockey net. In the cool darkness, I remembered family members and voices in the community remarking, "He's a natural." A polite way to say the sport is "in his blood."

Notes

[1] Sklar, Robert. *Movie-Made America: A Cultural History of American Movies.* Revised and Updated Edition (New York: Vintage Books, 1994) 346.

[2] Bloom, John and Michael Nevin Willard. "Introduction." *Sports Matters: Race, Recreation, and Culture* (New York: New York University Press, 2002), 8.

[3] *The Royale.* By Marco Ramirez, directed by Rachel Chavkin. (April 8, 2016. Newhouse Theater. New York) Performance.

[4] Rodriguez, Julio. "Documenting Myth: Racial Representation in Leon Gast's *When We Were Kings.*" *Sports Matters: Race, Recreation, and Culture.* Edited by John Bloom and Michael Nevin Willard. (New York: New York University Press, 2002), 209.

[5] Rodriguez 210.

[6] Fanon, Frantz. *Black Skin, White Masks* (New York: Grove, 1967), 1-2.

[7] Morrison, Toni. *Playing in the Dark: Whiteness and the Literary Imagination* (Cambridge, MA: Harvard UP, 1992), 38.

[8] Bazin, Andre. *What is Cinema? Vol. I.* (Berkeley: University of California Press, 1997), 102.

[9] Diawara, Manthia. "Black Spectatorship: Problems of Identification and Resistance." *Film Theory and Criticism.* 6th Ed. Edited by Leo Braudy and Marshall Cohen. (Oxford: Oxford University Press, 2004), 892.

[10] Diawara 894.

[11] A pin spot is a theatrical term and a type of lighting equipment. Pin spots produce a very narrow beam and thus a pin spot in a script calls for tightly illuminating an object or actor.

[12] Ramirez, Marco. *The Royale* (London: Oberon Books, 2015), 7.

[13] Ramirez 7.

[14] Post, Deborah Waire. "Cultural Inversion and the One-drop Rule: An Essay on Biology, Racial Classification, and the Rhetoric of Racial Transcendence." *Albany Law Review* 72.4 Winter 2009 (Albany, NY: Albany Law School Press), 918.

[15] Gates, Henry Louis. *The Signifying Monkey A Theory of African-American Literary Criticism* (Oxford: Oxford UP, 1988), 1586.

[16] Ramirez 10-11.

[17] Ramirez 12.

[18] Ramirez 15.

[19] Gilroy, Paul. *Against Race: Imagining Political Culture Beyond the Color Line.* (Cambridge, Mass: Belknap Press of Harvard University Press, 2000), 166.

[20] Diawara 894

[21] Diawara 894.

[22] Ramirez 26.

[23] Ramirez 49.

[24] Ramirez 49.

[25] Ramirez 50.

[26] Ramirez 58-9.

[27] Ramirez 77.

[28] Ramirez 79.

[29] Ramirez 81.

[30] Ramirez 81.

[31] Ramirez 90.

[32] Ramirez 91.

[33] Ramirez 91.

[34] Ramirez 94-5.

[35] Ramirez 101.

[36] Ramirez 102.

[37] Ramirez 110.

[38] Ramirez 117.

[39] Ramirez 116-7.

[40] Yu, Henry. "Tiger Woods at the Center of History: Looking Back at the Twentieth Century through the Lenses of Race, Sports, and Mass Consumption." *Sports Matters: Race, Recreation, and Culture.* Edited by John Bloom and Michael Nevin Willard. (New York: New York University Press, 2002), 339.

[41] Dyer, Richard. "White." *Film Theory and Criticism.* 6th Ed. Edited by Leo Braudy and Marshall Cohen. (Oxford: Oxford University Press, 2004), 733-4.

[42] When writing this essay for publication, Alshon Jeffrey was a Wide Receiver for the Chicago Bears and had not yet been suspended for performance-enhancement drug use. My brother and I spent our adolescence in the Chicago suburbs and are devoted Bear fans, as most Chicagoans are. We were conscious of representational concerns and specifically discussed purchasing a jersey of a black athlete as a gift for my son.

[43] I was born in the Bronx, NY. My first professional sports experience was attending a Yankees game in 1977. One of my earliest memories is chanting "Reggie, Reggie, Reggie" each time Reggie Jackson arrived at home plate to bat.

Works Cited

Bazin, Andre. *What is Cinema?* Vol. I. Berkeley: University of California Press, 1997. Print.

Bloom, John and Michael Nevin Willard. "Introduction." *Sports Matters: Race, Recreation, andCulture.* New York: New York University Press, 2002. 1-10. Print.

Diawara, Manthia. "Black Spectatorship: Problems of Identification and Resistance." *Film Theory and Criticism.* 6th Ed. Edited by Leo Braudy and Marshall Cohen. Oxford: Oxford University Press, 2004. 892-900. Print.

Dyer, Richard. "White." *Film Theory and Criticism*. 6th Ed. Edited by Leo Braudy and Marshall Cohen. Oxford: Oxford University Press, 2004. 733-752. Print.

Fanon, Frantz. *Black Skin, White Masks*. New York: New York, Grove, 1967. Print.

Gates, Henry Louis. *The Signifying Monkey A Theory of African-American Literary Criticism*. Oxford: Oxford UP, USA, 1988. Print.

Gilroy, Paul. *Against Race: Imagining Political Culture Beyond the Color Line*. Cambridge, MA: Belknap Press of Harvard University Press, 2000. Print.

Morrison, Toni. *Playing in the Dark: Whiteness and the Literary Imagination*. Cambridge, MA: Harvard UP, 1992. Print.

Post, Deborah Waire. "Cultural Inversion and the One-drop Rule: An Essay on Biology, Racial Classification, and the Rhetoric of Racial Transcendence." *Albany Law Review* 72.4 (Winter 2009). Albany, NY: Albany Law School Press. 909-920. Print.

Ramirez, Marco. *The Royale*. London: Oberon Books, 2015. Print.

Rodriguez, Julio. "Documenting Myth: Racial Representation in Leon Gast's *When We Were Kings*." *Sports Matters: Race, Recreation, and Culture*. Edited by John Bloom and Michael Nevin Willard. New York: New York University Press, 2002. 209-222. Print.

Sklar, Robert. *Movie-Made America: A Cultural History of American Movies*. Revised and Updated Edition. New York: Vintage Books, 1994. Print.

The Royale. By Marco Ramirez, directed by Rachel Chavkin. April 8, 2016. Newhouse Theater. New York. Performance.

Yu, Henry. "Tiger Woods at the Center of History: Looking Back at the Twentieth Century through the Lenses of Race, Sports, and Mass Consumption." *Sports Matters: Race, Recreation, and Culture*. Edited by John Bloom and Michael Nevin Willard. New York: New York University Press, 2002. 320-354. Print.

Lynching and Spectacle: The Burning and Desecration of Colin Kaepernick's Jersey

TRAVIS D. BOYCE AND
STEPHANIE M. BURCHETT

In Michael Stein's 1977 article "Cult and Sport: The Case of Big Red," the sociologist points out that sport is an integral component to American society. Using football at the University of Nebraska as the central example of the article, he theorizes that sport is not just recreational. He claims that sport is more than just a game because it intersects with society, thus creating "dramatic flair" or *spectacle*. This intersection between society and sports can consequently gain substantial media attention that rivals politics.[1] There are various examples in U.S. sport history (and even global history) where sport intersects with society in a way that mesmerizes or captures the attention of the public. Perhaps one of the most notable spectacles was the trial of Orenthal James (O.J.) Simpson, a Heisman Trophy winner. More than two decades ago, the nation was enthralled with the infamous Bronco chase and subsequent trial for murder (and acquittal) of Simpson. It was high drama to see in the courtroom a former collegiate All-American at the University of Southern California, and member of the National Football League (NFL) Hall of Fame. Simpson represented the antithesis of African American athletic activism. During his collegiate, professional, and post-athletic career, he was indifferent toward or remained silent on social issues impacting the African American community. Simpson elected to relish in his fame through his athletic accomplishments, lucrative endorsements, acting and broadcasting career, and overall acceptance by white America.[2] Despite these accomplishments, his downfall ironically was based on his arrogance. He'd had a history of domestic violence toward his wife, Nicole Brown Simpson. White Americans, who had enthusiastically propped up his career, lost their feelings of adoration when he began the murder trial. Undeniably, people were now riveted to the courtroom drama's "intriguing mix of celebrity, horror, race, and sensationalism."[3]

Sport in American society is more than a game. The intersectionality of sport and society provides a framework of understanding. Through this intersection, we can see that sports are important and also grasp the essence of society itself.[4] For example, in an article published in 2011 in the *Journal of Sport History* titled "Fuzzy Memories: College Mascots and the Struggle to Find Appropriate Legacies of the Civil War," author Megan Bever examines the importance of college mascots in relationship to both its respective university and state history. Perhaps one of the most controversial American collegiate mascots is the University of Mississippi's (Ole Miss) Colonel Reb, for the mascot's racist legacy of the Confederacy, chattel slavery, and violence (such as the riot in wake of the desegregation of the University of Mississippi in 1962). Bever further looks at the complexities of normalizing (through sport) problematic mascots such as Colonel Reb in a multicultural, integrated society.[5] Despite the contradictions, Ole Miss students, alumni, and fans (primarily whites) continue to romanticize Colonel Reb (now no longer the university's official mascot), the Confederate battle flag, and the song *Dixie*, because all three confederate symbols reflect their identity in terms of their heritage, university collegiate sports identity, and in various aspects of their daily lives.[6]

The intersectionality of sport and society in terms of spectacle has also been carefully dramatized in documentaries. In celebration of its thirtieth anniversary in 2009, ESPN (Entertainment and Sports Programming Network) released its first volume of thirty documentaries of sports-related stories since its founding in 1979. Unlike ESPN's *Best of Series* or *Sports Century* format (which specifically covers the best highlights from sporting events), the *30 for 30* series was designed to reinforce a sense of dramatic flair or spectacle of sport stories to its audience. As American Studies professor Travis Vogan notes, the ESPN *30 for 30* series "focus(es) on emotional narratives centered around events that were significant when they occurred but have since faded from public memory."[7] The success of the first volume of the *30 for 30* series in 2009 resulted in a continuation of the series that now includes a *30 for 30 Short*; a series of short films (15–30 minutes long), apart from its traditional regular series that is an hour or longer. Thought-provoking documentaries of sport-related stories captured the spectacle of sport and life. Among the strong lineup in the *30 for 30* series, the most notable documentaries that examine sport within the context of America's troubled racial history (vilification of African American male athletes) include *The U* (in 2009) and *The Fab Five* (in 2011).

In terms of America's racial history in relationship to sport, one must consider the social construct of how white Americans view sport. In 2016, history professor Jamal L. Ratchford noted:

> 1."...sports best represented American democracy . . . and the integrated sports represented the possibilities of American greatness."
> 2. "...black protest was seen as antithetical to the idea of sports as a nonpolitical space." Therefore, "black activism (this includes various aspects of self-determination) in sports was defined as un-American."[8]

The U and *The Fab Five* were situated in a post-integrated society in which the African American athletes who are featured in the documentary, in the eyes of white America, were "damned" because of their pursuit of self-determination. The athletes were "othered" as ungrateful men, spoiled thugs, or criminals, and more importantly, not one of us (Americans).

Professor Ratchford's examination of NBA (National Basketball Association) superstar LeBron James's controversial 2010 decision and aftermath to leave the Cleveland Cavaliers for the Miami Heat falls within this line of thinking. The controversial (*The*) *Decision*[9] debuted in front of a nationally televised audience, showing James's decision to leave the Cleveland Cavaliers for the Miami Heat during the summer of 2010. The Cleveland Cavalier's owner, Dan Gilbert, angrily penned an open letter to Cleveland's *The Plain Dealer*, framing James's decision to leave as "cowardly betrayal."[10] Reverend Jesse Jackson came to James's defense, noting James's right to self-determination and condemning Gilbert as merely a slave owner in distress who had lost his best slave.[11]

Cleveland fans condemned James, branded him as a traitor, and burned his jersey in effigy, acts that gained an incredible amount of attention in various media outlets, notably social media. Indeed, "celebratory violence" or "celebratory riots," as noted by comparative politics professor Andrei S. Markovits, is a European and American sport tradition that has been normalized and acceptable.[12] For example, it is common for sports fans to riot in jubilation by destroying public and private property if their respective team wins a pivotal game. In contrast to celebratory violence or riots, fans may also display outright violence to mark their displeasure toward their respective or opposing teams or individual athletes. Fan violence can be rooted in racial hatred, as seen in European football (soccer) toward black players such as Italian footballer Mario Balotelli and Kevin-Prince Boateng.[13] Markovits further explains that as opposed to American sports, where fan racial violence in the post-integration era is considered taboo, fan racial violence remains a fixture in the European sporting tradition where such violence, rhetoric, songs, and slogans are acceptable. Perhaps U.S. sports fans instead practice a quasi-covert form of racism disguised in a much more menacing and darker form of celebratory violence. The burning of an African American athlete's jersey in effect can be a reproduction of a lynching. A casual observer may dismiss the burning of James's jersey as merely fan displeasure at his leaving to play for another team.

But what if the athlete had questioned America's racial status quo (which is grounded in white supremacy), police brutality, and other forms of racial oppression? What if he or she refused to stand for the national anthem? That brings to mind Colin Kaepernick.

Prior to a 2016 NFL preseason game, former San Francisco 49ers quarterback Colin Kaepernick elected to sit as opposed to stand during the playing of the national anthem. (In the final preseason game on September 1, 2016 and subsequently during the regular season, Kaepernick modified his protest from sitting to kneeling.) He was protesting America's long, troubled history of racial discrimination and police brutality against communities of color. In the middle of a hostile election season, in which Donald Trump won the U.S. presidential election based primarily on the rhetoric of racism, white nationalism, fear, and xenophobia, Kaepernick's peaceful protest was met by angry fans creating photographs and videos of the burning of his jersey. These videos feature mostly white men (at times women and children) who proclaim their disgust with Kaepernick's protest coupled with the playing of "The Star-Spangled Banner." These videos have been posted to social media sites including YouTube, Instagram, and Facebook.

Burning the jersey of professional athletes and posting the video on social media websites is not a new trend. When a professional athlete moves to a new team or has a bad game, fans will often burn the player's jersey (for example, Golden State Warrior all-star forward Kevin Durant). However, the Kaepernick photos and videos set a precedent because they have similar characteristics to the lynching photographs created in the late nineteenth and early twentieth centuries. As historian Amy L. Wood clarifies, "lynching photographs . . . served to normalize and make socially acceptable, even aesthetically acceptable, the utter brutality of a lynching."[14] To be black and a lynching victim during the late nineteenth and early twentieth centuries meant to whites that a black person had violated the law by committing a violent crime, often that of assaulting (real or imagined) a white woman. Or the victim may have been simply perceived as a threat (behaved uppity) to the racial status quo. We argue that Kaepernick was perceived as a threat to the country's racial status quo. Therefore, the burning of Kaepernick's jersey in the twenty-first century was meant to evoke the same emotion as a lynching.

This article will first review the lynching photographs from a historical perspective. Next, we will discuss African American athletes taking unpopular political position by examining the life and times of Jack Johnson, the first African American heavyweight world-boxing champion (1908-1915). Johnson challenged the racial status quo and consequently encountered significant backlash during the nadir of race relations in the United States. Armed with that knowledge, the reader will be able to see that online videos and internet memes (a digital hate archive) strikingly reflect the intention to evoke the same emotion of fear found in the archive of postcards of lynching victims. Finally, we will underscore how online images of the burning and desecration of Kaepernick's jersey mimic photos of racial lynchings in this nation's history.

Lynching Photographs

In 1865, the American constitution was amended, to end the enslavement of African-Americans. The former confederate states[15] created state laws to permit racial segregation also known as the Jim Crow Laws. During this time, white supremacists used the act of lynching as an informal system of enforcement. These murderous accusations were to keep races separate, as more interactions between whites and blacks took place after slavery was abolished. Between the years of 1880 and 1930 approximately 4,697 lynchings took place in the United States. This act of violence became a form of racial terrorism, a means of consolidating white supremacist nationalism and a way to reinforce segregation.

These lynchings became spectacles[16]; often announced in the local newspaper beforehand, they were recorded by both amateur and professional photographers. These spectacles coincided with the invention of Kodak's Brownie Camera, which allowed photographs to be made with ease. This new technology let the everyday person create snapshots of their lives. Once a roll of film was completely exposed it could be turned into Kodak to be developed and printed. For 10 cents, postcards could be created of these snapshots. People attended lynchings with these cameras in hand and with the click of a button the lynching was documented and could be added to a family photo album, a remembrance of an event attended.

Professional photographers were active participants in documenting lynchings. The images they made were staged and occurred after the lynching and before the crowd would disperse. Photographer Lawrence Beitler of Indiana would pay for a spot in the crowd of the mob to document the end of these so-called "spectacle-lynchings." These photographs would then be sold as postcards and prints, as souvenirs, for spectators to take with them, to send to their friends or to hang on their walls as trophies (see Figure 2, *Photograph of Tom Shipp and Abe Smith*). These photographs were defined as "a tool of the mob, used to determine how a lynching should be pursued, announced, remembered, and understood."[17]

Identifiable crowds of white people surrounded the corpses and gazed through the camera at the viewer, some smiling and others with a righteous conviction.[18] These people did not flee the scene of these murderous events; they posed unafraid of the repercussions of participation, as if to say "look at what we caught today." The victims were objectified, in their anonymous depiction coupled with the crowds who showed no signs of remorse or sympathy, was a consistent characteristic in professional lynching photographs. Dora Apel explains: "Making a photograph became part of the ritual, helping to objectify and dehumanize the victims and, for some, increase the hideous pleasure. Photographs were souvenirs of lynching, keepsakes that could be shown as proof that one was there."[19] These images of the cruel torture and humiliation of African-Americans were intended to create fear in one audience while giving power to another.

Historically, these images freely circulated through the US Postal Service until 1908, through the southern states, to and from white supremacists, family members and also members of the community who spoke out against lynchings. The language used on these postcards personalized their messages which added to their already threatening presence.

On May 15, 1916, seventeen-year-old Jesse Washington was lynched in Waco, Texas. After confessing to the murder and rape of his neighbor in Robinson, Texas, his trial was announced, and during the reading of the verdict, a mob of people captured Washington.[20] Fred Gildersleeve, a professional photographer, was notified by the mayor of the upcoming lynching, and he documented the events of the day. Gildersleeve's photographs were made into postcards (see Figure 1) and sold after the event as souvenirs.[21] One of these postcards was purchased by a man named Joe, who inscribed a message on the back of the postcard to his parents. His message read "This is the barbecue we had last night my picture is to the left with a cross over it. Your Son, Joe."[22] In the photograph Washington's charred body is on display as two men gaze back at the viewers. Washington's lower body is covered, which was often done when a lynching victim was castrated. The image coupled with the text on the back points to the familial tradition of white supremacy. Joe wrote to his family to tell them of this event he experienced, showing proof that he was there and participated in an event that was compared with the pastime of an American BBQ. Dora Apel explains: "The card celebrates the intergenerational reproduction of white supremacist violence"[23].

Returning to Lawrence Beitler's *Photograph of Tom Shipp and Abe Smith*. The evening of August 7, 1930 three men were to be lynched but, as the photograph displays, only two became victims that evening. His neighbor who recognized and released him from the mob saved James Cameron, the third man who was to be murdered. Cameron's memory of the event is mostly presumed from Beitler's photograph.[24] Lynchings generally were not attended by African Americans, so their reference for them was from the photographs that circulated. Cameron recalls seeing the photograph from the lynching in the *Anderson Daily Bulletin*, as a prison guard shoved it in his face while he was sitting in his jail cell the next morning.[25] "The guard understood the image in the context as a threat, a demonstration of the power of white men and women believed it their right to wield over him."[26]

The photograph of Shipp and Smith was also found as an object, owned by a Klansman who had the photograph framed with locks of hair from one of the victims. It was later found by James Allen, an antique collector, who created a collection of 145 lynching photographs and postcards from private and personal collections. These objects were repurposed into a book called *Without Sanctuary*, which was published in 2000. Allen intended for these photographs to create a conversation about what he believed to be a forgotten part of American history. Susan Sontag discussed the collection of photographs in her book *Regarding the Pain of Others*. She explained that by looking at the extent of lynching photographs presented in *Without Sanctuary*, "it should help us understand such atrocities not as the acts of 'barbarians' but as the reflection of a belief system, racism, that by defining one people as less human than another legitimates torture and murder. But maybe they *were* barbarians. Maybe *this* is what most barbarians look like. (They look like everybody else.) That being said, one person's 'barbarian' is another person's 'just doing what everybody else is doing.'"[27]

From Lynchings to Character Deformation

By the 1940s lynchings decreased in the United States; however, the character assassination of African American activists or those who challenged traditional white spaces continued. In the political arena for example U.S. Supreme Court associate justice Clarence Thomas referred to the bombshell sexual harassment accusation lodged against him at his 1991 confirmation hearings as a high-tech lynching.[28] In the sporting world, the media, politicians and mainstream Americans condemned American sprinters John Carlos and Tommie Smith as militants when they raised their fists (in protest) during the playing of the national anthem during the 1968 Olympics medal ceremony.[29] The dramatic flair and spectacle of sport in contemporary life in the United States speaks to the importance of how sport is deeply connected with issues of society such as racism. Colin Kaepernick is connected to America's legacy of racism. We will situate him in the "bad nigger" archetype.

In Al-Tony Gilmore's biography of the controversial heavyweight-boxing champion Jack Johnson (1878–1946), Gilmore examines the historical importance of the *bad nigger* archetype. This term is rooted in American chattel slavery; a bad nigger "was one who refused to submit to his shackles without active resistance and . . . was willing to fight the system."[30] In a post-emancipation context, this person was black and bravely and unapologetically challenged the racial status quo. The term describes someone who refuses to submit to white authority. In this context, Kaepernick can be seen as embodying the characteristics of a bad nigger. He refused to stand for the national anthem in order to condemn law enforcement for its brutal practices against communities of color. He played a key position on the team that was historically reserved for whites and embodied the essence of white masculinity. He refused to go along with the safe and conventional standards of behavior as a professional athlete, to stay out of politics and just play the game. On social media, there is a plethora of Kaepernick critics. They claim that he has never experienced oppression because he is a multimillion-dollar athlete.

Critics framed him as either an opportunist or simply ungrateful to a nation that has given him an opportunity to be a well-paid professional athlete.

In the world of U.S. sport history (particularly in contemporary sport), history might shine a light on some other supposedly bad niggers: boxer Muhammad Ali (1942–2016); 1968 Olympians Tommie Smith and John Carlos; the University of Miami football team during the 1980s; the 1991 University of Michigan's Fabulous Freshman Five; former Chicago Bulls prolific shooter and NBA champion Craig Hodges (b. 1960); and basketball star Allen Iverson (b. 1975), among others. All, in their unique ways, frightened white America as they challenged the racial status quo. They all suffered the consequences such as a damaged reputation or a loss of career and livelihood. NBA hall of famer Allen Iverson, for example, lives in infamy in many sectors of society for his condemnation and initial refusal to comply with a controversial mandatory dress code.

The dress code was born in an early regular season game in November of 2004, when members of the Indiana Pacers brawled with members of the Detroit Pistons. Famously known as "The Malice in the Palace," Indiana held a 97-82 lead with less than a minute in the game. During a dead ball, Indiana forward Ron Artest (b. 1979) charged into the stands after a fan threw an object at him. Various fights ensued among the players and fans on the arena floor and in the stands. NBA Commissioner David Stern (b. 1942), fearing that the predominately African American sport would lose its white fan base, introduced a mandatory dress code. The code required business casual as opposed to baggy clothes, excessive jewelry, and baseball caps. Stern saw the code as a matter of public relations, to soften the NBA's image. He wanted to draw ratings and public interest from an already declining fan base.[31] Iverson was one of the most vocal critics of the dress code, believing that the dress code was inherently racist as it specifically targeted African American fashion. Stern threatened players who failed to comply. He promised fines, suspensions, and ultimately expulsion from the league.[32] Iverson had "a history of trouble." In 1993, Iverson was accused of assaulting a white woman with a chair during a racially charged melee in a Hampton, Virginia bowling alley. Iverson had been a two-star athlete in football and basketball, but lost all of his division-won offers and served four months (of a fifteen-year sentence) in state prison. Virginia Governor Douglas Wilder (b. 1931) pardoned him; furthermore, Georgetown University's basketball coach John Thompson, Jr. (b. 1941) offered him a scholarship. *ESPN 30 for 30 series* covered this in a 2010 documentary, *No Crossover: The Trial of Allen Iverson*. So he entered the NBA in 1996 with that already-tarnished reputation. He maintained a negative image throughout his career due to encounters with the law, and a poor relationship with the media. The NBA dress code controversy was the cherry on top that reinforced Iverson's bad image. The mandatory dress code was met with approval from various members of the NBA community. Those in favor of the dress code included former NBA all-star and commentator Charles Barkley, former Philadelphia 76ers coach Larry Brown (b. 1940), and former Los Angeles Lakers coach and now New York Knicks president Phil Jackson (b. 1945). Brown was quoted to have been so embarrassed by his players' appearance that he sent them back to their hotel. Moreover, Jackson stated, "The players have been dressing in prison garb the last five or six years . . . all the stuff that goes on, it's like gangsta, thuggery stuff."[33] Under the guise of a dress code policy, nightclub and bar owners in recent years both in the United States and Europe have systematically barred African American patrons.[34] Iverson retired in 2013. During the summer of 2016, he was inducted into the NBA Hall of Fame, where he symbolically passed the torch to Kaepernick. However, to understand Kaepernick, and the concepts of lynching and spectacle, one must understand the original unrepentant athlete in terms of modern sport history: Jack Johnson, the first African American heavyweight champion of the world.

It was not until April 5, 1915 in Havana, Cuba, that Jack Johnson, the then-undisputed champion, lost by knockout in the twenty-sixth round to "White Hope" Jess Willard. Throughout Johnson's seven-year reign, promoters and members of the media had sought out and recruited a series of white fighters framed as "The White Hope" to challenge Johnson, with the intention of redeeming the white race.[35] Since the 1880s, this championship title symbolically represented "whiteness, masculinity, and nationalism" in the United States. [36] Recall that the Reconstruction era followed the American Civil War (1865–1877). During this time, the African American majority and their Republican allies, armed with the right to vote, controlled the politics in the former confederate states.[37] Through political mudslinging, violence, and intimidation, white Americans (under the banner of the Democratic Party and vigilante groups such as the Ku Klux Klan, the Red Shirts, and the White League) successfully overturned radical reconstruction[38] and put in place state-sanctioned Jim Crow laws that would last for generations. By the 1890s, when Reconstruction was completely toppled, Southern state governments held conventions to disenfranchise African Americans. White Americans from both the North and the South reconciled their differences (based on the American Civil War fought a generation prior). They mutually agreed that Reconstruction and the enfranchisement of African Americans was a bad idea for whites and thus carried out the systematic oppression of African Americans. This oppression included violence such as lynchings/race riots, voting suppression, and de facto/de jure racial segregation.[39] At South Carolina's 1895 Constitutional Convention, U.S. Senator Benjamin Tillman declared, "My Democracy means white supremacy. I and those who have backed me will not join forces with the negro. . . . All the offices in the world are not worth such a price."[40] The Tuskegee Institute (in Alabama) reported over 4,500 documented lynchings nationwide between 1880-1964 and more specifically, there were approximately 1,500 lynchings during the progressive era (1900–1917), which occurred during the rise and fall of Jack Johnson.[41] This act of violence was racial terrorism designed to maintain the racial status quo. As Dora Apel and Michelle Shawn Smith state in their 2007 book, *Lynching Photographs*, "Scholars and activists have sought to explain lynching as a form of racist terrorism and racialized economic warfare, a means of consolidating white supremacist nationalism, and a way of reinforcing segregation."[42]

Jack Johnson was born in the middle of this political and social maelstrom, in 1878 in Galveston, Texas, a year after the collapse of Reconstruction. He came of age and successfully held the world's heavyweight boxing title during the era of Jim Crow and America's low point in race relations. Unlike many African Americans who carefully walked the line in terms of racial etiquette during the early twentieth century, Johnson unapologetically flaunted his wealth by wearing expensive, tailor-made suits; driving fast, expensive cars; drinking champagne; and smoking cigars. Furthermore, he lived in all-white neighborhoods, displayed no deference to whites, and had sexual relationships with white women—all while easily beating a series of "white hopes" thrown at him.[43] Morehouse College President Dr. Benjamin E. Mays (1894–1984) frankly put it, "Johnson's victory was hard on the white man's world. . . . Jack Johnson committed two grave blunders as far as whites were concerned: He beat up a white man and he was socializing with a white woman—both deadly sins."[44] Indeed, the United States was a hostile political environment where Johnson's mere existence could have gotten him killed. Miraculously, Johnson was never physically harmed by a mob during his boxing career. There were threats made against him, and unpleasant encounters with the law, whether it was a speeding ticket, being jailed for an illegal fight, or even the more serious: violating the controversial, racially motivated Mann Act of 1910. In wake of the death of his first wife in 1912, Johnson was arrested in Chicago for the alleged kidnapping of Lucille Cameron, a nineteen-year-old white prostitute, who would later become his wife. While waiting to make bail, a fellow white inmate called for his lynching. Furthermore, after his arraignment, Johnson was met (but protected) by an angry white mob calling for his death. He received threatening letters from people across the country, and the media harshly condemned him. It was reported that two southern white ministers called for his death.[45] As reported in the *Chicago Daily News*, an unfazed Johnson appeared in court a half-hour late, accompanied by an entourage of bodyguards and a cigar in his mouth.[46]

While angry mobs did not have direct access to Johnson, they did target African Americans during his reign as champion. Following Johnson's fights, race riots were common throughout the country. For example, on July 4, 1910, Johnson soundly defeated former world heavyweight boxing champion Jim Jeffries (1875–1953). The Johnson–Jeffries fight was a highly anticipated fight that had gained considerable national and international attention.[47] Six years prior, Jeffries decided to retire as the undisputed heavyweight-boxing champion, rather than to fight a black man. Racial tensions across the country were high.[48] In the eyes of white Americans, a Johnson victory symbolized a peril to the status quo. It was as if whites were face-to-face with the second emancipation of African Americans.[49] White Americans across the country were vexed about Johnson's victory because it threatened their sense of supremacy. The nation experienced a surge of attacks on African Americans. Al-Tony Gilmore (b. 1946) notes that in every state in the American south, there were documented incidents of racial unrest. In Norfolk, Virginia, white servicemen attacked African Americans. In Chattanooga, Tennessee, white Mississippi soldiers attacked African Americans. Furthermore, in Richmond, Virginia, a white man attacked two unsuspecting African American men in wake of Johnson's victory.[50] In 1910, there were approximately sixty-seven documented lynchings of African Americans in the United States. In Dallas, Texas, four months before the Johnson–Jeffries fight, Allen Brooks, a sixty-five-year-old African American, was lynched. Accused of assaulting a white girl under the age of three, Brooks was helpless as an armed mob of 10,000 removed him from police custody and immediately hanged him outside the courthouse.[51]

As the unapologetic athlete Jack Johnson went through his career, he endured character assassination, government conspiracy, censorship, and Hollywood propaganda. Using his relationships with white women and his violation of the Mann Act as a weapon, the media and government officials launched a series of negative stories to sully Johnson's character. For example, South Carolina governor Coleman Blease used veiled threats of violence to those who would dare do it in his state and made it clear that this was about protecting the white woman from the black brute.[52] The federal government successfully convicted Johnson under the Mann Act, despite Lucile Cameron's refusal to incriminate Johnson. Fearing the possibility of race riots, Congress abolished the distribution of fight films across state lines in 1912. This ruling hurt fight promoters and Johnson's ability to capitalize. His last fight was at age 67. He died the next year, in an auto accident while racing away from a diner that refused him service.

In 1915, D.W. Griffith released the film *The Birth of a Nation*. This movie retold the American Civil War and Reconstruction era through the ideology of white supremacy: the Ku Klux Klan were the heroes, and African Americans were lazy, corrupt, and capable of being the "black brute rapist."[53] In the film, Gus, characterizing the black brute rapist, meets his demise at the hands of the Klan.[54] The movie set off more violence perpetrated by whites. When Johnson finally lost the championship in April of 1915, white supremacy was redeemed.

Similarities between athletes Jack Johnson and Colin Kaepernick are glaring. They both occupy sports positions that embody the notion of whiteness, masculinity, and nationalism. They both live unapologetically and have received much criticism for that stance. For example, the role of a quarterback (both on and off the field) is supposed to demonstrate "leadership, intelligence, and poise."[55] In 2003, radio host Rush Limbaugh claimed that African Americans had an innate inability to play quarterback. He blamed the media for giving African American quarterbacks unearned positive reviews. Limbaugh was subsequently terminated as an ESPN analyst (Hartmann).[56] Limbaugh's claim was debunked when David Niven did a content analysis comparing media coverage of African American versus white quarterbacks. The study showed that the media, in general, treated both racial groups fairly.[57] Yet it is hard to dismiss the power and impact to the public of Limbaugh's line of thinking. While there have been African American quarterbacks in collegiate and NFL history, they are underrepresented in the broader context of integrated football history. Matthew Bigler and Judson Jeffries further note in their article "'An Amazing Specimen': NFL Draft Experts' Evaluations of Black Quarterbacks" that the lack of African American quarterbacks is a reflection of systemic and structural racism. Promising African American quarterbacks at the high school and collegiate ranks are either discouraged from playing the position or not given adequate time to develop into a pro-style quarterback. Such development is essential to being successful in the NFL. Moreover, people hold racial stereotypes that black athletes are not intelligent or strategic. These stereotypes play into systemic and structural racism resulting in the dearth of African American quarterbacks.[58]

By the start of the 2016 season, Colin Kaepernick had defied the odds and was on track to be a long-term and productive NFL quarterback. The season prior, he'd had a shoulder injury, yet the former University of Nevada standout was off to a great start in his professional career. He was on track of eventually winning a Super Bowl by leading the San Francisco 49ers to two consecutive National Football Conference (NFC) championship games. Kaepernick was at the top of his career and, to a casual observer, had no incentive to violate the American idea of sport by protesting in a "nonpolitical space."[59] Kaepernick, in effect, had traded his status of the leader of team and the mythology of the quarterback to the lowly status of the bad nigger. Kaepernick critics attacked his character and questioned his patriotism.

For example, Fox Sports' commentator Colin Cowherd (b. 1964), who already had a record of criticizing Kaepernick, condemned the San Francisco 49ers front office for trading veteran quarterback Alex Smith (b. 1984; a proverbial white hope) and replacing him with the up-and-coming Kaepernick. Cowherd praised Smith for his work ethic, resiliency, and dedication to professional football. He criticized Kaepernick for his protests, lack of professionalism, and perceived narcissism.[60] Cowherd perhaps believes that sport is not the appropriate arena to protest. Rather in sports, one simply plays the game. In another example, former Fox News commentator and conservative pundit Bill O'Reilly (b. 1949) discredited Kaepernick's form of protest and questioned his patriotism.[61] Another critic was Johnny Joey Jones (b. 1987). Appearing on Fox News's *On the Record*, Jones, a retired marine veteran and a double leg amputee due to injuries sustained in combat, also questioned Kaepernick's patriotism. The veteran compared Kaepernick's life with his service and subsequent injuries.[62] While Jones acknowledged the presence of racism in this country and that not all Americans are racist, he did not mention America's structural racism (racial profiling, housing discrimination, and so on) that is designed to maintain the racial status quo. Above all, Kaepernick is likely protesting this structural racism. Perhaps the most provocative and notable critic of Kaepernick was President Donald Trump (b. 1946). The 2016 NFL season began in an already hostile, divisive presidential election season. Trump used the Kaepernick controversy to score political points with a segment of his voter base who were white, critical of the Black Lives Matter Movement, and subscribers of right-wing ideologies such as ethnonationalism, anti-immigration, and law and order. Trump immediately jumped on the Kaepernick controversy in late August by stating that Kaepernick should either respect the flag or leave the country.[63] At a campaign rally in late October 2016 on the campus of the University of Northern Colorado, Trump blamed Kaepernick for NFL's low television ratings. Trump's merely invoking Kaepernick's name was met by a resounding boo and heckling from the Trump audience (Carbonated TV; Right Side Broadcasting).[64]

In spite of Kaepernick's critics, there were many who openly supported him. For example, retired NBA player and hall of fame inductee Kareem Abdul-Jabbar (b. 1947) came to Kaepernick's defense and offered thoughtful, smart commentary in terms of race, sports, social protest, and the perceptions of patriotism. In an opinion piece published in the *Washington Post*, Abdul-Jabbar challenged his readers to consider that Kaepernick's form of protest was just as patriotic as one who may only embrace the aesthetic symbols of America or gets teary eyed at the playing of the national anthem. Kaepernick, according to Abdul-Jabbar, embodies patriotism, as he is willing to sacrifice his career and livelihood for a worthy and moral cause. He links Kaepernick to courageous athletes of the past such as Muhammad Ali, Tommie Smith (b. 1944), John Carlos (b. 1945), Jim Brown (b. 1936), and Bill Russell (b. 1934) for risking their livelihood in the support of black lives. Abdul-Jabbar further pointed out, "One of the ironies of the way some people express their patriotism is to brag about our freedoms, especially freedom of speech, but then brand as unpatriotic those who exercise this freedom to express dissatisfaction with the government's record in upholding the Constitution."[65] Despite this defense of Kaepernick, the election of Donald Trump has emboldened his supporters to harass anyone who challenges the racial status quo.

"Colin Kaepernick spewed his hate for America. Now America is roaring back..."

Video Response to Colin Kaepernick

The idea of just doing what everybody else is doing, as referenced by Sontag in the lynching photographs section of this paper, draws parallels to the videos that were being created in response to Kaepernick's protest. Facebook user, Shane White, from Alabama was one of the first San Francisco 49er's fans to create a video burning Kaepernick's jersey in effigy, while playing The Star Spangled Banner. After a monologue he removes his hat, places his hand over his heart, and stands at attention to a burning Kaepernick jersey suspended from a tree (see Figure 3).[66] The video went viral. Breitbart, a self-described conservative news and opinion website, shared Mr. White's video on Facebook with the headline "Colin Kaepernick spewed his hate for America. Now America is roaring back..."[67] The post received over 7,000 likes and was shared by other Facebook users over 700 times.

There were Facebook users who shared the video accompanied with hostile comments regarding Kaepernick. Mike Peeples, from Abilene, Texas wrote the following: "Too bad he wasn't in the jersey at this time."[68] Gary Evertsen, from Spring Creek, Nevada noted, "Him and Obama are at the top of my shit list and I have a gift I wish I could give them soon."[69] Both of these users also have many posts on their public Facebook pages that match this rhetoric. Their response to the Breitbart post is an example of how similar language, referenced on the postcards of lynchings, was used with the shared videos to evoke fear or hate.

Others quickly followed suit and started publishing their own videos to YouTube. The majority of the videos have white, identifiable men, who gaze through the camera and speak directly to the viewer about their disapproval of Kaepernick's actions. Their language is filled with hateful rhetoric and they refer to burning the jersey as if they were burning a person. In one video, by LRG LIVIN, an unidentified man points to a fire on his grill, where the jersey is being destroyed and exclaims, "That's what happens to people who sit during the national anthem."[70] This rhetoric is also vocalized in a video of three people, one stating, "Kaepernick can burn."[71] Other videos show entire families with children, who made s'mores from the fire where they have just burned his jersey while waving the American flag as the national anthem plays in the background. These actions that surround this object, this stand-in for the body of Colin Kaepernick, are visually relatable to the characters and objectification of the subject in lynching photographs. The rhetoric of these videos is also similar to the language used on the backs of the lynching postcards. Using everyday rhetoric, as "here is the BBQ we had last night" to "let's make us some s'mores"[72]

Conclusion

The burning and desecration of Kaepernick's jersey in these videos mimics photos of racial lynchings in America's history. By reviewing the characteristics of lynching photographs from a historical perspective, it is evident that the YouTube videos strikingly reflect the rhetoric and intention to evoke the same emotion of fear intended in the creation and circulation of lynching photographs. Similar characters are present in the videos including the actions of burning objects, effigies of the body, coupled with language that is similar to the language used on the backs of lynching postcards.

Imagery created to empower one group of people while making another group of people vulnerable is nothing new but the ways in which images are being shared to pass along the message have changed significantly with the internet and social media. Created with cell phones instead of film cameras and distributed through social media, the videos, as the photographs did in *Without Sanctuary*, reflect a belief system happening in the present day. Social media allows us to share, like, and publicly terrorize using current technology. This public access allows us to watch and look at, a subsection of people whose belief systems are a reflection of our contemporary society. Thus, creating an archive, that is trackable, measurable and contributing to forming history from our time.

We assume that we live in a post-racial, integrated society. This article has shown evidence that racial issues are present in sport. While the desecration of Kaepernick's jersey has declined since his initial protest in late 2016, the overt and dog whistle rhetoric both online and in the mainstream media has remained constant. By the 2017-18 season, Kaepernick was in effect blackballed from the league.[73] In solidarity, many NFL players showed their support for Kaepernick and his cause by kneeling during the national anthem. This created further polarization in the United States among fans and nonfans alike. At a campaign style rally in late September 2017, President Donald Trump referred to the predominately black protesting athletes as "sons of bitches" and encouraged NFL owners to terminate their contracts.[74]

When athletes challenge the racial status quo, what are the social and economic consequences? This discourse includes the present-day story of Colin Kapernick, who has encountered video backlash to his human rights protest. The backlash is reminiscent of the rhetoric of the lynching photographs. Also, the rebukes against Kaepernick very much reflect the character assassination of boxer Jack Johnson. With this context in mind, the Kaepernick videos are an example of the use of imagery to create fear, using the technology of our time.

Figure 1. Postcard of Jesse Washington's lynching, Waco, Texas, 1908.

Figure 2. Lynching of Thomas Shipp and Abram Smith, as photographed by Lawrence Beitler, 1930.

Figure 3.Video still image of Shane Hall as he burns Colin Kaepernick's jersey. Courtesy of Breitbart News.

Notes

[1] Michael Stein, "Cult and Sport: The Case of Big Red," *Mid-American Review of Sociology* 2(2), 1977: 30–31.

[2] *O.J.: Made in America*, dir. Ezra Edelman, perf. OJ Simpson (archival footage), ESPN, Disney, 2016.

[3] Cydney Adams, "June 17, 1994: O.J. Simpson White Bronco Chase Mesmerizes Nation," CBS 17 June 2016. Accessed 1 February 2017. http://www.cbsnews.com/news/june-17-1994-o-j-simpson-car-chase-mesmerizes-nation/.

[4] Allen Guttmann's 2003 article "Sport, Politics and the Engaged Historian" published in the *Journal of Contemporary History* 38 (3) explores aspects of this, 363 to 375.

[5] Megan L. Bever, "Fuzzy Memories: College Mascots and the Struggle to Find Appropriate Legacies of the Civil War," *Journal of Sport History,* 38 (3), 2011: 454–456.

[6] Stuart Stevens, "What College Football Means in the South: A Story of a Father Son Son—And the Odes to Dixie and the Civil War that Have Been Tied to Ole Miss Football Traditions for Years," *The Atlantic*, 15 Sept. 2015. Accessed 1 February 2017. https://www.theatlantic.com/politics/archive/2015/09/what-college-football-means-in-the-south/405283/

[7] Travis Vogan, "30 for 30," *Journal of Sport History*, 38 (1), 2011: 126. www.jstor.org/stable/10.5406/jsporthistory.38.1.125.

[8] Jamal L. Ratchford, "The LeBron James Decision in the Age of Obama," *From Jack Johnson to LeBron James: Sports, Media, and the Color Line*, ed. Chris Lamb (Lincoln, NE: The University of Nebraska Press, 2016) 582–602.

[9] Henry Abbott, "LeBron James' Decision: The Transcript," ESPN, 8 July 2010. Accessed 1 February 2017. http://www.espn.com/blog/truehoop/post/_/id/17853/lebron-james-decision-the-transcript.

[10] Michael Lee, "Dan Gilbert Letter: Cavaliers Owner Unloads on LeBron James," *The Washington Post*, 9 July 2010.

[11] Ratchford 582–602.

[12] Andrei S. Markovits, "Sports Fans Across Borders: America from Mars, Europe from Venus," *Harvard International Review*, 33 (2), 2011: 19.

[13] Wright Thompson, "When the Beautiful Game Turns Ugly: A Journey into the World of Italy's Racist Soccer Thugs," *ESPNFC & ESPN The Magazine*, 5 June 2013.

[14] Amy Louise Wood, *Lynching and Spectacle: Witnessing Racial Violence in America, 1890–1940* (Chapel Hill, NC: The University of North Carolina Press, 2009) 75.

[15] The confederate states included: Alabama, Arkansas, Florida, Georgia, Louisiana, Mississippi, North Carolina, South Carolina, Texas, Tennessee, Virginia; the states were founded in 1861 and dissolved in 1865 after the American Civil War.

[16] Spectacles are regarded as events of a performance or public show with visual impact.

[17] Dora Apel and Michelle Shawn Smith, *Lynching Photographs* (Los Angeles, CA: University of California Press, 2007), 14.

[18] Apel and Smith 24.

[19] Apel and Smith 15.

[20] Amy Louse Wood, *Lynching and Spectacle:Witnessing Racial Violence in*

America.(Chapel Hill: The University of North Carolina Press, 2009), 41.

[21] Body parts of the victims were also included as part of the souvenir sales following lynchings.

[22] James Allen, *Without Sanctuary* (Santa Fe, NM: Twin Palms, 2000).

[23] Apel and Smith 25.

[24] Apel and Smith 18.

[25] Apel and Smith 18.

[26] Apel and Smith 20.

[27] Susan Sontag. *Regarding the Pain of Others* (New York: Farrar, Straus, Giroux, 2009) 73.

[28] Henry Vance Davis, "The High-Tech Lynching and the High-Tech Overseer: Thoughts from the Anita Hill/Clarence Thomas Affair." *The Black Scholar*, 22 (1/2), 1991: 27.

[29] J. Peterson, "A 'Race' for Equality: Print Media Coverage of the 1968 Olympic Protest by Tommie Smith and John Carlos," *From Jack Johnson to LeBron James: Sports, Media, and the Color Line*, ed. Chris Lamb (Lincoln, NE: The University of Nebraska Press, 2016), 332-356.

[30] Al-Tony Gilmore, *Bad Nigger! The National Impact of Jack Johnson* (Port Washington, New York/London: Kennikat Press, 1975), 13.

[31] Zack Graham, "How David Stern's NBA Dress Code Changed Men's Fashion," *Rolling Stone* 4 November 2016.

[32] Jamie Wilson, "NBA's 'No Bling' Dress Code Prompts Racism Accusations," *The Guardian* 30 October 2005; Rachel Alicia Griffin and Bernadette Marie Calafell, "Control, Discipline, and Punish: Black Masculinity and (In)visible Whiteness in the NBA," *Critical Rhetorics of Race*, ed. Michael G. Lacy and Kent A. Ono (New York: New York University Press, 2011), 127.

[33] Wilson.

[34] Katherine Perlata, "EpiCentre Club Accused of Denying Entrance to Black Patrons," The *Charlotte Observer* 19 September 2016; Hugh Muri, "How Dodgy Door Policies Keep Black People Out of Night Clubs," *The Guardian* 6 July 2016.

[35] Hutchinson 501–521.

[36] Hutchinson 24.

[37] Justin Behrend, *Reconstructing Democracy: Grassroots Black Politics in the Deep South After the Civil War* (Athens, GA: The University of Georgia Press, 2015), 6.

[38] *See* Elaine Frantz Parsons, *Ku Klux: The Birth of the Klan during Reconstruction* (Chapel Hill, NC: The University of North Carolina Press, 2016); LeeAnna Keith, *The Colfax Massacre: The Untold Story of Black Power, White Terror, & The Death of Reconstruction* (Oxford & New York: Oxford University Press, 2008); Carole Emberton, *Beyond Redemption: Race, Violence, and the American South after the Civil War* (Chicago: The University of Chicago Press, 2013).

[39] Bruce E. Baker, *What Reconstruction Meant: Historical Memory in the American South* (Charlottesville, VA: University of Virginia Press, 2007), 70–71.

[40] Michael Perman, *Struggle for Mastery: Disenfranchisement in the South, 1888–1908* (Chapel Hill, NC: The University of North Carolina Press, 2001), 97.

[41] Amy Kate Bailey and Stewart E. Tolnay, *Lynched: The Victims of Southern Mob Violence* (Chapel Hill: The University of North Carolina Press, 2015), 5; Russell T. Wigginton, *The Strange Career of the Black Athlete: African Americans and Sports* (Westport, CT & London: Praeger, 2006), 36–37.

[42] Dora Apel and Michelle Shawn Smith, *Lynching Photographs* (Los Angeles,

CA: University of California Press, 2007), 16.

[43] Denzil Batchelor, *Jack Johnson and His Times* (London: Phoenix Sports Books, 1956); Wigginton 35–40.

[44] Benjamin E. Mays, *Born to Rebel: An Autobiography* (New York: C. Scribner's Sons, 1971), 19.

[45] Gilmore 97, 107.

[46] Gilmore 14–15.

[47] Batchelor; Wigginton, 80–87; *Unforgiveable Blackness: The Rise and Fall of Jack Johnson*, dir. Ken Burns, perf. Jack Johnson (archival footage), PBS, DVD, 2004.

[48] Gilmore 59–72.

[49] Gilmore 60.

[50] Gilmore 59–72.

[51] "Dallas Mob Hangs Negro from Pole at Elks' Arch: Fights Way into Courtroom and Takes Allen Brooks from Armed Officers," *The Dallas Morning News* 4 March 1910. *Note:* A postcard and photo of Brooks's lynching can be found in James Allen's *Without Sanctuary: Lynching Photography in America*.

[52] Gilmore 107.

[53] Melvyn Stokes, *D.W. Griffith's* The Birth of a Nation: *A History of "The Most Controversial Motion Picture of All Time"* (New York: Oxford University Press, 2007).

[54] Wood 106.

[55] Matthew Bigler and Judson L. Jeffries, "'An Amazing Specimen': NFL Draft Experts' Evaluations of Black Quarterbacks." *Journal of African American Studies*, 12 (2), 2008: 122.

[56] Hartmann.

[57] David Niven, "Race, Quarterbacks, and the Media: Testing the Rush Limbaugh Hypothesis," *Journal of Black Studies, 35(5)*, 2005: 690–692.

[58] Bigler and Jeffries 122–127.

[59] Ratchford 585.

[60] Colin Cowherd, "Colin Kaepernick Is Showing You How Unappreciated Alex Smith Is." Online video clip. YouTube, 17 October 2016.

[61] Fox News, "O'Reilly: Kaepernick Missing the Big Picture of His Country." Online video clip. YouTube, 15 September 2016. Web, 1 February 2017.

[62] Fox News, "Vet Who Lost Legs Has Message for Kaepernick." Online video clip. YouTube, 29 August 2016. Web, 1 February 2017.

[63] TMZSports, "Donald Trump: If Kaepernick Doesn't Like America...G(e)t Out," online video clip, YouTube, 29 August 2016. Web, 1 February 2017.

[64] Carbonated TV, "Donald Trump Blames Colin Kaepernick for NFL's Poor Ratings," online video clip, YouTube, 31 October 2016. Web, 1 February 2017. To see the full speech see Right Side Broadcasting, "Full Speech: Donald Trump Rally in Greeley, CO," online video clip, YouTube, 30 October 2016. Web, 1 February 2017.

[65] Kareem Abdul-Jabbar, "Abdul-Jabbar: Insulting Colin Kapernick Says More about Our Patriotism than His," *The Washington Post* 30 August 2016.

[66] The PolitiStick, "49ers Fan Burns Colin Kaepernick's Jersey to National Anthem," YouTube, uploaded by The PolitiStick, 27 August 2016, https://www.YouTube.com/watch?v=-HkMmL4EC7o. **Note**: This video is a re-share of Shane White's videos that is still available online. This has been reported in various mainstream news sources such as the *Washington Post* and the *New York Daily News*. See Cindy Boren, "Colin Kaepernick protest has 49ers fans burning their

jerseys," *The Washington Post*, 28 August 2016; Andy Clayton, "Video: Angry 49ers fan burns Colin Kaepernick shirt after QB's refusal to stand for national anthem," The New York Daily News, 28 August 2016. It was also shared by the rightwing news source Breitbart. Shane White's Facebook page, where the original video is posted, is no longer available.

[67] Breitbart, "Colin Kaepernick Spewed His Hate for America. Now America Is Roaring Back," 28 August 2016, 7:58 p.m. Facebook post. https://www.facebook.com/Breitbart/posts/10157648033390354

[68] Peeples, Mike. "Too Bad He Wasn't in the Jersey at the Time," 29 August 2016, 12:11p.m.
Facebook post. https://www.facebook.com/mrace4u2c **Note**: Mr. Peeple's shared and commented on said post on August 29, 2016 at 12:11 pm. Mr. Peeple's Facebook profile is publically accessible to Facebook users.

[69] Evertsen, Gary. "Him and Obama Are at the Top of My Shit List and I Have a Gift I Wish I Could Give Them Soon," 28 August 2016, 10:19 p.m. Facebook post.
https://www.facebook.com/gary.
evertsen.5?lst=42103618%3A1440191990%3A1481344738. **Note**: Mr. Evertsen's shared and commented on said post on August 28, 2016 at 10:19 pm. Mr. Evertsen's Facebook profile is publically accessible to Facebook users.

[70] LRG LIVIN, "Kapernick Jersey Burning," YouTube, uploaded by LGR LIVIN, 28 August 2016, https://www.YouTube.com/watch?v=NfBMiSyadFg **Note**: On August 28, 2016. An unknown man who goes by the username LGR LIVIN posted a video on the social media platform YouTube of him burning Kaepernick jersey on what appears to be a personal grill.

[71] Bdp711, "Fans Burn Kaepernick Jersey," YouTube, uploaded by Bdp711, 28 August 2016, https://www.YouTube.com/watch?v=MSZ0iuc_uy0. **Note**: On August 28, 2016, an individual with the username bdp711 posted a video on the social media platform YouTube. The video highlights three unknown people burning Kaepernick's jersey while holding the American flag noting that, "Kaepernick can burn."

[72] Blizzard 1203, "Farewell to kaepernick s'mores," YouTube, uploaded by blizzard 1203, 30 August 2016, https://www.YouTube.com/watch?v=zSaCGSOo7_I **Note**: On August 30, 2016, an individual with the username blizzard 1203 posted a video on the social media platform YouTube. The video depicts an unidentified woman with three children. They are burning Kaepernick's jersey followed by making s'mores.

[73] Although Colin Kaepernick appears to have been blackballed from the NFL and likely will not play again, he has enjoyed success off the field. He has created a platform (Know Your Rights Camp) that addresses social justice and equality, won adoration from the international community, and most notably appeared on the December 2017 front cover of GQ (Gentleman's Quarterly Magazine) as its *Citizen of the Year*.

[74] President Donald Trump used the national anthem protests during 2017-18 NFL season as a political weapon (through twitter and at campaign style rallies) to appeal to his base. Most recently, President Trump took the field at the 2018 College Football Playoff National Championship game and stood for the national anthem symbolically as a rebuke to those who protested the national anthem.

Works Cited

Abbott, Henry. "LeBron James' Decision: The Transcript." ESPN, 8 July 2010, http://www.espn.com/blog/truehoop/post/_/id/17853/lebron-james-decision-the-transcript. Accessed 1 February 2017.

Abdul-Jabbar, Kareem. "Abdul-Jabbar: Insulting Colin Kaepernick Says More About Our Patriotism Than His." *The Washington Post*, 30 August 2016, https://www.washingtonpost.com/posteverything/wp/2016/08/30/insulting-colin-kaepernick-says-more-about-our-patriotism-than-his/?utm_term=.bfbdede17c1a. Accessed 1 February 2017.

Adams, Cydney. "June 17, 1994: O.J. Simpson White Bronco Chase Mesmerizes Nation." CBS, 17 June 2016, http://www.cbsnews.com/news/june-17-1994-o-j-simpson-car-chase-mesmerizes-nation/. Accessed 1 February 2017.

Allen, James. *Without Sanctuary*. Santa Fe, NM: Twin Palms. 2000.

Apel, Dora, and Shawn Michelle Smith. *Lynching Photographs*. Los Angeles: University of California Press, 2007.

Baker, Bruce E. *What Reconstruction Meant: Historical Memory in the American South*. Charlottesville, VA: University of Virginia Press, 2007.

Bailey, Amy Kate, and Steward E. Tolnay. *Lynched: The Victims of Southern Mob Violence*. Chapel Hill, NC: The University of North Carolina Press, 2016.

Batchelor, Denzil. *Jack Johnson and His Times*. London: Phoenix Sports Books, 1956.

Bdp711. "Fans Burn Kaepernick Jersey." *YouTube*, uploaded by Bdp711, 28 August 2016, https://www.YouTube.com/watch?v=MSZ0iuc_uy0.

Behrend, Justin. *Reconstructing Democracy: Grassroots Black Politics in the Deep South After the Civil War*. Athens, GA: The University of Georgia Press, 2015.

Bever, Megan L. "Fuzzy Memories: College Mascots and the Struggle to Find Appropriate Legacies of the Civil War." *Journal of Sport History*, 38(3), 2011: 447–463. www.jstor.org/stable/10.5406/jsporthistory.38.3.447.

Bigler, Matthew, and Judson L. Jeffries. "'An Amazing Specimen': NFL Draft Experts' Evaluations of Black Quarterbacks." *Journal of African American Studies*, 12(2),2008: 120–141.

Blizzard 1203. "Farewell to kaepernick s'mores." *YouTube*, uploaded by bBizzard 1203, 30 August 2016, https://www.YouTube.com/watch?v=zSaCGSOo7_I

Breitbart. "Colin Kaepernick Spewed His Hate for America. Now America Is Roaring Back..." 28 August 2016, 7:58 p.m. Facebook post.

Carbonated.TV. "Donald Trump Blames Colin Kaepernick for NFL's Poor Ratings." Online video clip. YouTube, 31 October 2016. Web, 1

February 2017.

Cowherd, Colin. "Colin Kaepernick Is Showing You How Unappreciated Alex Smith Is." *YouTube*, uploaded by Colin Cowherd, 17 October 2016, https://www.YouTube.com/watch?v=CxQA2znHiDo

"Dallas Mob Hangs Negro from Pole at Elks' Arch: Fights Way into Courtroom and Takes Allen Brooks From Armed Officers." *The Dallas Morning News*, 4 March 1910, http://www.dallasnews.com/news/photos/2013/03/03/today-in-dallas-photo-history-1910-allen-brooks-lynched-in-downtown-dallas-by-angry-mob. Accessed 1 Feburary 2017.

Davis, Henry Vance. "The High-Tech Lynching and the High-Tech Overseer: Thoughts from the Anita Hill/Clarence Thomas Affair." *The Black Scholar*, vol. 22, no. ½, 1991: 27-29.

Emberton, Carol. *Beyond Redemption: Race, Violence, and the American South After the Civil War*. Chicago: The University of Chicago Press, 2013.

Evertsen, Gary. "Him and Obama Are At the Top of My Shit List and I Have a Gift I Wish I Could Give Them Soon." 28 August 2016, 10:19 p.m. Facebook post.

Fox News. "O'Reilly: Kaepernick Missing the Big Picture of his Country." *YouTube*, uploaded by Fox News, 15 September 2016, https://www.YouTube.com/watch?v=FSS9QfGBNno .

Fox News. "Vet Who Lost Legs Has Message for Kaepernick." *YouTube*, uploaded by Fox News, 29 August 2015, https://www.YouTube.com/watch?v=FpsM6zoSPuE .

Graham, Zack. "How David Stern's NBA Dress Code Changed Men's Fashion." *Rolling Stone*, 4 November 2016, http://www.rollingstone.com/sports/features/david-sterns-nba-dress-code-legacy-w448591. Accessed 1 February 2017.

Gilmore, Al-Tony. *Bad Nigger! The National Impact of Jack Johnson*. Port Washington, New York/London: Kennikat Press, 1975.

Griffin, Rachel Alicia, and Bernadette Marie Calafell. "Control, Discipline, and Punish: Black Masculinity and (In)visible Whiteness in the NBA." *Critical Rhetorics of Race*. Ed. Michael G. Lacy and Kent A. Ono. New York: New York University Press, 2011, 117–138.

Guttmann, Allen. "Sport, Politics and the Engaged Historian." *Journal of Contemporary History*, 38(3), 2003: 363–375. www.jstor.org/stable/3180642.

Hartmann, Douglas. "Rush Limbaugh, Donovan McNabb, and 'A Little Social Concern': Reflections on the Problems of Whiteness in Contemporary American Sport." *From Jack Johnson to LeBron James: Sports, Media, and the Color Line*. Ed. Chris Lamb. Lincoln, NE: The University of Nebraska Press, 2016: 501-521.

Hutchinson, Phillip J. "Framing White Hopes: The Press, Social Drama, and the Era of Jack Johnson, 1908-1915." *From Jack Johnson to LeBron James: Sports, Media, and the Color Line*. Ed. Chris Lamb. Lincoln, NE: The University of Nebraska Press, 2016: 19– 51.

Keith, LeeAnna. *The Colfax Massacre: The Untold Story of Black Power, White*

Terror, & The Death of Reconstruction. Oxford & New York: Oxford University Press, 2008.

Lee, Michael. "Dan Gilbert Letter: Cavaliers Owner Unloads on LeBron James." *The Washington Post,* 9 July 2010. http://voices. washingtonpost.com/wizardsinsider/2010/07/cavaliers-owner-dan-gilbert-un.html. Accessed 1 February 2017.

LRG LIVIN. "Kaepernick Jersey Burning." *YouTube,* uploaded by LGR LIVIN, 28 August 2016, https://www.YouTube.com/ watch?v=NfBMiSyadFg.

Markovits, Andrei S. "Sports Fans Across Borders: America from Mars, Europe from Venus." *Harvard International Review,* 33(2), 2011: 17–22. www.jstor.org/stable/42763469.

Mays, Benjamin E. *Born to Rebel: An Autobiography.* New York: C. Scribner's Sons, 1971.

Muri, Hugh."How dodgy door policies keep black people out of night clubs." *The Guardian* 6 July 2016, https://www.theguardian. com/uk-news/2015/jul/06/dodgy-door-policies-black-people-nightclubs-discrimination. Accessed 1 February 2017.

Niven, David. "Race, Quarterbacks, and the Media: Testing the Rush Limbaugh Hypothesis." *Journal of Black Studies, 35(5),* 2005: 684–694.

O.J.: Made in America. Directed by Ezra Edelman, performed OJ Simpson (archival footage), ESPN, Disney, 2016.

Parsons, Elaine Frantz. *Ku Klux: The Birth of the Klan during Reconstruction.* Chapel Hill, NC: The University of North Carolina Press, 2016.

Peeples, Mike. "Too Bad He Wasn't In the Jersey at the Time." 29 August 2016, 12:11 p.m. Facebook post.

Perlata, Katherine. "EpiCentre Club Accused of Denying Entrance to Black Patrons." *The Charlotte Observer,* 19 September 2016, http:// www.charlotteobserver.com/news/business/article102776532. html. Accessed 1 February 2017.

Perman, Michael. *Struggle for Mastery: Disenfranchisement in the South, 1888-1908.* Chapel Hill, NC: The University of North Carolina Press, 2001.

Peterson, Jason. "A 'Race' for Equality: Print Media Coverage of the 1968 Olympic Protest by Tommie Smith and John Carlos." *From Jack Johnson to LeBron James: Sports, Media, and the Color Line.* Ed. Chris Lamb. Lincoln, NE: The University of Nebraska Press, 2016: 332-356.

The PolitiStick. "49ers Fan Burns Colin Kaepernick's Jersey to National Anthem." *YouTube,* uploaded by The PolitiStick, 27 August 2016, https://www.YouTube.com/watch?v=-HkMmL4EC7o .

Raiford, Leigh. "Photography and the Practices of Critical Memory." *History and Theory, 48(4).* Dec. 2009: 112–129.

Ratchford, Jamal L. "The LeBron James Decision in the Age of Obama." *From Jack Johnson to LeBron James: Sports, Media, and the Color Line.* Ed. Chris Lamb. Lincoln, NE: The University of Nebraska Press, 2016: 582-602.

Right Side Broadcasting. "Full Speech: Donald Trump Rally in Greeley, CO." *YouTube,* uploaded by Right Side Broadcasting, 30 October

2016, https://www.YouTube.com/watch?v=aMZsKq99hdk .

Sontag, Susan. *Regarding the Pain of Others*. New York: Farrar, Straus, Giroux, 2009.

Stein, Michael. "Cult and Sport: The Case of Big Red." *Mid-American Review of Sociology, 2(2)*, 1977: 29–42.

Stevens, Stuart. "What College Football Means in the South: A Story of a Father Son Son — And the Odes to Dixie and the Civil War that Have Been Tied to Ole Miss Football Traditions for Years." *The Atlantic*, 15 September 2015, https://www.theatlantic.com/politics/archive/2015/09/what-college-football-means-in-the-south/405283/. Accessed 1 February 2017.

Stokes, Melvyn. *D.W. Griffith's* The Birth of a Nation: *A History of "The Most Controversial Motion Picture of All Time."* New York: Oxford University Press, 2007.

Thompson, Wright. "When the Beautiful Game Turns Ugly: A Journey into the World of Italy's Racist Soccer Thugs." *ESPNFC & ESPN The Magazine*, 5 June 2013, http://www.espn.com/espn/feature/story/_/id/9338962/when-beautiful-game-turns-ugly. Accessed 1 February 2017.

TMZSports. "Donald Trump: If Kaepernick Doesn't Like America…Get Out." Online video clip. YouTube, uploaded by TMZSports 29 August 2016, https://www.YouTube.com/watch?v=kwDs4AlYYF0 .

Unforgiveable Blackness: The Rise and Fall of Jack Johnson. Directed by Ken Burns, performance by Jack Johnson (archival footage), PBS, DVD, 2004.

Vogan, Travis. "30 for 30." *Journal of Sport History, 38(1)*, 2011: 125–127. www.jstor.org/stable/10.5406/jsporthistory.38.1.125.

Wigginton, Russell T. *The Strange Career of the Black Athlete: African Americans and Sports*. Westport, CT/London: Praeger. 2006.

Wilson, Jamie. "NBA's 'No Bling' Dress Code Prompts Racism Accusations." *The Guardian* 30 October 2005, https://www.theguardian.com/world/2005/oct/31/usa.americansports. Accessed 1 February 2017.

Wood, Amy Louise. *Lynching and Spectacle: Witnessing Racial Violence in America, 1890–1940*. Chapel Hill: University of North Carolina, 2009.

Wortham, Jenna. "How an Archive of the Internet Could Change History." *New York Times Magazine*, June 21, 2016.

The Devil and Len Bias:
How Politicians, Players and Pushers
Made the 1986 Crack Scare and the
Modern War on Drugs.

MICHAEL J. DURFEE

At approximately 7:00 p.m. on June 17, 1986, twenty-two-year-old basketball star Len Bias was selected as the number two overall pick in the NBA Draft by the Boston Celtics. Following the euphoria of draft night, Bias and his father James flew to Boston to sign a multimillion dollar endorsement deal at Reebok headquarters. After meeting with Reebok brass and representatives from the Boston Celtics, Len and James flew home to Washington D.C. The whirlwind of interviews, meetings, autograph signings and T.V. appearances meant two things: Len had finally made it; and James needed a nap.

Unlike James, his ebullient young son remained eager to celebrate with his college teammates at nearby University of Maryland. With that, Len leapt into his newly-leased Nissan 380ZX sports car at 11:00 p.m. and headed for campus. He and his roommates ate crabs and then drove to a nearby liquor store, where the night manager sold him malt liquor and a fifth of cognac. Bias autographed his receipt for the manager, careful to include "30," his new Celtics number. At roughly 3:00 a.m., Bias returned to Washington Hall where he shared a suite with teammates Terry Long and David Gregg. Bias also returned with his childhood friend Brian Tribble and several grams of cocaine. After waking up both Long and Gregg, the four young friends partied into the early morning.[1]

At 6:32 a.m. the frantic 911 call from Brian Tribble came in. Tribble attempted to explain to the dispatcher that Bias had gone into seizures, "This is Len Bias. You have to get him back to life. There's no way he can die. . . . It's an emergency. It's Len Bias, and he just went to Boston and he needs some assistance. . . . This is Len Bias. You have to get him back to life. There's no way he can die. Seriously, sir. Please come quick."[2]

At 8:50 a.m. on June 19, 1986, Bias was pronounced dead at Leland Memorial Hospital in Maryland from cocaine-related cardiac arrest. Bias's death proved timely for the broader agenda of politicians from both parties who spearheaded the call for a national mobilization against "crack" cocaine, as well as the drug's dealers and users.[3] The groundswell of support from Congressmen and Senators alike to take action against the perceived crack crisis had actually begun in early May, prior to Bias' death, but lacked public awareness and support. The agenda was clear however: a unified, dramatized, forceful attack to be made upon popular opinions and attitudes regarding drug use had been issued on no uncertain terms.[4] These American politicians were thus ready when at 8:50 a.m. on June 19, 1986, Len Bias delivered the ultimate weapon to fight the War on Drugs.

Len Bias (left) and Brian Tribble (right) outside of a Barbershop in their Landover, Maryland neighborhood.

In the summer of 1986, politicians – Democrats and Republicans alike – successfully manufactured a nationwide crack scare: a major problem in urban communities was portrayed as a problem that threatened every town and village of the United States. Certainly, crack took an incredible toll on specific urban communities such as New York City, Miami, Los Angeles, and Chicago to name just a few. However, evidence suggests that crack never posed a legitimate threat nationwide, remaining far from the ubiquitous scourge imagined by congressional committees and popular media of the period.[5]

Instrumental to popular perceptions regarding the dangers of crack became the tragedy, and unique political opportunity, surrounding the death of Len Bias. The specific place in time and space occupied by Bias's death is one key to understanding why this flashpoint in contemporary history proved so pivotal.[6] Facing the prospect of a crucial midterm election in November, Democrats and Republicans both searched for an emotionally charged issue to galvanize electoral support. Bias's death generated the proverbial "juice" to the War on Drugs and provided a compelling storyline for campaign sound bites. By invoking Bias's death as a cautionary tale, politicians could effectively conjure up a powerful fear-based discourse regarding the threat of pervasive drug abuse in America.[7]

Also, central to understanding the media and political phenomena which followed Bias's death are popular representations of Bias and his vilified childhood friend Brian Tribble. Major national media outlets, politicians, and other primary movers in the War on Drugs all portrayed these two young men on vastly different terms. Bias and Tribble shared more similarities than they did differences, but their respective political utility in the War on Drugs drove a wedge between them in popular culture. While Bias came to be the physical personification of the individualist, New Right "culture of triumph" in the 1980s, coverage of Brian Tribble depicted a highly dangerous, racialized, "menace to society" representative of the underclass and a burgeoning hip-hop culture.[8] Certainly, Senators and Congressmen of the *Select Committee on Narcotics Abuse and Control*, and columnists from the *NY Times, LA Times,* and *Washington Post* all pointed to Len Bias as *the* casualty of the drug war. However, it is clear that Brian Tribble, and the countless others like him, were also casualties in the War on Drugs.

In the post-civil rights era, a rising New Right helped push explicit issues of race to the background of popular and political discourse. In its place, conservatives discussed issues of poverty, crime, drug abuse, and a failing education system through the lens of class and culture, making their policies appear less grounded in race. Instead of pointing their fingers at blacks in general, conservative politicians strategically pointed to the developing underclass as the locus of moral decline and urban crisis. In short, a more discrete, sophisticated brand of institutional and structural racism supplanted the direct and overt racism of previous decades in the post-civil rights era.[9]

Both Len Bias and Brian Tribble serve as a powerful case in point for this contention. By heaping praise upon the more acceptable Christian student-athlete Bias, the Right could excuse themselves from the table of bigotry and hate. By condemning a thug drug-dealer like Brian Tribble, the Right simply condemned the deviant behavior and moral repugnance of the underclass, not African-Americans as a whole. In the hands of a media increasingly warm to conservative rationale, the whole sobering story – in all its details – served to reinforce popular conservative ideology. Len Bias, a Horatio Alger of his generation, had pulled himself up by his bootstraps, out of the ghetto of Landover, Maryland where he was born, by way of his hard work, determination, Christian values, and upright moral character. Brian Tribble, typical of the underclass, learned from the wisdom of his misspent youth to sell drugs. His inherent moral failings had remanded him to a life of crime, unstable and tenuous at best. More importantly, Tribble's moral defects became an overwhelming negative influence upon Bias, dragging him back down to the depths from whence he came. With that, Len Bias overdosed on cocaine presumably provided by his childhood friend. Brian Tribble placed the subsequent 911 call notifying the authorities that his best friend lay dead on his dorm-room floor.[10]

In addition to the rise of the New Right, the curious circumstances of Len Bias's death also revealed the ways in which Democrats and Liberalism continued to change in response to a shifting social and political landscape. Desperate to prove that they could be hard on drugs and crime, as well as to regain their electorate, Democrats joined Republicans in the War on Drugs. A deliberate public struggle between both parties followed as they attempted to embrace the drug issue as their own. Amidst this struggle, Democrats found themselves culturally outmaneuvered by Republicans. Long the party which came to the aid of poor urban minorities, Democrats regularly hung their hat on issues of urban blight. In the Crack Era, drug warrior Democrats uncomfortably portrayed a more aggressive posture, what one columnist E.J. Dionne later referred to as "Kojak Liberalism."[11]

The death of Len Bias however, allowed conservatives to effectively steal the issue on their own terms. The New Right was able to adopt Bias as a martyr, simultaneously representing its alleged progress in terms of race as well as their ability to protect the country against the mushrooming prospect of drug abuse and moral decline. In turn, this allowed an environment in which both Democrats and Republicans mounted aggressive attacks upon the underclass without raising eyebrows nationwide. After all, Congress was merely addressing the concerns of grassroots organizations in cities like New York, Los Angeles, and Oakland. As the War on Drugs escalated, politicians pushed closer to passing new, increasingly harsh drug reform as each side struggled to champion the issue. California Congressman Tony Coelho unpacked this phenomenon best as he told a local newspaper that, "the chemistry to create an issue was all there, and Bias lit it."[12]

Much has been made about the rise of the New Right and the War on Drugs. Many historians have argued that the War on Drugs served as a vehicle for legislators and prominent national media outlets to wage war upon the underclass.[13] While this portion of the historical narrative is compelling, previous histories often ignore or dismiss the bipartisan nature of crack-era drug reform. Too often, Democrats are excused or ignored for their heavy-handed role in the War on Drugs. Democrats – particularly Charles Rangel – embraced the Len Bias opportunity and used it to advance their own individual political agendas. Democrats and Republicans cast out Len Bias into the broader public periphery as both a martyr and a warning against the dangers of drug abuse. For

Republicans, this situation fostered a coherent continuation of established priorities such as family values, the restoration of order, and urban disinvestment. For Democrats, the picture remains less linear. For Rangel and other Democrats representing urban constituents, Bias presented an opportunity to win much-needed resources for cities and an opportunity to protect the majority of urban citizens who worked, paid their taxes, and abided the law. Questioning whether the Reagan administration planned to continue policies of benign neglect, leading Democrats had goaded Reagan to get more serious about drugs in urban communities long before the Bias overdose.

On the whole, scholars of history, sociology, medicine, and drug policy almost uniformly argue that drug use – particularly the abuse of crack – became associated with the underclass. Implicit in this association was the understanding that the underclass largely represented African-American urban poor, in addition to other disadvantaged minorities. Most scholars cast blame exclusively upon Conservative Republicans under the Reagan administration for the advancement of public policy which effectively crippled the underclass of urban communities. Sociologists Craig Reinarman and Harry G. Levine do acknowledge the role of Democrats in the War on Drugs albeit sparingly in their authoritative work, *Crack in America: Demon Drugs and Social Justice*. Mainly, they cite the "conservative ideological environment" as responsible for broader problems of poverty and increasing inequality. Furthermore, they suggest that "competition between political parties in a conservative context contributed significantly to the making of the crack scare".[14] According to Reinarman and Levine, Democrats found the collective War on Drugs to be an opportunity to appear more Conservative, hard on drugs, and to recapture a portion of their electorate. Additionally, a similar case is made by historian David Courtwright who argues that the legislative process became a competition for toughness points in which Democrats had little choice but to go along.[15]

How did the War on Drugs become an acceptable opportunity to gain more votes in the eyes of Democrats? Or, to put it more broadly, how had both parties reached a place where conservatives had begun to dictate the rules of play? Uniformly, scholars have ignored the work done by the Len Bias opportunity in this instance as well as the deeper historical roots connecting Liberalism to law and order politics. The death of Len Bias arrived at an explosive crossroads of time and space, representing a tipping point of sorts. Both Len Bias and Brian Tribble help us to see the cultural mechanics of this seismic shift. As race faded to the background in the post-civil rights era, a new institutionalized racism emerged.[16] Crack dealers became synonymous with the underclass and a deviant hip-hop culture in its infancy. While Len Bias became the poster boy for the War on Drugs, Brian Tribble served as the poster boy for everything that was wrong with America's urban centers and ghettos – the underclass.

By the end of the Bias affair in mid-summer 1986, the New Right had been largely successful in portraying the underclass as a morally deficient, pathologically deviant segment of the population to blame for their own circumstances.[17] The death of Len Bias and subsequent representations of Bias as well as Tribble served to advance this commonly held belief. Thus, Democrats were presented with a decision to make. They could either publicly unpack the myth that the underclass was solely to blame for their inequitable exigencies – or – Democrats could choose to play in the backyard of the New Right out of desperation. Democrats chose the latter, engaging in sensationalized rhetoric, fear-mongering, and draconian legal measures to combat the modern urban crisis.

This chapter will proceed in three basic sections. Section one traces the political maneuvering which shifted the War on Drugs from a crusade of the Right to conventional wisdom over the course of a few months in 1986. Strict attention will be paid to the role of the *Select Committee on Narcotics Abuse and Control*, chaired by Democrat Charles Rangel. Section two will deal with popular representations of Len Bias and Brian Tribble. Representations of both Bias and Tribble were carefully and strategically packaged by politicians and prominent national media outlets. Each served a specific political function in advancing the War on Drugs. In section three, I will further evaluate the role of race in the post-civil rights era as well as the legacy of both Bias and the Anti-Drug Abuse Act of 1986. Additionally, section three will serve as a space for reflection upon the dangers of individual political opportunism in an atmosphere of crisis and panic. More broadly, what Lisa Miller aptly refers to as the "perils of federalism"[18] will be addressed. As grassroots activists won more attention and notoriety for their issue, they were increasingly squeezed out of the process at the state and national level. Thus, the activists who first identified the problem of crack-cocaine and worked tirelessly to mitigate its effects in their community were increasingly rendered voiceless and invisible. As such urban communities were portrayed by national media and Congress as complicit in, or apathetic to the purported evils of the crack trade. The consistent grassroots activism of groups in areas hit hardest by crack such as the Bronx suggests an entirely different reality.

Creating Reality: *The Politics of a Manufactured Crisis*

By 1986, Democrats had lost three of the last four presidential elections, as well as their majority status in the Senate. Two years prior, Ronald Reagan carried forty-nine states with unprecedented ease in the 1984 presidential election. His opponent, Walter Mondale, was only able to win the District of Columbia and his home state of Minnesota by a small margin. All told, the overwhelming popular vote issued a clear mandate of the people. "Reagan Democrats" and the Silent Majority had spoken. By 1986 it was clear to Democrats that they must eschew perceptions that they were soft on crime and drugs. Thus, Democrats seemed determined to project the image of firm support for any anti-drug and crime bills which came across the House floor.

Emblematic of the attempt to give the party's image regarding drugs and crime a facelift, the predominantly Democratic *Select Committee on Narcotics Abuse and Control* took center stage in the summer of 1986 as crack exploded onto the national scene.[19] Despite lacking concrete knowledge of the scope and severity of the crack problem in the United States, both politicians and national newspapers such as the *New York Times, LA Times, and Washington Post* all employed hyperbole and sensationalism, inspiring a national panic surrounding the dangers of crack.[20]

As early as May, politicians of the Select Committee – most of whom were Democrats – began to frame the crack issue as they railed against the perceived atmosphere of social acceptability for drug use in the broader American public. Democrat Jim Wright:

> Instead of sending out the message of "Caveat Emptor" – let the buyer beware – proliferating stories involving rock stars, movie idols, athletes, television personalities seem to give drug use a sometimes subtle but always seductive stamp of apparent approval. This creates an atmosphere of social acceptability, particularly among the impressionable young that enables drug use and abuse to permeate and corrode American Society.[21]

African-American activist Reverend Jesse Jackson attended the second session of the hearings and emphasized the lack of public awareness: "The first step in solving our drug problem is to recognize it as a problem, which most Americans do not."[22] Jackson went on to claim that "America still has not really come to grips with how drugs are affecting our youth."[23] Moreover, later in the hearing Jackson identified a growing sentiment amongst politicians of the *Select Committee* that sought to induce panic amongst the general public: "So far we have not been able to get the sense of alarm, sense of emergency, the sense of immorality, sense of un-Americanism and all the other great phrases that makes us jump about this dope situation."[24] Here, Jackson proves prophetic in his ability to foreshadow events that would follow in the summer of 1986; events which were largely engineered by the very committee to whom he was speaking.

Tired, and perhaps desperate in their attempts to overturn what they perceived to be blatant disregard for long suffering urban communities predicated upon race, liberal politicians sought to call attention to such long-standing issues. In 1984, Charles Rangel wrote about the need to "target" dealers and addicts in *Justice Quarterly*: "Are streets are more dangerous because of the illegal trafficking by violence-prone dealers and the presence in many communities of large numbers of addicts . . .

There can be little doubt that there is a relationship between drugs and crime."[25] In the same piece, Rangel attacks the Reagan Administration for scaling back both treatment and enforcement funding to "save money in a time of worrisome deficits."[26] In a sign of rhetoric to follow in the Crack Era, Rangel also sloppily compares nonviolent drug crimes to rape: "I have no patience with those who say that the law is at fault. Legalize drugs, they say, and drug crimes will disappear. Would they use the same logic to repeal the laws against rape?"[27] Referencing too much benign neglect, Rangel argued that too many on the Right had fostered a spirit of "defeatism in some quarters"[28] with respect to the War on Drugs.

Politicians of the Select Committee believed that a general level of social acceptability surrounding drugs pervaded American society as late as May and early June of 1986. Despite an acknowledged lack of public support, men such as Jim Wright, Charles Rangel, and several others discussed the need for a unified effort to manipulate public understandings and attitudes around crack: "Nothing could demand a greater priority in our scale of national values than the terrible growing menace of drug abuse and the illicit traffic in narcotics. Nothing less than our national security in the ultimate analysis is at stake."[29]

Almost uniformly, politicians looking to advance the case for the War on Drugs framed discussion around values and security. Drugs, drug users, and drug dealers were to be understood as dangerous as well as inherently and pathologically immoral. Charles Rangel's statements in the same hearing best embody this specific effort: "I agree with you that we have to turn it [national drug problem] around. It is a moral question, a family question, a community question."[30] In addition to the emphasis on morality and family values, members of the Select Committee like Jim Wright hoped to create an environment of drug intolerance: "What we need is to deglamorize drugs through an aggressive public education campaign. Towards this end, celebrities, public officials, and ordinary citizens alike should get organized to help dramatize the drug crisis and popularize the state of being drug-free as the condition of social acceptability."[31]

The desire to dramatize the drug crisis led the Select Committee to fully embrace the power of hyperbole. Jim Wright at once coined crack dealers the "Grim Reapers of the modern age," while Charles Rangel referred to crack as "the modern Medusa," quipping that with crack, "one look and you're caught."[32] In a particularly telling moment at the end of one committee hearing, Rangel provided a window of insight into potential electoral leverage to be gained for Democrats by beating Republicans to the drug issue: "But one of the biggest problems we have with this Administration is that they have not admitted to the scope of the problem . . . how we take advantage of it, I do not know."[33] Rangel's comment suggests that Democrats hoped to position themselves as pioneers in the assault upon crack before mid-term elections in November. However, the lack of public support left politicians such as Rangel confounded as they openly wondered how to harness the potential of the growing crack problem.

Less than a month later, the high-profile death of Len Bias would offer a unique opportunity for the Select Committee. On the day of Bias's passing, the *Boston Globe* received more calls inquiring about his death than they had received for any other incident since the assassination of President John F. Kennedy.[34] In the thirty days following the Bias tragedy, seventy-four national evening news segments featured cocaine and crack-cocaine abuse and addiction.[35] In the months leading up to the November elections a handful of national newspapers and magazines produced roughly a thousand stories discussing crack. On August 11, 1986, *Newsweek* reported that, "nearly everyone now concedes that the plague is all but universal"[36] when reflecting upon the growing prospect of crack abuse in the United States. By September 20, *Time* called crack "the Issue of the Year."[37] Furthermore, *Time* and *Newsweek* each devoted five cover stories to crack and the perceived "drug crisis" in 1986. In the spring of 1986, when popular media "discovered" crack, the percentage of the public identifying "drugs" as the "number one problem facing the nation" climbed from 3 percent to 13 percent in just three months.[38] While the specter of crack and crack abuse had permeated national media circles prior to Len Bias's death, what followed belied any proponent of the War on Drug's wildest imaginings.[39]

As an identifiable tipping point, the death of Len Bias allowed politicians as well as prominent national media outlets to exacerbate – if not manufacture – widespread panic. As quickly as July, public opinion surrounding the drug issue mobilized in contempt of drugs, drug users, and drug dealers. Popular public opinion, as well as sensationalized rhetoric from Democrats, Republicans, and media outlets all served to complement each other, further heightening a sense of panic and crisis. As rhetoric and public outcry against the drug problem intensified, politicians scrambled to champion the issue as their own.

Following their traditional July 4th recess, the House of Representatives returned in mid-July for a series of hearings regarding the "Crack-Cocaine Crisis." What emerged from these hearings were the seeds of the Anti-Drug Abuse Act of 1986. Although initiated by Republicans, both Democrats and Republicans soon invoked Bias as a symbol for the War on Drugs. More specifically, Bias became not only a victim, but a martyr for supporters of the War on Drugs. Lastly, as the rhetoric of politicians intensified, a language of combat became commonplace. By consistently framing the War on Drugs as out-and-out combat, politicians effectively exaggerated the pervasiveness and threat of crack abuse nationwide. Furthermore, this language of combat began to identify an enemy – the underclass. By increasingly associating the underclass with crack abuse and crime, politicians began their campaign against the urban poor which would ultimately culminate in the Anti-Drug Abuse Act of 1986.

In an early July Select Committee hearing – this time on "Trafficking and Abuse of 'Crack' in New York City" – Charles Rangel entered opening remarks: "Today only a few short months later, we have returned to this because of another epidemic threatening our cities, our towns and villages, that of crack, a purified, inexpensive, concentrated form of cocaine, whose popularity has been spreading like wildfire across the country."[40] Rangel continued as he argued, "crack is invading our towns," calling for the need to "combat this deadly menace . . . jeopardizing the very foundations of our institutions."[41] If such hyperbole were not enough, Governor of New York Mario Cuomo proceeded to identify it as "fashionable" while simultaneously engaging in this very practice: "It is fashionable, as we have seen today, and as we will continue to see throughout this hearing, it is fashionable now to talk of the problem of substance abuse and narcotics addiction as an epidemic. Tragic and ugly episodes like the deaths of two young athletes dramatize for us a menace that has existed, that has spread, that has grown more devastating and pervasive for a couple of decades."[42]

Cuomo's remarks point to the way many of crack's critics used Bias as a symbol in the War on Drugs. Dr. Jerome H. Jaffe, Director of the National Institute on Drug Abuse was called before the *Select Committee* to lend his expertise to the issue of crack abuse in July. Entrusted with the responsibility of creating and disseminating the nation's anti-drug campaign, Jaffe commented that "the tragedy of two healthy and promising sports stars dying from cocaine has produced perhaps more exposure to the real dangers of cocaine than we have purchased through Government efforts in the last year."[43] Jaffe also stated that: "The message that 'cocaine kills' is something that I think is being started from the tragedy of Len Bias and other sports people."[44] Perhaps more interesting were Jaffe's comments regarding the Institute's ability to surmise how quickly the crack problem was spreading and how pervasive use had become: "I think it would be fair to say that we do not have any accurate estimate at this time. . . . The difficulty is that crack appeared within a year, so it is very hard to tell about actual crack use."[45] Coincidentally, no further dialogue was pursued on the matter of actual crack use throughout the nation.

In search of a moral to the developing story of that 1986 summer, Peter Rodino Jr. of New Jersey offered his own personal sentiments: "with the recent cocaine-related deaths of Len Bias and Don Rogers, our Nation has once again learned the hard way about the dangers of our national drug epidemic. The lesson is clear: drug abuse can hit anyone, no matter how promising and successful. It also tells another unfortunate fact—that our Nation is losing the war on drugs."[46] Rodino could not be clearer about the ways in which politicians sought to use Len Bias in the

War on Drugs. As a cautionary tale, Bias warned the nation against the ubiquitous danger of drugs as they had taken the life of an impeccably conditioned, morally upright, Christian athlete.

While Len Bias emerged as a martyr, anti-crack crusaders painted other young black men — the underclass - as enemies of the state. Crack abuse and crack dealing was also tied to violent crime by politicians in late summer and early fall. Congressman James Scheur, for example claimed that:

> It is probably more responsible for school failure, for defeat in life for young kids, especially minority kids, than any other phenomenon in our society. It is a truism that drug addiction is responsible for perhaps a half — 55 or 60 percent of the violent crime in our urban centers, so it is a destabilizing fact in urban life, but it is a crippling and disabling event in the life of millions of our kids.[47]

A more direct link of crack addiction to violent crime was made in the same hearing by Congressman Mel Levine of California: "Crack addiction often leads to violent and criminal behavior to support the habit. . . . The victimization produced by crack addiction is infinite. Desperate addicts will steal, sell their possessions, and even sell themselves to buy more crack."[48] Perhaps even more to the point, Senator Patrick Moynihan addressed the Senate regarding his alleged concern for the young black male:

> It seems to me that we cannot ignore the fact that when we talk about drug abuse in our country, in the main, we are talking about the consequences it has for young males in inner cities, for whom drug use is an aspect of a generally abused, wasted and ruined life, and indeed, ruinous to those in the community around them. Any society that is really serious about drug abuse will be serious about that class of young males. It has been growing. It has reached proportions that threaten to bring about the destruction of whole communities and cities across the nation.[49]

Here, Moynihan - an often criticized proponent of the very idea of an "underclass" and "culture of poverty" - succinctly generalizes and targets young black males of the underclass without explicitly mentioning race.[50] Instead, Moynihan emphasizes issues of culture and class. As politicians from both sides of the aisle continued to echo the statements of Senator Moynihan, a picture of the underclass as the enemy in the War on Drugs began to crystallize.

Riding the wave of an unforeseen media bonanza surrounding the death of Len Bias and subsequent crack scare throughout the summer of 1986, politicians had successfully mobilized public support behind the War on Drugs. Moments after Moynihan closed his remarks about the danger of drugs and young inner-city males, Senator Strom Thurmond commented on the shifting tide of public opinion: "We are beginning to see a fundamental change in the attitude of the American people toward the use of illegal drugs. Across the country individual citizens, private organizations, community groups, public agencies are all working to reestablish a moral climate in which drug use is not just illegal, but socially and ethically unacceptable."[51]

By late September, the consensus among politicians that the American public had come to demand harsher penalties on drugs had arrived. In the following month, the War on Drugs would be forever changed by the passage of the Anti-Drug Abuse Act of 1986. Democrat Jim Wright of Texas first introduced House Resolution 5484 in Congress on September 8, 1986. House Resolution 5484, which would later be known as the Anti-Drug Abuse Act of 1986 was drafted in less than a month, and passed through Congress with almost no opposition. The official vote was 378 supporting votes to a paltry 16 votes in opposition of the Resolution. Ronald Reagan signed the Act into law on October 27, 1986, less than a month before midterm elections.

Coming out "hard" on drugs, both parties engaged in a game of political chicken, each increasing proposed punitive measures as they struggled to champion the issue for their respective party. While Reagan himself initially proposed a 20:1 ratio with regards to penalties of mandatory time served for crack cocaine versus powder cocaine related offenses, the final result became the 100:1 ratio which largely remains to this day. This means that mandatory penalties for crack cocaine are one-hundred percent more severe than those attached to powder cocaine offenses.[52] The *Washington Post* perhaps offered the most honest critique of this dangerous game of political posturing:

> Beneath the sheen of bipartisan cooperation that accompanied House passage of the anti-drug bill last week, there was much jockeying for advantage on what is seen as an emotion-laden political issue. In the end, strategists for the two parties settled for a joint effort, hoping to check the opposition's attempt to capture the issue as its own.[53]

While the jockeying of both parties escalated the punitive measures of what is often referred to as the "Len Bias Law," the Anti-Drug Abuse Act of 1986 ultimately boiled down to one common denominator.[54] As Representative Robert Dorman of California explained to reporters, "it all came down to one man not dying in vain."[55] That man was Len Bias.

Photo of Univerity of Maryland basketball star Len Bias.
Photograph by the *Washington Post*, courtesy of Getty Images

Both Len Bias and Brian Tribble grew up in the notably disadvantaged urban community of Landover, Maryland, not far from the nation's capital. By way of their exceptional basketball talents, both earned full athletic scholarships to attend the University of Maryland. In his sophomore year, however, Tribble suffered a career-ending knee injury and subsequently dropped out of classes. While the truth of the matter remains mere speculation, it appears that Tribble began to sell high-grade cocaine shortly after he left the university as a student.

Bias was lucky enough to remain healthy and flourished on the basketball court, earning All-American and ACC Player of the Year honors during the 1985-86 season. His high-flying exploits seemed an infinite highlight reel of dunks and acrobatic maneuvers that captured the attentions and enthusiasms of basketball fans and casual sports fans alike. By the night of his death, Bias had become a household name and appeared poised to become the next NBA icon to join the ranks of Michael Jordan, Magic Johnson, and Larry Bird. Despite hazy details, we know that Bias celebrated on that fateful night with his childhood friend Brian Tribble, along with teammates Terry Long and David Gregg. Regardless of what happened in the interim, we also know without question that the draft-night revelry ended with Len Bias dead due to complications from cocaine use. As Bias lay dead, his friend Brian Tribble placed a now infamous 911 call to authorities desperate for help.

Tribble may have been the one that lived that night, but he too suffered a death of sorts. In the days and weeks that followed, Brian

Tribble would prove a convenient scapegoat for politicians and media alike. The stereotype embodied by Brian Tribble – a drug dealer – intimately linked him with the underclass. His perceived moral deficiencies and social deviance added significant fuel to the fire as Tribble faced criminal charges in a public trial stemming from the events leading to Bias's death. In the ensuing months, Brian Tribble became an effective tool for crusaders in the War on Drugs to reinforce discursive links between drug abuse, drug dealers, and the underclass. Despite his roots in the same underprivileged neighborhood as Tribble, and his close personal relationship with the eventual villain in this narrative, Len Bias came to embody a much different stereotype for conservatives. As the physical personification of the New Right's ideology of individualism and competition, Bias embodied the "culture of triumph" which marked the decade.[56] Because of this, representations of Len Bias as a martyr and victim of the drug war were politically useful for both Democrats and Republicans.

It is hard to overstate the physical presence of Len Bias. His stature was at once overwhelming and slightly unbelievable. Prior to the advent of serious weight-training programs, personal trainers, supplements and steroids, Bias stood out amongst the most impressive of athletes. Certainly, other attributes such as Bias's religiosity, charming personality, and determined disposition all made his case compelling. However, it is perhaps his profound physical stature which first strikes any passive witness to the Bias tragedy. Exactly how could a man of such size, strength, and impeccable physical conditioning fall victim to a few grams of powdered cocaine? Defying all elementary logic, drugs had killed the once seemingly invincible Len Bias.

Treatment of Bias by journalists, television pundits, and politicians belies typical coverage of young African-Americans of his generation. Although Bias fit the cultural script of a drug user (young, black, underprivileged) constructed by politicians and the media, he was not treated as such. One explanation for the Bias exception seems to be that his fame as an "accepted" African-American entertainer/sports sensation provided politicians with an opportunity to capitalize on his personal tragedy.[57] This dynamic is best explained in Spike Lee's quintessential Crack Era movie *Do The Right Thing*. In a dialogue between Spike Lee's character Mookie, a pizza delivery man, and his young boss Pino, the son of the Italian pizza shop's owner, Mookie questions Pino's use of the word "nigger." In response, Mookie asks Pino about his favorite musician, comedian, and sports star. Pino quickly lists Prince, Eddie Murphy and Magic Johnson. When prodded to explain how he can look up to three black stars and still use racial slurs, Pino responds, "They're different." When asked how they are different, Pino responds: "They're not niggers."[58]

By emphasizing his positive traits and triumphal narrative prior to his fatal encounter with cocaine, drug warriors were able to reinforce New

Right ideology while publicly defending a young African-American. *The Washington Post* described Bias as an icon for the bootstrap ethic praised by Conservatives, "Bias seemed to make lies come true. He beat the odds."[59] Constantly, the public was reminded that Bias was a good son, student, teammate, and Christian. Perhaps most famously, the public learned of how Lonise Bias, Len's mother found the names of all of his Maryland teammates inscribed on the front cover of his Bible.[60] Instead of portraying Bias as an active participant, and perhaps even an enemy in the War on Drugs, drug warriors used Bias as a cautionary tale which sent the message that drugs could ruin the country's best and brightest with one solitary indiscretion. Alongside slogans such as "Just say NO" and "Crack is whack," the simple phrase "Remember Len Bias" came into being.[61]

Among the onslaught of statements made by politicians following his death, Republican Senator Mack Mattingly of Georgia typified what became the norm: "The death of Len Bias, for example, and the fact, widely broadcast by the media, that drugs can kill even the strong has resulted in a national outcry."[62] Republican Congressman Benjamin Gillman in similar sentiments advanced the case for Bias as a martyr, "and it took the tragic death of Len Bias, that fine young man who was about to reach the pinnacle of his career, to see his life snuffed out by this poison that has reached our nation."[63] In a concerted, strategic effort, the image of Len Bias as both victim and martyr in the War on Drugs crept into popular memory. Treated as a fallen hero rather than a menace to society, Len Bias became a casualty in the War on Drugs in the eyes of the American public. Furthermore, Bias represented a casualty of the perceived drug epidemic which could potentially encroach upon the upper and middle class. Indeed, his overdose did not occur on the streets of Landover, Maryland – but rather – on a college campus largely populated by middle and upper-class white students. Demonstrating the effort to cement Bias's place as a victim rather than an active combatant in the War on Drugs crossed party lines, New York Democrat David Patterson lamented that Bias "was an obvious victim."[64]

Immediately after his death, national media outlets portrayed Bias as a religious, likable, highly-motivated young athlete who had fallen victim to bad influences. After joking that Bias was an innocent, harmless kid whose only vice had been ice-cream, University of Maryland coach Lefty Driesell commented that, "Leonard was a kind person. He was a Christian."[65] Focusing on his immense talents and well-documented affable personality, drug war crusaders and major media outlets positioned Bias as a victim whose unlimited potential was stolen by the dangerous specter of crack in America. Activist and Reverend Jesse Jackson even called Bias "a rose of our generation."[66]

Helping insulate conservatives from any possible ties to racist public policy, Len Bias became an acceptable martyr and victim for the War on Drugs. Furthermore, Len Bias provided the largely Democrat-driven Select Committee with the opportunity they thought they had been looking for to demonstrate their new stance on drugs. However, Bias may have ultimately served to co-opt Democrats to carry out the discreet, sophisticated policy agenda of the New Right. As Bias became an acceptable martyr for both parties to rally around, condemning a thug like Brian Tribble became an apparently acceptable form of racism due to its emphasis on culture and class. Ultimately, Tribble could be condemned for his behavior and hedonistic lifestyle rather than his race, even if race remained the elephant in the room.

Only well after his death in 1987 did rumblings begin to circulate about the other side of Len Bias. Although much remains murky regarding the habits and behavior of Bias in the months and years leading up to his death, rumors of Bias's frequent drug use, poor grades, womanizing and partying with Brian Tribble at posh night clubs began to surface almost a full year after his death.[67] While underlying political agendas may have assured that the ugly truth regarding Len Bias's personal demons remained largely suppressed, every unsightly detail which could be linked to Brian Tribble found itself under the microscope of public opinion. Because of his own specific political utility to the primary movers in the War on Drugs, Brian Tribble endured a much different fate from that of Len Bias.

As a representative of the underclass, Brian Tribble embodied what Senator Howell Heflin of Alabama referred to as: "The lowest form of subhumans found on this Earth, peddlers of human misery, greed-soaked mutants who wage this war without a passing thought given to the tragedy they bring to their fellow man. Although this country has declared war on drugs, it is the drug pushers and smugglers who declared war on humanity."[68] By reifying the drug dealer as a sub-human villain out of a comic strip, politicians like Heflin vehemently and enthusiastically pointed the finger at Brian Tribble and the underclass.

As he publicly bore the blame for Bias's death, Tribble was the only person brought to trial. Charges for both Terry Long and David Gregg were dropped in exchange for their testimony against Tribble. Although Tribble was acquitted of all charges because of a lack of evidence, he remained convicted in the eyes of the public. Rather than put the drug use and deviant behavior of Len Bias on trial, crusaders in the War on Drugs implicated and condemned Brian Tribble for Bias's death in the court of public opinion. For politicians seeking to link Tribble to the underclass, Tribble fit the archetype: criminal, poor, and uneducated. Using cultural descriptors to identify Tribble and associate him with the underclass, both the media and politicians presented Tribble as a common street thug. Commenting on Tribble and the "bad crowd" of friends surrounding Bias, one columnist described "losers who were drifting away from athletic success with lackluster college basketball careers and using drugs."[69] The prosecution in the Tribble case went to great lengths to emphasize his lifestyle, behaviors, and selfish materialism rather than his race.[70]

Among other things, the prosecution highlighted Tribble's taste for expensive automobiles, designer clothes, and gold jewelry. Prominently figuring into their case was the Mercedes-Benz owned by Tribble and the expensive high-rise apartment near the University of Maryland which he rented for $699 a month.[71] How, asked the prosecution, could a man of Tribble's means acquire such material wealth?

In addition to the prosecution, the actions of the court judge reinforced perceptions of Tribble as a dangerous member of the criminal underclass. Unlike David Gregg and Terry Long, Brian Tribble was arrested and handcuffed. While Gregg and Long were not considered "flight risks" by the judge because of their status as college students, Tribble's warrant included a lofty bail meant to keep him from leaving custody. With no official evidence to support his claim, Prince George County's State Attorney, John Marshall declared that, "It seems pretty clear to us that Tribble is the person that brought the drugs into the room."[72] Despite being exonerated in the court of law, Brian Tribble had been fingered by law enforcement, popular media, and consequently, the American public for his role in the Bias tragedy.

While Brian Tribble can easily be reduced to a passing cultural trope surrounding drug dealers and minority urban youth, he is emblematic of significant developments of the period which often go overlooked by scholars of drug policy and contemporary American history. According to renowned cultural critic Nelson George: "Hip-hop music, the NBA, and crack dealing became central parts of the American consciousness in the 1980s . . . defining both possibility and cool for young black males stuck in the hood."[73] Perhaps Brian Tribble once harbored dreams of playing in the NBA alongside Bias. However, after his knee injury Tribble was presumably left with one option if he still wanted to gain respect, success, and material wealth. Famed rapper and lyricist Notorious B.I.G. perhaps explained Tribble's quandary best, "Because the streets is a short stop, either you're slingin' crack-rock, or you got a wicked jump-shot."[74] Tribble had the jump-shot, but his knees failed him. Ultimately, he turned to a life of crime.

As the general detachment of generations of young black males from the legitimate job market continued to solidify,[75] Brian Tribble became one of a cadre of young urbanites that learned to embrace the oppositional identity embodied in an emerging hip-hop culture. Realizing that the system was not designed for them, these young men adopted an organic critique of dominant culture through hip-hop and its accompanying lifestyle. While critics have traditionally bashed hip-hop for its violence, misogyny, and avid materialism, its value in channeling feelings of frustration, disenchantment, and even empowerment must be acknowledged.[76]

Conspicuously absent from both the prosecution's case and the broader public discourse were the behavior and consumption patterns of Bias himself. While drug warriors fixated on the flashy clothes and gold jewelry of Brian Tribble and others like him, they ignored the fact that Bias dressed and behaved similarly. Before his death, Bias already began to settle into the trappings, lifestyle and grueling pace of a professional athlete. He had an ankle-length fur coat, a Nissan 380ZX sports car, and a gold bracelet with diamonds spelling "L-E-N." Additionally, Bias had earned failing grades in three classes and dropped two others in his last semester. Much like Brian Tribble, Len Bias had effectively dropped out of school prior to graduation.[77]

For the purposes of the immediate crack scare and its consequences, Tribble remained a thug and thug only. His direct link to the underclass allowed politicians to make the underclass synonymous with drug abuse and drug dealing. Conversely, Bias's perceived connections to individual triumph, moral fiber, and hard work all helped to reinforce the prominent Conservative narrative of individual accountability. Bias had succeeded up until his death by way of his Christianity, determination, and adherence to a higher moral code. Tribble on the other hand had failed immeasurably due to his inherent moral deficiencies and pathological disposition for criminal behavior. In the summer and fall of 1986, both Len Bias and Brian Tribble served as political vehicles to advance the agenda on the War on Drugs. While the fame of Len Bias provided the impetus to get the ball rolling in the War on Drugs, Brian Tribble also proved useful in his ability to trace the locus of drug abuse and drug dealing back to the underclass. Ultimately, the fallen star of Len Bias and the defiance of Brian Tribble were both necessary for politicians and media outlets to successfully manufacture the crack scare of 1986.

As Race Recedes: *The New Right and Forces of Institutional and Structural Racism in the Post-Civil Rights Era*

Much of the struggle surrounding issues of race, culture, and class in the 1980s is best encompassed by the polarizing views of policy writer Charles Murray on the Right and sociologist William Julius Wilson on the Left. Murray represents the new wave of conservatism under the Reagan Administration with his support for decreased spending on social programs, and professed belief in the spirit of self-enrichment.[78] Wilson, on the other hand, points to the structural racism inherent in the 1980s, emphasizing the profound negative impact this new brand of racism had upon urban communities.

Ultimately, figures like Len Bias and Brian Tribble found themselves in the crossfire of such polemic debates. Their respective political utilities for conservative cultural crusaders lent themselves kindly to Murray's argument that the inherent "self-destructive" nature of the underclass was responsible for economic and class inequalities. The very notion that both Bias and Tribble were personally responsible for their assumed positions along the social hierarchy devoid of any external forces—lends credence to the argument of the New Right that individuals determined their own fate regardless of social, cultural and economic barriers.[79]

Countering the conservative argument, Wilson contends that consistent structural racism seen in the post-civil rights era was largely responsible for the existence of the underclass. Furthermore, Wilson argues that the "self-defeating behaviors" of the underclass are functions of poverty itself. Similar to Thomas Sugrue's argument that urban ghettoes become a "self-perpetuating stigma," Wilson reads deviant behavior such as criminal activity, single-parenthood, welfare dependency, and drug use as symptoms of joblessness and economic disadvantage rather than products of moral deficiency. Ultimately, a better understanding of poverty can be reached through the lens of hip-hop culture. While they do not acknowledge it by name, Reinarman and Levine strike at the root of a problem which still exists today: "Rather than a culture of poverty, the violence, crime, and substance abuse of the inner city can be understood as manifestations of a 'culture of resistance,' a culture defined by its stance against mainstream, white, racist and economically exclusive society. This culture of resistance, however, results in greater oppression and self-destruction."[80] Despite providing an increasingly culturally viable outlet, hip-hop culture often results in counter-productive behavior. Furthermore, in its ugliest moments, hip-hop culture serves to reinforce the undue negative stereotypes and convictions of the New Right.

At first glance, Bias's death should be unsurprising given the broader narrative of the War on Drugs: Young black male falls into life of fast success, drug use and materialism; surrounded by fast cars, fast women, and easy access to high-grade cocaine. Young black male overdoses and dies due to his own moral deficiencies. Big deal.

However, at second glance policy-makers, politicians, media pundits and columnists alike all saw the opportunity presented by the Bias case. With no small measure of precision, these primary movers in the War on Drugs turned Len Bias into a martyr for the ensuing crisis. Bias became a cautionary tale which effectively delivered the message that this could happen to any young American – white or black – rich or poor. Conversely, any legitimate war must frame public support against an identifiable enemy, preferably, an enemy that can be safely depicted as somehow less than human and undeserving of sympathy and compassion.[81] Brian Tribble and the inherently lazy, pathologically criminal, morally deficient underclass became the enemy of the War on Drugs. As with any enemy, the underclass found themselves systematically targeted and devastatingly attacked in the summer of 1986.

The Anti-Drug Abuse Act of 1986, the product of the crack scare which ensued that summer sounded the death knell of the underclass. The ramifications of this legislation have had long-lasting, profound effects upon the underclass. Highlighted by the minimum sentencing of crack-related crimes, The Anti-Drug Abuse Act has now eviscerated two, and sometimes even three generations of underclass families.[82] Its legacy, as well as the legacy of Len Bias must stand as a testament to the dangerous prospects of political opportunism in the throes of national crisis.

The Bias saga and passage of the Anti-Drug Abuse Act of 1986 also offer yet another warning against the "perils of federalism." In her work by the same name, Lisa Miller examines how local grassroots organizations find their causes co-opted at the state and national level. Through the haze of federalism, grassroots positions are often parsed for political convenience – and worse – often silenced or obscured entirely. While Miller analyzes grassroots efforts towards gun control, I argue the same applies to grassroots activists in the Crack Era. As national media and congress took control of the political football of crack, they took what they needed from grassroots messaging and ignored portions less complimentary to their respective political agendas.

More specifically, Congress on the Left and Right eschewed prescriptions from grassroots organizations for specific forms of cooperative community policing, structural reform, aid to cities, and genuine empowerment of local residents to help work against crack and crime. They also rarely mentioned the years of painstaking work that grassroots organizations undertook to raise local and national awareness to their plight. Instead urban communities were portrayed as monolithic in their complicity of the burgeoning crack trade. Urban residents were also portrayed as hapless victims again in need of saving by the federal government. To be sure, grassroots organizations needed and aggressively pursued help in finding their salvation. They did not however intend to be written out of the process. Grassroots activists were a clear asset in understanding and mitigating problems of poverty, drug use, and rising crime. Their value, and in many cases, their mere existence was consistently overlooked at the federal level.

As we move forward and attempt to undo the brutal legacy of the Anti-Drug Abuse Act of 1986 and the public policy of the New Right, we must heed the warnings offered by the narrative of Len Bias and the crack scare of 1986. As politicians from both parties scrambled to champion the drug issue as their own, the focus remained on individual gains that could be made before the upcoming November midterm elections. Rather than effecting enduring, positive change, politicians postured and positioned themselves as "hard" on drugs and crime. Politicians and the popular public alike widely supported harsher judicial penalties for drug dealers and users in 1986. The federal drug-control budget increased fivefold between 1986 and 1993.[83] Budgetary priorities and prison construction signaled the triumph of an unabashed enforcement approach. Over the course of Ronal Reagan's tenure as President the nation's prison population nearly doubled between 1980 and 1988 tallying 627,402 American citizens incarcerated.[84] Our current prison population has now mushroomed to over 2 million citizens as the prison industrial complex has become a growth industry amidst a period of grave economic recession.

To borrow from scholar Michel Foucault, it is important to remember that law does not work simply through the prohibition of crime but also through the production of criminality. The cultural script borne out of 1986 produced criminals and assumed that young black men like Brian Tribble were the worst kind of criminals, drug pushers. Several scholars have depicted the drug game as a form of bootstrap capitalism, even calling it "the free market's answer to deindustrialization."[85] Viewed as an alternative survival strategy under a rapidly changing postwar economy, psychoactive commerce can rightfully be seen as a deliberate, profit-driven process rather than a pathological deviance.

By and large, treating drug abuse as more of a public health issue than a criminal justice matter might provide a step in the right direction. American drug policy targets the individual drug user and drug pusher, emphasizing arrests and incarceration rather than focusing on the social setting and economic inequality which perpetuate the distribution and use of illicit drugs. Using local police tactics to deal with a global drug problem is both naïve and wrongheaded. Until the United States recognizes the fundamental mistakes of an enforcement approach and embrace harm reduction, the War on Drugs will continue to be ineffective and economically burdensome.

The cultural script of 1986 effectively produced new brands of criminality, heavily intensifying the modern War on Drugs. Reagan-style drug warriors cemented into popular imaginations a new vision of drug users and pushers based on small truths magnified through the lenses of fear, racism, and class prejudice. As one scholar lamented, "Utility was out, symbolism was in."[86] Demonstrating the new zeal of an unabashed enforcement approach, one DEA agent brashly boasted "We aren't here to solve the drug problem. We're here to put bad guys in jail."[87] Presently, the modern War on Drugs has ceased to be tied exclusively to drugs at all. Over time, the War on Drugs has evolved into a "reelection, crime-prevention, revenue-transferring, culture-war omnibus."[88] Undoubtedly, the Anti-Drug Abuse Act of 1986 held unforeseen, far-reaching, and unintended consequences which affected our society profoundly. The narrative which played out in the summer of 1986 and subsequent drug legislation which followed bear witness to the power of panic and fear, as well as to the power of government to manufacture crisis in the wake of national tragedy.

Notes

[1] Harrison and Jenkins, "Maryland Basketball Star Found Dead at 22."

[2] Tribble, 911 Transcript.

[3] See U.S. House of Representatives. *Select Committee on Narcotics Abuse and Control: Hearing on "Drug Abuse Education", Hearing on "The Crack Cocaine Crisis", Hearing on "Trafficking and Abuse of "Crack" in New York City", Hearing on "The Federal war on Drugs: Past, Present and Future".* (Washington, D.C.: 5/20/86, 5/21/86, 7/15/86, 7/18/86, 10/3/86).

[4] U.S. House of Representatives. *Select Committee on Narcotics Abuse and Control: Hearing on "Drug Abuse Education."* (Washington, D.C.: Jim Wright [D – Texas], 5/20/86).

[5] U.S. Sentencing Commission "Report on Cocaine and Federal Sentencing Policy."

[6] By the "space" occupied by Len Bias I am referring to the cultural space which allowed Len Bias to transcend boundaries of race and class. Due to his stature as a successful, Christian, mainstream athlete Bias became a martyr for the War on Drugs, rather than a menacing enemy – the fate left to his friend Brian Tribble.
For examples of this treatment see Dean Baguet, "Bias: Portrait of a Star Fallen into Bad Company."

[7] See U.S. House of Representatives. *Select Committee on Narcotics Abuse and Control, Select Committee on Children, Youth, and Families: Hearing on "The Crack Cocaine Crisis", Hearing on "Trafficking and Abuse of "Crack in New York City."* (Washington, D.C.: Dr. Jerome H. Jaffe, Peter Rodino Jr. [D – New Jersey], Mario Cuomo [D – New York], Lawton Chiles [D – Fla], David Patterson [D – New York], 7/15/86, 7/18/86).

[8] For examples of this treatment see Dean Baguet, "Bias: Portrait of a Star Fallen into Bad Company," *Chicago Tribune*, 20 July 1986; Keith Harriston, "Tribble Trial Shows Other Side of Local Guy Who Made Good," *Washington Post*, 31 May 1987.

[9] For examples of similar work please see Donald Critchlow. *The Conservative Ascendancy: How the GOP Right Made Political History.* Cambridge: Harvard University Press, 2009; Robert O. Self. *All in the Family: The Realignment of American Democracy Since the 1960s.* New York: MacMillan, 2012; Ronald Story and Bruce Laurie. *The Rise of Conservatism, 1945-2000* (Boston: Bedford/St. Martin's, 2008), 21.

[10] Harrison and Jenkins, "Maryland Basketball Star Found Dead at 22."

[11] E.J. Dionne, "Saving Cities: Is Kojak Liberalism the Answer?" *The Washington Post* 15 June 1993; Carlo Rotella. "The Case against Kojak Liberalism," *The Wire: Race, Class, and Genre*, ed. Liam Kennedy and Stephen Shapiro (University of Michigan Press, 2012): 113-129. Per Dionne, Kojak Liberalism embodied the spirit of Television Cop Kojak played by Telly Savalas: "who was tough as nails but had a heart of gold." Dionne argued that cities like New York had spent too much money on social programs and not enough money on "putting cops on the street." Dionne explained the position as one that "accepts that poverty causes crime, but it also holds that crime causes poverty." Kojak Liberals were to be "unabashed in saying that when it comes to priorities, law enforcement and crime prevention get top billing." Perhaps most interesting is the framing of crime of "freedom from crime" as a "basic civil rights issue." David Dinkins—a Kojak Liberal—expressed this sentiment in his inaugural mayoral address.

[12] Elwood 48.

[13] Significant work which supports these contentions include: Michelle

Alexander. *The New Jim Crow: Mass Incarceration in the Age of Color Blindness.*
New York: The New Press, 2013; Nancy Campbell. "Regulating 'Maternal
Instinct': Governing Mentalities of Twentieth-Century U.S. Illicit Drug Policy."
Journal of Women in Culture and Society 1999, Vol. 24, no. 4. (Chicago:
University of Chicago Press, 1999); Nancy Campbell. *Using Women* (New
York: Routledge, 200); David Courtwright. *Dark Paradise: A History of Opiate
Addiction in America* (Cambridge: Harvard University Press, 2001); Crutis
Marez. *Drug Wars: The Political Economy of Narcotics* (Minneapolis: University
of Minnesota Press, 2004); David Musto. *The American Disease: Origins of
Narcotic Control* (Oxford: Oxford University Press, 2000); Craig Reinarman and
Harry G. Levine. *Crack in America: Demon Drugs and Social Justice* (Berkeley:
University of California Press, 1997); Vesla Mae Weaver. "Frontlash: Race
and the Development of Punitive Crime Policy." *Studies in American Political
Development.*
[14] Reinarman and Levine 78.
[15] David Courtwright. *Dark Paradise: A History of Opiate Addiction in America*
(Cambridge: Harvard University Press, 2001).
[16] Story and Laurie 21.
[17] Conspicuously absent in Congressional Hearings, public rhetoric, and
national media reports were grassroots activists seeking to "take back" their
streets and change their situation on the ground. Most certainly, a clear
acknowledgement of these active citizens and their persistent activism presents
a different picture of urban communities as a whole.
[18] Lisa Miller, *The Perils of Federalism: Race, Poverty and the Politics of Crime
Control* (Oxford and New York: Oxford University Press, 2008).
[19] The Select Committee on Narcotics Abuse and Control began as a panel
established on a temporary basis in 1977 to deal with the national drug
problem. As the heroin epidemic of the 1970s faded from view, the Committee
also played less of a public role until the summer of 1986. In 1993 the House of
Representatives refused to reauthorize the Committee, signaling a temporary
referendum upon harsh drug policy approved between 1986 and 1992.
[20] Reinarman and Levine 25-33. Crack was a major problem in cities such as
NYC, LA, Miami, Washington D.C., Baltimore, Philadelphia, etc. However, the
scope and severity of the problem was largely unknown because of its relatively
new appearance on American streets as well as the difficulty differentiating
between cocaine and crack-cocaine. Undoubtedly Crack had become a major
problem in select urban communities by May of 1986. *To say that a concerted
effort among politicians as well as national media successfully
manufactured a crack scare in 1986 is not to ignore the reality of the
issue.*
[21] U.S. House of Rep. Drug Abuse Education.
[22] U.S. House of Rep. Drug Abuse Education.
[23] Ibid.
[24] Ibid.
[25] Rangel 281.
[26] Ibid.
[27] Ibid.
[28] Ibid.
[29] U.S. House of Rep. *Drug Abuse Education.*
[30] Ibid.
[31] Ibid.
[32] Ibid.
[33] Ibid.
[34] Barnicle "Some Things Don't Add Up."
[35] Baum 226.
[36] Qtd. in Reinarman and Levine 4.

[37] Reinarman and Levine 20.

[38] Fink "Don't Forget the Hype."

[39] In May, 1985 the *New York Times* published their first article on crack. By November of 1985 the newspaper had assigned a full-time reporter—Jane Gross—to cover the drug beat. Between July and September of 1986, the *Times* printed a monthly average of 103 articles, hitting its peak the month before passage of the 1986 Anti-Drug Abuse Act, in September, with 169 articles.

[40] U.S. House of Representatives. *Select Committee on Narcotics Abuse and Control, Hearing on "Trafficking and Abuse of 'Crack' in New York City"* 2.

[41] Ibid. 3.

[42] U.S. House of Rep. *Trafficking and Abuse of 'Crack' in NYC.* Don Rogers, a safety for the Cleveland Browns, died of a cocaine overdose seven days after Bias. Rogers' death received much less media attention and scrutiny because he was a less identifiable public figure. Although he was a successful athlete, Rogers ultimately presented a less compelling narrative than the Bias incident and was treated accordingly by columnists, politicians, and other media outlets.

[43] U.S House of Representatives. *Select Committee on Narcotics Abuse and Control, Hearing on "The Crack Cocaine Crisis"* 53.

[44] Ibid. 56.

[45] Ibid. 39.

[46] Ibid. 95.

[47] Ibid. 52.

[48] Ibid. 107.

[49] U.S. Senate. *Congressional Record, Friday, September 26, 1986.*

[50] Moynihan became well known and heavily criticized for his 1965 report: *The Negro Family: The Case for National Action.* Popularly known as the "Moynihan Report," this document borrows from Oscar Lewis' "culture of poverty" trope, claiming that the underclass represented pathological deviance which was both systemic and self-perpetuating. Mainly, the report has been criticized for its "blame the victim" approach by liberal scholars and policymakers.

[51] U.S. Senate. *Congressional Record, Friday, September 26, 1986.* Thurmond's reference of an effort to "reestablish a moral climate" is indicative of the Right's claims to "traditional morality" in opposition to the sex, drugs, rock n' roll, and war protestors of the 1960s and 70s.

[52] For example, distribution of five grams or more of crack, worth an estimated $125 mandated a five-year prison sentence. Conversely, an individual must be convicted of distributing 500 grams or more of powder cocaine, worth an estimated $50,000 to qualify for a similar sentence. This disparity has been highly controversial and well-publicized due to the disproportionate tendency of racial minorities to use the much cheaper and readily available crack cocaine versus powder cocaine.

[53] "The War on Drugs: Congress Finds a Crisis."

[54] For an example please see: Scott Goldstein, "Man Convicted in Heroin Death under Len Bias Law," *The Boston Globe* 13 May 2005.

[55] "Congress Finds a Crisis."

[56] The "culture of triumph" which pervaded 1980s conservative ideology is closely associated with the power of the individual to triumph over adverse socioeconomic circumstances by way of strong moral character and hard work. Along this same vein, victims of socioeconomic obstacles were compared against personal success stories (exceptions) like Bias. Their inability to reach these same heights marked their inherent moral deficiencies and laziness. Please see: Ronald Story and Bruce Laurie. *The Rise of Conservatism, 1945-2000* (Boston: Bedford/St. Martin's, 2008), 21.

[57] Much work by S. Craig Watkins supports this contention via his use of the trope "model minorities." For more on this please see: S. Craig Watkins. *Representing: Hip Hop Culture and the Production of Black Cinema.* Chicago:

University of Chicago Press, 1998.

[58] Spike Lee. *Do The Right Thing.* 40 Acres and a Mule Filmworks. 1989.

[59] Milloy, "Cocaine Victim Len Bias Beat the Odds and Blew It."

[60] Gildea, "Driesell: Bias ACC's Best Ever."

[61] Vescey, "Using Len Bias as a Different Kind of Role Model."

[62] Senate Congressional Record 26 Sept 1986.

[63] House of Representatives *Select Committee on Nacrotics Abuse and Control* 3 Oct 1986.

[64] House of Representatives *Select Committee on Narcotics Abuse and Control* 18 July 1986.

[65] McMullan, "Bias Receives Final Ovation."

[66] Smith 35.

[67] Harrison, "Tribble Trial Shows Other Side of Local Guy Who Made Good."

[68] Senate Congressional Record 26 Sept 1986.

[69] Baguet, "Portrait of a Star Fallen into Bad Company."

[70] It is important to note that the presence of a court reporter is not mandatory in grand-jury proceedings. Thus, there are no official records of the Tribble hearings. The sources consulted are from primary newspaper accounts of the hearings. Despite this gap in the archive, newspapers uniformly confirm attempts by the prosecution to paint Tribble as a drug-dealing street thug.

[71] Pressley, "Questions Surround Bias's Final Hours."

[72] Baguet, "Bias: Portrait of a Star Fallen into Bad Company."

[73] George 200.

[74] "Things Done Changed."

[75] See Thomas Sugrue, *Origins of the Urban Crisis* (New Jersey, Princeton University Press, 1996), 147.

[76] Please see Curtis Marez, *Drug Wars* for treatment of narco-corridos and rap music as an emerging counternarrative to the War on Drugs. Marez argues that hip-hop culture, and others like it, intentionally invert traditional power hierarchies, glamorizing the deviant subaltern hero – the drug dealer.

[77] Goldstein and Kinzie, "Bias Death Still Ripples Through Athlete's Academic Lives."

[78] "Reaganomics" of the era helped to substantially widen the gap between the rich and poor. In 1986, the U.S. Census Bureau announced that the gap between rich and poor Americans was more pronounced that year than it had been in four decades. This gap reflected racial disparities as well: the poverty rate for blacks was nearly three times that for white Americans. Please see: The Food and research Action Center, Washington D.C., "Analysis of 1986 Poverty Data," 3 July 1987; The U.S. Census Bureau, "Historical Poverty Tables: Table 2."

[79] Murray 9-11.

[80] Reinarman and Levine 64.

[81] Please see David Courtwright, *Dark Paradise* for his treatment of harsh drug legislation. Courtwright argues that draconian legislation is easier to pass if the perceived target of said laws is of lower status and/or deviant. Fears about the nation's future (the youth) often fuel support for legislation of this manner.

[82] For more on the consequences of said legislations see Marc Mauer, "Intended and Unintended Consequences: State Racial Disparities in Imprisonment," *Thomas M. Cooley Law Review,* 16:47 (1999).

[83] Courtwright 76.

[84] McCoy 445.

[85] Schneider 203.

[86] Courtwright 175.

[87] Ibid. 176.

[88] Ibid. 179.

Works Cited

Barnicle, Mark. "Some Things Don't Add Up." *Boston Globe* 20 June 1996.

Baguet, Dean. "Bias: Portrait of a Star Fallen into Bad Company." *Chicago Tribune,* 20 July 1986.

Baum, Dan. *Smoke and Mirrors: The War on Drugs and the Politics of Failure.* Boston: Little, Brown and Company, 1997.

Courtwright, David. *Dark Paradise: A History of Opiate Addiction in America.* Cambridge, MA: Harvard University Press, 2001.

Elwood, Wilson. *Rhetoric in the War on Drugs: The Triumphs and Tragedies of Public Relations.* Westport, Conn.: Praeger Press, 1994.

Fink, Mikah. "Don't Forget the Hype: Media Drugs and Public Opinion." www.fair.org, Accessed 4/19/2010.

Foucault, Michel. *Power.* New York: The New Press, 2001.

George, Nelosn. *Elevating the Game: Black Men and Basketball.* Lincoln, NE: University of Nebraska Press, 1999.

Gildea, William and Dave Sell. "Dreisell: Bias Acc's Best Ever." *The Washington Post* 20 June 1986.

Goldstein, Amy and Susan Kinzie. "Bias Death Still Ripples Through Athlete's Academic Lives." *Washington Post* 19 June 2006.

Harrison, Keith. "Tribble Trial Shows Other Side of Local Guy Who Made Good." *Washington Post* 31 May 1987.

Harrison, Keith and Sally Jenkins. "Maryland Basketball Star Found Dead at 22." *The Washington Post* 20 June 1986.

Lee, Spike. *Do The Right Thing.* 40 Acres and a Mule Filmworks. 1989.

MacMullan, Jackie. "Bias Receives Final Ovation." *Boston Globe* 24 June 1986.

McCoy, Alfred. *The Politics of Heroin: CIA Complicity in the Global Drug Trade.* Chicago: Lawrence Hill Books, 2003.

Miller, Lisa. *The Perils of Federalism: Race, Poverty, and the Politics of Crime Control.* Oxford and New York: Oxford University Press, 2008.

Milloy, Courtland. "Cocaine Victim Len Bias Beat the Odds and Blew It." *The Washington Post* 3 July 1986.

Murray, Charles. *Losing Ground: American Social Policy, 1950-1980.* New York: Basic Books, 1984.

Pressley, Sue. "Questions surround Bias's Final Hours; Accounts of Fatal Night Vary." *Washington Post* 29 June 1986.

Rangel, Charles. "Combatting Drug Abuse and Trafficking: Some New Directions." *Justice Quarterly* 277 (1984), 277-287.

Reinarman, Craig and Harry G. Levine. *Crack in America: Demon Drugs and Social Justice.* Berkeley, CA: University of California Press, 1997.

Schneider, Eric. *Smack: Heroin and the American City.* Philadelphia: University of Pennsylvania Press, 2008.

Smith, C. Fraser. *Lenny, Lefty and the Chancellor: The Len Bias Tragedy and the Search for Reform in Big-Time College Basketball.* Baltimore: The Bancroft Press, 1992.

Story, Ronald and Bruce Laurie. *The Rise of Conservatism, 1945-2000.*

The Devil and Len Bias

Boston: Bedford/St. Martin's, 2008.

"The War on Drugs: Congress Finds A Crisis." *Washington Post* 14 September 1986.

Tribble, Brian. 911 Dispatch Transcript. College Park, Maryland, 19 June 1986.

Sugrue, Thomas. *The Origins of the Urban Crisis.* Princeton, NJ: Princeton University Press, 1996.

U.S. House of Representatives. *Select Committee on Narcotics Abuse and Control: Hearing on "Drug Abuse Education."* (Washington, D.C.: Jim Wright [D – Texas], 5/20/86).

U.S. House of Representatives. *Select Committee on Narcotics Abuse and Control, Hearing on "The Federal War on Drugs: Past, Present, and Future"* (Washington, D.C.: Benjamin Gillman [R – NJ], 10/3/86)

U.S. House of Representatives. *Select Committee on Narcotics Abuse and Control, Hearing on "Drug Abuse Education."* (Washington, D.C.: Reverend Jesse Jackson, 5/21/86]

U.S House of Representatives. *Select Committee on Narcotics Abuse and Control, Hearing on "The Crack Cocaine Crisis"* (Washington D.C.: Dr. Jerome H. Jaffe, 7/15/1986)

U.S. House of Representatives. *Select Committee on Narcotics Abuse and Control, Hearing on "Trafficking and Abuse of 'Crack' in New York City"* (Washington D.C.: Senator David Patterson [D – NY], 7/18/1986)

U.S. House of Representatives. *Select Committee on Narcotics Abuse and Control, Hearing on "Trafficking and Abuse of 'Crack' in New York City"* (Washington D.C.: Charles Rangel [D – NY], Mario Cuomo [D – NY], 7/18/1986)

U.S. House of Representatives. *Select Committee on Narcotics Abuse and Control, Hearing on "The Crack Cocaine Crisis"* (Washington D.C.: Peter Rodino Jr. [D – NJ], 7/15/1986)

U.S. House of Representatives. *Select Committee on Narcotics Abuse and Control, Hearing on "The Crack Cocaine Crisis"* (Washington D.C.: James Scheur [D – NY], 7/15/1986)

U.S. Senate. *Congressional Record, Friday, September 26, 1986* (Washington, D.C.: Senator Howell Heflin [D – ALA])

U.S. Senate. *Congressional Record, Friday, September 26, 1986* (Washington, D.C.: Senator Patrick Moynihan [D –NY])

U.S. Senate. *Congressional Record, Friday, September 26, 1986* (Washington, D.C.: Senator Strom Thurmond [R – SC])

U.S. Senate. *Congressional Record, Friday, September 26, 1986* (Washington, D.C.: Senator Mack Mattingly [R – GA])

United States Sentencing Commission. "Report on Cocaine and Federal Sentencing Policy." http://www.ussc.gov/report-cocaine-and-federal-sentencing-policy-5. Retrieved 5/7/13.

Vescey, George. "Sports of the Times: Using Len Bias as Different Kind of Role Model." *The New York Times* 21 June 1987.

Wallace, Christopher A.K.A. Notorious B.I.G. "Things Done Changed." *Ready to Die.* Bad Boy Records, 1994.

Wilson, William Julius. *The Truly Disadvantaged: The Inner City, the Underclass, and Public Policy.* Chicago: Chicago University Press, 1987

Women and the Business of Dragon Boat Sport: Overcoming Obstacles and Reaching for Success
An Interview with Penny Behling of Dynamic Dragon Boat Racing

Raúl Fernández-Calienes

Women are a central part of the sport of Dragon Boating all around the world.[1] Female dragon boaters participate at every level, from athletes to team captains and coaches, to sport executives, to event organizers and company owners.[2] In fact, with increasing frequency in recent years, major media outlets such as *Forbes, Time, National Geographic, Sports Illustrated,* and many others are featuring both the sport of dragon boating and the women in this sport.[3] This article features an interview with the only woman owner of a dragon boat event production company in the United States: Penny Behling, of Dynamic Dragon Boat Racing.[4]

A former newspaper reporter, Behling changed careers in the late 1990s and early 2000s, and since then has become a leading figure at regional and national levels in the sport of dragon boating in the U.S. She went from producing a few local dragon boat festivals in Tennessee to growing her business to produce many more events in many other states and hiring two strong female managers.[5] During that period, she was elected the founding President of the Southeast Region Dragon Boat Association (SRDBA)[6] – one of the four regional bodies of the United States Dragon Boat Federation (USDBF)[7] - and she achieved widespread recognition for producing the 2010 U.S. Dragon Boat Club Crew National Championships, one of the official qualifying events for the World Championships.[8]

Behling presents her own story, from her early days struggling to break into the industry to her perseverance in the face of intense personal and business challenges, to her groundbreaking work successfully raising millions of dollars for charity.[9] The questions and answers that follow cover such areas as her origins in the sport, an overview of her company, a typical "dragon boat day," leadership qualities essential for effectiveness, some of her greatest challenges in life and in the sport, sources of strength upon which she has drawn, her greatest achievements (so far!), her life's legacy, and why – in such a highly competitive business – her company is different and successful.

With illustrations from her own experience producing almost thirty festivals per year and races all across the country, this interview presents Behling's perspectives on subtle and not-so-subtle hurdles and hindrances as well as strategies for success and fulfillment.

The tremendous growth of her company, and the great popularity both she and her company enjoy – are a testament to her remarkable business model and ability to break down barriers and to overcome obstacles.

Interview

Question 1: How did you first hear about the sport of dragon boating, and what drew you to it?

I knew nothing about the sport until I met Wendy Lambert, who started a race in Knoxville, Tennessee, in 2003. She convinced me to attend "dragon boat camp" with her two years later, around the same time she asked me to quit my job to become her business partner.

The diversity of the sport drew me in for the long run. Boredom in the sport of dragon boat racing is unlikely. There are so many things to learn, from the paddling technique, to steering, to race officiating. And with this sport, you feel like you never conquer perfection.

Once you hear about dragon boat racing and become involved in this world of sport and community, there is no turning back from it. There is much more to it than a great day on the water. There are different and interesting ways to experience the sport for both team members and spectators. Whether you've paddled in a festival or regatta, or you paddle regularly in a dragon boat, you feel connected to it. That's the beauty of it – from the moment you pick up a paddle, you love dragon boat racing!

Traditional Hong Kong style dragon boats are 46-feet long, with 10 seats and 20 people. A drum seat in front of the first two paddlers (seated beside each other) holds a drummer – you want the smallest, loudest, most rhythmic person you can find. A steerer guides the boat with the steering oar in back. These 22 people make up a dragon boat team. The stroke is unlike any other (the most similar is outrigger canoe) and is taught in practice sessions.

With origins dating back 2,300 years, dragon boat racing is a unique cultural event featuring adrenaline-pumping action. Teams rave about the excitement, friendly competition, and community spirit surrounding the sport. All ages, skill levels, and physiques perfect their stroke and timing for the ultimate teamwork experience!

Every paddler plays a specific role. They sit next to each other, and against the gunnel, to balance the boat as they paddle. The strokers occupy the front three seats of the boat, while the fourth seat is a transition place where, ideally, the paddlers have rhythm and power. Then, seats four, five, and six consist of the "engine room," where the largest and strongest team members sit. The last four rows of a dragon boat are filled with strong paddlers who are also typically shorter and able to paddle faster. Paddlers at this location in the dragon boat are considered "rockets," because the water is moving faster past them, from the first 14 seats since they're scooping water back. The paddlers are taught to watch up the middle of the boat and two seats across – when that paddler has his or her paddle up in the air, ready to engage the water, it's the cue for the person watching to get his or her paddle up as well. While the drummer keeps the rhythm for most of the boat, it can be difficult to hear on race day. It's also a very visual sport, and if everyone is watching the right person, magic absolutely can happen in a dragon boat. Teams have to follow the strategy and then execute. The team members in the front must paddle in perfect timing as an example for the back half of the boat. When the power from the middle is mixed with the speed and capabilities of the athletes in the back, a dragon boat can glide quickly through the water like a bullet.

Teams feel a connection to the racing. They feel connected to the experience. People love it – the thrill, the teamwork, the adrenaline, the interaction in the boat – everything. People are drawn to this sport, to each other in a setting that exemplifies human connectivity on a level comparable to nothing else. As dragon boaters say, "What happens in a dragon boat stays in the dragon boat." People who never thought of themselves as athletes can thrive in a dragon boat. People who are athletes discover a challenging alternative to general sports. That's why once you get involved in this sport, it's hard to let it go.

Question 2: When and how did you get started in dragon boating?
Wendy and I attended our first dragon boat camp in April 2005 as paddlers. I was terrible at it the first four or five sessions. My timing was horrible. I watched myself on video, which confirmed what the coach was telling me: I was way off pace. It took me some time to get it, but eventually I did better. It probably took me a good year to fully develop a paddling style and then another year to competently steer and coach. It has been a learning process to discover all things dragon boat over the years.

Question 3: What do you think of the new international rule about the specific number of women paddlers in a dragon boat during a race? Does this rule help overcome any obstacles?

I think the new rule is great for the sport on a competitive racing level. It levels the playing field. For our purposes, working with clients offering races for local corporate and community teams, we suggest they implement an eight-female rule, which was the previous international rule. We now communicate to the client that eight or ten is an option. All of them prefer to stay with the eight-female rule because they say it is often difficult for teams to find women to fill the paddler slots. Some clients actually bypass the rule altogether, and either eliminate the female rule, or reduce the number. For example, some clients only require four female paddlers.

I think so many women are accustomed to overcoming obstacles, this is just another in a long line of those obstacles.

Question 4: How do you describe your dragon boat company?

Dynamic Dragon Boat Racing ("Dynamic") has established itself as a nationally respected dragon boat event company with a reputation for managing quality dragon boat races. Dynamic's clientele has doubled in the past three years. In eleven years of business, we've been part of events that have resulted in more than $4 million raised for charity so far. A combination of unique services and excellent customer service leads to success rates in event involvement and fundraising for our clients. Most clients net, on average, $50,000 from this event, with some making $250,000-plus. The individual paddler is the focal point of a dragon boat race. Each one contributes to the team, and each has the capability to raise money for the cause. We understand how to help you build relationships to retain paddlers as annual participants. For example, in its first year, The Fuse Project raised more than $100,000 in 2014, and last year, more than $160,000. There are many other success stories associated with our work; we strive to share this approach with all of our clients. Dynamic connects clients, sharing information online to offer advice about event enhancements that have worked for them. The more we all put into this event, the better it is for everyone.

My business, Dynamic Dragon Boat Racing, primarily focuses on the festival aspect of the sport. Most clients are non-profit organizations hosting a dragon boat festival to raise money through sponsorship sales, team registration fees, and pledges. In 2012, dragon boat races yielded nearly $500,000 for clients Dynamic served. In 2013, races Dynamic managed netted more than $1 million for charities. In just three short years, that fundraising number has jumped to $4 million for various charities across the country. People love unique avenues to give back to their community, and the beauty of dragon boat racing is that almost anyone can do it. Most people enjoy competing. When you create opportunities for connecting on that level while giving back to the community, people will respond.

Question 5: What is a "typical" dragon boating day for you?

Dragon boat planning really begins from the time a client calls for a bid. We help them think through details of what it takes realistically to produce a dragon boat race. Sometimes, that includes corresponding through e-mails, phone calls, and conference calls with various event organizers. It may even involve a site visit. We encourage client prospects to attend a race we manage so they can see for themselves the equipment and services they can expect.

We arrange the contract, based on the client's needs and scope of their race. It is typically a seamless process. We then work with our subcontractor list of steerers and race officials to schedule staffing for each race. We arrange staffing for steerers, unless they are driving, and pay them a stipend to work each day and for lodging, food, and per diem on food they purchase while traveling.

In advance of the race, we communicate with our clients on logistics, including use of venue, water logistics and safety, sponsorship, and team solicitation as well as share information from other success stories to help in fundraising efforts.

We arrive at each venue the week leading up to the race. Two or three coaches are available to coach corporate and community teams for one-hour-long practice sessions. While an hour doesn't seem like long, it is amazing sometimes how quickly you can show a team how to paddle together in a quick timeframe.

Before racing, we set a racecourse, using colored buoys to help steerers navigate lanes during racing. Sometimes, we set the course the day before and sometimes the day of (due to barge traffic, etc.). If needed, a racecourse can be set in two hours or less.

On race day, there are a variety of tasks and organization required. This is when we set up the finish line equipment, dress the boats with heads and tails for the ornamental effect, drums, drum seats, racing numbers, life jackets, and paddles in place as well as placing the boats in their proper location for loading.

Once racing begins, we manage all race logistics. This includes making sure racing is efficient, with heats starting on time and ending on time, all equipment is working properly, every staff member is doing his or her job, and everyone is having a good time.

After the event, we immediately debrief with the client to cover each detail related to the day. We decide to stick with what worked, and improve any challenges or unforeseen situations.

Question 6A: What are some skills or qualities that are essential to be effective in this sport?

Dragon Boat racing has been described as organized chaos. That is quite accurate. So, to be successful in the sport, you have to understand how to control the chaos. Leadership qualities for this sport include a strong sense of organization, combined with the ability to handle the unexpected at any given time.

Question 6B: What are some skills or qualities that are essential to be effective in this business?

There is a constant learning curve in running a business because there are always lessons, and you can either learn or burn. Owning a business means you're always open to change. If you're not adapting, you're not growing. The first thing a business needs is a leader. Anyone following must respect the leader and be willing to go above and beyond to get the job done. If not, then the leader isn't effectively playing his or her role.

Question 7A: What have been some of your greatest challenges in life in general?

I view challenges as opportunities. I generally try to come out on the other side of a challenge with the opportunity to turn it into a positive.

I didn't have the best childhood. Unfortunately, it was marred with emotional, physical, and sexual abuse. Because of these experiences, I developed a drive and determination to overcome challenges. My greatest obstacle in life was changing my thought process regarding my own knowledge and capabilities. Instead of believing I couldn't do something, or listening to someone say I can't do it, I turned around the psychology and decided to prove that I can. Thanks to that foundation, and after many years of trial and error, for the most part, I can now shut out negativity and use any doubt as a motivator to make the impossible happen.

Now, when I encounter people who underestimate me because I'm a woman, or because they take one look at me and doubt that I'm strong, I think it's funny. I don't have to say a word, or take offense, considering it's their problem and not mine. All I have to do is show what I'm capable of, and if they're still talking, then they clearly aren't the person I need to impress. There will always be certain people who refuse to work with me simply because I'm a woman, and they, for whatever reason, refuse to work with any woman. I would much rather work with clients who respect me for my knowledge and my talent. We end up getting so much more out of it that way.

Question 7B: What have been some of your greatest challenges specifically in the sport?

Strategically planning for all things related to both the sport and the business has been one of the biggest challenges of working in this field. Running a business is like predicting the future. You don't know what is going to happen, but you have to plan for it anyway.

Question 8: Why did you decide to buy out your business partner, and what were some of the barriers in the transaction?

The business was not profitable at the time (late 2009), and someone had to go. She had children, plus any traveling was tough for her, since she was a single mother at the time. It was hard for her to let the business go, for various reasons, but primarily, because she started it. She knew it was the right thing to do, but it was very difficult. It took months to work everything out, but in the end, it all worked out for the best, and she is still involved with the sport and works some of our festivals as subcontract labor.

Question 9: Why did you decide to expand the business from just a few races to now about thirty per year?

The expansion was a gradual result of steady growth. In the past six years, we have tripled our clientele. My original goal when I restructured the business was to create a market for myself so that potential clients found me, and I didn't have to sell myself to them. That happened much quicker than I imagined thanks to successful client fundraising and word of mouth. The result has been phenomenal growth.

Question 10: What were (or are) some of the obstacles in the expansion?

While business growth is wonderful, it brings logistical challenges. You can't do more without acquiring more – whether it be more equipment, more staff, or more services – you can't grow without also making it feasible to accept the extra work.

Question 11: How do you sustain that kind of growth in only a few years with quality and longevity?

I was determined from the outset of executing a new business plan in 2010 to build a company that does not have to create business, but attracts clients seeking a viable fundraising option because the company's reputation is that good. Now, it's only a matter of always delivering the best, and continuing to be true to my word, and to the client. We enjoy good working relationships; in my view, we are partner experts in our respective fields who collaborate on a great event. When the client looks good, my company is commended. If the opposite happened, the quality of my services and longevity of my business would be at risk. My staff takes pride in creating an atmosphere of community while having fun and making optimal use of individual talents. Like a dragon boat team synchronizing on the water, a typical Dynamic-staffed dragon boat race is just as well known for proficient organization as it is for unprecedented charity fundraising.

Question 12: What are some of the expectations (both positive and negative) that people have of you?

I expect a lot from myself, so naturally, people expect a lot from me. That's not a bad thing, but at the same time, perfection is hard to achieve. I make mistakes, just like anyone. I find the sooner I fix it, apologize, and move on, the better. I certainly prefer to exceed expectations, and that is my goal. Usually, the expectations we deal with involve money. Producing a dragon boat race is not inexpensive, and it takes effort, so sometimes, the negative expectations include being comfortable enough to say no to business. If the client isn't so willing to invest the time or money then maybe that client isn't the right fit. I've learned to allow my reputation to speak for itself. As long as the quality of our services continues to be high then it will be easy enough to fulfill expectations.

Question 13: How have you overcome obstacles, and what sources of strength have you drawn upon to face each of the aforementioned challenges?

One thing about obstacles – whether you like it or not – they're coming. Considering we manage events for a living, I feel like I always expect obstacles. Something always seems to happen to change plans. Some examples we see: weather, loud sound system on race day, boats or obstacles in the racecourse, people disrupting race officials while they're trying to work, participants getting drunk on race day, and lots of other random acts.

Question 14: What are some of your greatest achievements in the sport of dragon boating, in your business, and in your life?

Taking a business with five clients in 2010 to thirty in 2016 is a huge accomplishment that I never expected to achieve. Other than that, helping teams believe they can win is the best reward. Giving back is my legacy. It makes me feel like I'm contributing something bigger than myself to the world.

Question 15: What message do you have for other women who may choose to participate in the sport of dragon boating or the dragon boat business?

Dragon Boat racing is a great sport for women! Some of the best dragon boat paddlers are women. Some of the best steerers are women as well. Women bring a renewed kind of focus to the sport. For example, when I line up a boat full of men and women, I often like to put men in the front to set the pace. I prefer to put women behind the men in order to keep the timing on track, and sort of control all the testosterone the men are bringing to the boat. Women often win races. Anyone can dragon boat, but women bring the intensity, heart, and soul that the sport needs.

Question 16: You are in a highly competitive business that includes companies from both the U.S. and Canada. What makes your organization different – and successful?

Some of my clients who researched and communicated with other companies have told me they chose my company because they believed I would invest a personal stake in the success of their dragon boat race. In the words of a client in Tuscaloosa, Alabama, "I felt like you cared." That sentiment is obvious on race day as well. I encourage potential clients to see a Dynamic event so they can experience the atmosphere and efficiency, and to help them make a well-informed decision.

The growing competitive market of dragon boat racing inspires me to work harder to keep current clients and attract new event partners. As the field evolves, I've focused on two philosophies going forward: (1) No one else is Dynamic. We will follow *our* business model, which will maintain current growth trends while creating new revenue streams;

and (2) With a combination of experience and an innate sense of people, Dynamic has fine-tuned the art of marketing itself and a sport that is beginning to capture the pulse of America.

Dynamic Dragon Boat Racing hopes to capitalize on its simple approach to giving clients and their paddling participants the time of their lives while helping them accomplish their own goals.

Conclusion

The stories of Dynamic Dragon Boat Racing generally, and Penny Behling specifically, provide us with a number of concepts, which we will summarize using keywords, from which we can draw lessons.

Join – Behling *joined* dragon boating, and she discovered a true team sport. Beginners, professionals, youth, elders, cancer survivors, differently-abled persons, blind persons, and many others participate actively in this sport (see, e.g., Storm 2008, McCausland 2010, Barned-Smith 2013), and they transcend their differences to become "one" on the boat. The lists in the Resources section below (e.g., International Dragon Boat Federations; Official IDBF Affiliate Festivals) show numerous events, groups, and locations where people can join the sport (cf. Wei 2011) and enjoy the benefits of joining with others. Behling teaches us that joining is one of the first steps toward success.

Listen – Behling *listened* to her first coach, and her form improved dramatically; to her friend, who invited her into the business, and her life changed dramatically; to veteran businesspeople, who advised her along the way, and she succeeded; to herself, when she bought out her business partner, and she gained independence; and to the community, when she adapted her business from pure profit to community fundraising, and she raised millions of dollars for charity. She shows us that listening is one of the secrets of success.

Persist – Behling *persisted* in the face of severe personal and business obstacles, despite negative comments by others, through criticism and doubt – and she is doing well. She reminds us of the many examples of people in dragon boating who persist against the odds – and succeed (cf. McKenzie 1998; Kent 2002; Weiner 2012).

Adapt – Behling *adapted* to changing circumstances, to a total company restructure, to logistical challenges, to rapid company growth – and her business is thriving. By the thousands, dragon boaters are adapting to the draw of an ancient and simultaneously modern, global sport – one that is very well known throughout Asia but still comparatively new in the West. As a result, the sport is growing very rapidly all around the world (cf. Bower 2006).

Reach – Behling *reached* beyond what she initially thought she ever could achieve, and she has succeeded beyond her wildest dreams. She reached out – first to help herself and then to help others – and in the process, she has helped thousands of people to overcome obstacles and reach for success.

Notes

[1] See much more detail in the resources listed in the References, such as the lists of periodicals, international federations, and Official International Dragon Boat Federation (IDBF) Affiliate Festivals across the globe in Appendix A.

[2] The category of "Women" is one of the major racing divisions of most dragon boat federations around the world; for more information, see the list of International Dragon Boat Federations in the References. Also, in 2014, the International Breast Cancer Paddlers Commission Participatory Festival, held in Sarasota, Florida, hosted more than 100 women's teams from all around the globe. Further, for many years, women have served as senior officers and executives of dragon boat federations in many countries; see, for example, the female presidents, vice presidents, secretaries, etc., of the International Dragon Boat Federation (IDBF 2017, 2016, 2016b, 2011), the European Dragon Boat Federation (EDBF 2017), the Pan American Dragon Boat Federation (PADBF 2017), and the United States Dragon Boat Federation (USDBF 2017).

[3] Stories also have appeared in other media outlets, such as *Boston Globe, Chicago Tribune, New York Times, Washington Post, Business Times* (Singapore), *Financial Times* (London), *Le Monde* (Paris), *Mail & Guardian* (Johannesburg), *South China Morning Post* (Hong Kong), *The Times of India* (Delhi), and many others; see Chakrabortyl 2016; "Dragon Boat Race" 2016; Flannery 2016; Mc-Cormick & Guise 2016; Singh 2016; Wong 2016; Hooi 2015; Correal 2014; Pavan 2013; Barned-Smith 2013; Grossfeld 2013; Wei 2011; Wertheim 2010; Sindane 2008; Bower 2006; Lloyd 1991.

[4] For more information, see the Dynamic website (www.racedragonboats.com) as well as the Dynamic pages on Facebook, LinkedIn, Twitter, and YouTube: www.facebook.com/racedragonboats/; www.linkedin.com/in/ racedragonboats; twitter.com/racedragonboats; www.youtube.com/channel/UCEOtE6iCLzJRSaW-gQjz17pA

[5] Three of the four members of senior management at Dynamic Dragon Boat Racing are women: Ms. Behling, a project management consultant, and a financial management consultant.

[6] The Southeast Region Dragon Boat Association (SRDBA) covers the states of Florida, Georgia, Alabama, Mississippi, South Carolina, North Carolina, Kentucky, and Tennessee.

[7] The United States Dragon Boat Federation (USDBF) is the governing body for dragon boat sport in the U.S.A. For more on the history of the sport of dragon boating in the United States, see Fernández-Calienes 2013.

[8] The International Dragon Boat Federation (IDBF) is the world governing body for dragon boat sport.

[9] From its founding through July 2016, Dynamic Dragon Boat Racing has raised more than $4 million for charity; see question four; see also Dynamic Dragon Boat Racing 2017.

Works Cited, Frther Readings, & Resources

Books

Barker, Pat. *Dragon Boats A Celebration*. Weatherhill, 1996.

Chan, Arlene, and Susan Humphies. *Paddles Up! Dragon Boat Racing in Canada*. Dundurn Press, 2009.

Fernández-Calienes, Raúl, and Penny Behling, eds. *Reaching for Life: Breast Cancer Survivors and Dragon Boat Sport*. Vol. 1-2. Dynamic Dragon Boat Racing, 2010.

Shum, Tyrone. *The Dragon Boats Quickstart*. Dragonglobe, 2008.

Tocher, Michelle. *How to Ride a Dragon: Women with Breast Cancer Tell their Stories*. Key Porter Books, 2002.

Academic Theses and Dissertations

Byrer, Beth Kathleen. *Breast Cancer Survivors' Decisions to Participate in a Physical Activity Group*. Master of Science Thesis. Purdue University, 2012.

Grace, Matthew James. *Geography, Cancer and Dragon Boats: Ethnographic Explorations of Breast Cancer Dragon Boating in the Lake District, UK*. Doctor of Philosophy Thesis. University of Exeter, 2012. ore.exeter. ac.uk/repository/handle/10871/10503. Accessed 10 Feb. 2017.

Storm, Kim. *The Survivor Sistership Dragon Boat Team: A Phenomenological Study of Breast Cancer Survivors*. Dissertation for the Degree of Doctorate in Education. Graduate School of Education, St. Mary's University of Minnesota, 2008.

Articles (Academic)

Fernández-Calienes, Raúl. "Bob Morro: International Rowing and Dragon Boat Racing Executive and Official." *Journal of Multidisciplinary Research*, vol. 5, no. 3, Fall 2013, pp. 71-78.

Kent, Heather. "Mr. Dragon Boat." *Canadian Medical Association Journal*, vol. 167, no. 9, 29 Oct. 2002, p. 1048. www.cmaj.ca/ content/167/9/1048.2.full. Accessed 10 Feb. 2017.

McCartney, Glenn, and Linda Osti. "From Cultural Events to Sport Events: A Case Study of Cultural Authenticity in the Dragon Boat Races." *Journal of Sport & Tourism*, vol. 12, iss. 1, 7 Aug. 2007, pp. 25-40. dx.doi.org/10.1080/14775080701496750. Accessed 10 Feb. 2017.

McCausland, Linda L. "Dragon Boat Racing: Life after Breast Cancer Treatment." *The American Journal of Nursing*, vol. 110, no. 10, Oct. 2010, pp. 48-54. doi: 10.1097/01.NAJ.0000389677.80144.2f. Accessed 10 Feb. 2017.

McKenzie, Donald C. "Abreast in a Boat: A Race against Breast Cancer." *Canadian Medical Association Journal,* vol. 159, no. 4, 25 Aug. 1998, pp. 376-78. www.cmaj.ca/content/159/4/376.full.pdf. Accessed 10 Feb. 2017.

Mitchell, Terry L., and Eleanor Nielsen. "Living Life to the Limits: Dragon Boaters and Breast Cancer." *Canadian Women's Studies-Les cahiers de la femme,* vol. 21, no. 3, Jan. 2002, pp. 50-57. cws.journals. yorku.ca/index.php/cws/article/view/6620/5808. Accessed 10 Feb. 2017.

Sabiston, Catherine M., et al. "Psychosocial Experiences of Breast Cancer Survivors Involved in a Dragon Boat Program: Exploring Links to Positive Psychological Growth." *Journal of Sport and Exercise Psychology,* vol. 29, no. 4, Sept. 2007, pp. 419-38. www. purdue.edu/hhs/hk/sportpsych/publications/Sabiston%20et%20 al%202007.pdf. Accessed 10 Feb. 2017.

Unruh, Anita M., and Natalie Elvin. "In the Eye of the Dragon: Women's Experience of Breast Cancer and the Occupation of Dragon Boat Racing." *Canadian Journal of* Occupational Therapy, vol. 71, no. 3, June 2004, pp. 138-49. doi: 10.1177/000841740407100304. Accessed 10 Feb. 2017.

Weiner, Janet. "Once a Taboo, Exercise Becomes Post-Cancer Surgery Rehab Tool: How Researchers Literally Rowed Past Traditional Medical Wisdom." *LDI Health Economist [Leonard Davis Institute of Health Economics, University of Pennsylvania],* May 2012, pp. [1-2]. www.ldihealtheconomist.com/he000025.shtml. Accessed 10 Feb. 2017.

Articles (Popular)

"AIMS on Course to get IOC Recognition." *Dragon Sport News,* April 2016, p. 4.

Barned-Smith, St. John. "Blind Dragon Boat Team Prepares to Race in the National Harbor Regatta." *Washington Post,* 23 Aug. 2013. www.washingtonpost.com/local/blind-dragon-boat-team-prepares-to-race-in-the-national-harbor-regatta/2013/08/23/ ffc02588-0b7e-11e3-8974-f97ab3b3c677_story.html. Accessed 10 Feb. 2017.

Bower, Amanda. "Racing the Dragon: How a New Industry is Working to Turn a 2,000-Year-Old Chinese Team Sport into the Next Big Thing." *Time Magazine,* 28 May 2006. content.time.com/time/ magazine/article/0,9171,1198916,00.html Accessed 10 Feb. 2017.

Chakrabortyl, Ajanta. "40th Dragon Boat Races Promises Excitement." *The Times of India,* 7 June 2016. timesofindia.indiatimes.com/ City/Kolkata/40th-dragon-boat-races-promises-excitement/ articleshow/52635809.cms. Accessed 10 Feb. 2017.

"China Commemorates Dragon Boating with an Annual National Day." *Dragon Boat International,* vol. 17, Oct. 2008, p. 10.

Correal, Annie. "New York Today: Dragon Boats Return." *New York Times,* 8 Aug. 2014.

cityroom.blogs.nytimes.com/2014/08/08/new-york-today-dragon-boats-return/?_r=0. Accessed 10 Feb. 2017.

"Dragon Boat Race." *Financial Times,* 9 June 2016. www.ft.com/content/f91d30cf-0b96-3584-aaa5-6553fcde5427. Accessed 10 Feb. 2017.

Flannery, Russell. "Greater China Bourses Closed for Dragon Boat Festival." *Forbes,* 9 June 2016. www.forbes.com/sites/russellflannery/2016/06/09/greater-china-bourses-closed-for-dragon-boat-festival/#1467d1306c7e. Accessed 10 Feb. 2017.

Gitlin, Beth (Ask a Business Expert). "Ask a Biz Expert: Dragon Boating a Lot like Business." *Florida Today,* 1 May 2014. www.floridatoday.com/story/money/ small-business/ask-business-expert/2014/05/01/ask-biz-expert-dragon-boating-lot-like-business/8576281/. Accessed 10 Feb. 2017.

Grossfeld, Stan. "Crossing the Dragon Boat Finish Line." *Boston Globe,* 16 June 2013. www.bostonglobe.com/sports/2013/06/16/crossing-dragon-boat-finish-line/gxlEw1kz7EsAfBj3k0ZnwO/story.html. Accessed 10 Feb. 2017.

Hooi, Joyce. "Dragon Boats Rule the Waters of Marina Bay." *The Business Times* (Singapore), 8 June 2015. www.businesstimes.com.sg/life-culture/dragon-boats-rule-the-waters-of-marina-bay/. Accessed 10 Feb. 2017.

"The IDBF Dragon Boating Family and the Olympic Flame Get in Contact Again for London 2012." *Dragon Boat International,* vol. 28, Dec. 2012, p. 8.

LaVerde, Donna M. "Surviving Breast Cancer Can Mean the Painful Loss of Support Group Friends." *Washington Post,* 19 Nov. 2012. www.washingtonpost.com/national/health-science/surviving-breast-cancer-can-mean-the-painful-loss-of-support-group-friends/2012/11/17/51f1548e-1d4c-11e2-b647-bb1668e64058_story.html. Accessed 10 Feb. 2017.

"Live Web TV Coverage of Dragon Boating in Szeged." *Dragon Boat International,* vol. 29, Dec. 2013, p. 4.

Lloyd, Barbara. "Dragon Boat Regatta on the Hudson." *New York Times,* 4 Aug. 1991. www.nytimes.com/1991/08/04/sports/boating-dragon-boat-regatta-on-the-hudson.html. Accessed 10 Feb. 2017.

"The Long and Winding Road to Becoming an Olympic Sport." *Dragon Boat International,* vol. 20, July 2009, p. 6.

McCormick, Mark, and Michael Guise. "Schuylkill River: Dragon Boat Coach Hype Mattingly Brings Survivor's Spirit to Racing." *Philadelphia Neighborhoods,* 22 Mar. 2016. philadelphianeighborhoods.com/2016/03/22/schuylkill-river-dragon-boat-coach-hype-mattingly-brings-survivors-spirit-to-racing/. Accessed 10 Feb. 2017.

Pavan, Benoît. "A Annecy, les Dragon Ladies rament contre le cancer." *Le Monde* (Ed. Global), 10 Mai 2013. www.lemonde.fr/sport/article/2013/05/09/a-annecy-les-dragon-ladies-rament-contre-les-cancer_3174611_3242.html?xtmc=dragon_boat&xtcr=2. Accessed 10 Feb. 2017.

Sindane, Lucky. "Paddling in New Directions." *Mail & Guardian,* 23 May 2008. mg.co.za/article/2008-05-23-paddling-in-new-directions. Accessed 10 Feb. 2017.

Singh, Harminder. "Way of the Dragon: All You Need to Know about the Hong Kong Dragon Boat Festival." *South China Morning Post,* 4 June 2016. www.scmp.com/news/hong-kong/education-community/article/1964246/way-dragon-all-you-need-know-about-hong-kong. Accessed 10 Feb. 2017.

Wertheim, Jon. "Pretty in Pink: Cancer Survivors Form Top Dragonboat Racing Team." *Sports Illustrated,* 6 Aug. 2010, n.p. www.si.com/more-sports/2010/08/06/dragon-boat. Accessed 10 Feb. 2017.

Wei, Christine. "Top 8 Dragon Boat Festivals in North America." *National Geographic,* 10 June 2011. intelligenttravel. nationalgeographic.com/2011/06/10/top-8-dragon-boat-festivals-in-north-america/. Accessed 10 Feb. 2017.

Wong, Grace. "Popular Dragon Boat Races Promote Literacy." *Chicago Tribune,* 24 June 2016. www.chicagotribune.com/news/ct-dragon-boat-literacy-met-20160624-story.html. Accessed 10 Oct. 2016.

Organization Documents

Dragon Boat Canada – Bateau-Dragon Canada. *Rules of Racing.* Jan. 2016. media.wix.com/ugd/2364d1_eb88c00871c8473d 867f5cc7423544fe.pdf

Dynamic Dragon Boat Racing. 2017. www.racedragonboats.com

European Dragon Boat Federation. 2017. www.edbf.org/

International Dragon Boat Federation. 2017. www.idbf.org/

_____. *Competition Regulations 2016.* 2016a. www.idbf.org/

_____. *Rules of Racing 2016.* 2016b. www.idbf.org/

_____. *Minutes of the 13ᵗʰ Meeting of the IDBF Members Congress Held in Tampa, Florida, USA.* 2011. www.idbf.org/

Pan American Dragon Boat Federation. 2017. www.panamdragonboat. org/

United States Dragon Boat Federation. 2017. www.usdbf.org/

Archival Materials

International Dragon Boat Federation. *IDBF Congress Minutes.* 2003-2017. www.idbf.org/library.php

Pan American Dragon Boat Federation. *PADBF Congress Minutes.* 2007-2017. www.panamdragonboat.org/

Periodicals

Dragon Boat International: The News Magazine of the International Dragon Boat Federation www.idbf.org/mag_DBI.php

Dragon Boat Magazine www.dragonboatmag.com

Dragon Sport News: An e-Magazine for Dragon Boaters Worldwide www.erdba.net/uploads/1/2/5/5/12550343/idbf-dragon-boat-news-april2016.pdf

IDBF Club Crew World Championship Bulletins
IDBF World Dragon Boat Racing Championship Bulletins
m.idbf.org/news.php
International Breast Cancer Paddlers Commission Newsletter
www.ibcpc.com/Newsletters.htm
Keeping Abreast
www.abreastinaboat.com

Blogs
Dragon Boat Globe
www.dragonglobe.com
Dragon Boat Sport
www.facebook.com/DragonBoatPaddling/

International Dragon Boat Federations
International Dragon Boat Federation (IDBF)
www.idbf.org
Asian Dragon Boat Federation (ADBF)
adbfdragon@126.com
Dragon Boat Federation of Africa (DBFA)
n.a.
European Dragon Boat Federation (EDBF)
www.edbf.org
Oceania Dragon Boat Federation (ODBF)
www.facebook.com/OceaniaDBF
Pan American Dragon Boat Federation (PADBF)
www.panamdragonboat.org/

Official IDBF Affiliate Festivals

Alcan Dragon Boat Festival Canada
Auckland Dragon Boat Festival (Aotearoa) New Zealand
Banyoles International Dragon Boat Festival Spain
Celebes International Dragon Boat Festival Indonesia
Chinese Bicentennial Ltd Dragon Boat Festival Trinidad & Tobago
Dragon Boat Israel, Ohalo Boating Club Israel
Győr International Dragon Boat Festival Hungary
Hong Kong International Races Hong Kong
Istanbul Dragon Festival Turkey
Labuan International Sea Challenge Malaysia
Limmasol International Dragon Boat Races Cyprus
Macau International Festival Races Macau
Miami Hong Kong Dragon Boat Festival U.S.A.
Musi Triboatton International Festival Indonesia
Nantes Atlantique Dragon Boat Festival France
New York Hong Kong Dragon Boat Festival U.S.A.
Padang International Dragon Boat Festival Indonesia
Panama Chinese Cultural Centre Dragon Boat Festival Panama

Penang International Dragon Boat Festival Malaysia
Prague International Dragon Boat Races Czechoslovakia
Putrajaya International Dragon Boat Festival Malaysia
Rouen AFCDB Dragon Boat Festival France
Sabah International Dragon Boat Races Malaysia
Stanley International Festival Races Hong Kong
Tampa Bay International Dragon Boat Festival U.S.A.
Thailand International Swan Boat Races Thailand
Tim Horton's Ottawa Dragon Boat Festival Canada
Toronto International Festival Races Canada
Vladivostok Governor of Primorye International Cup Russia

Ethnicity, Culture, Religion and Sport: Sectarianism as an Obstacle to the Development of Sport in Cape Town, South Africa during the First Half of the Twentieth Century

FARIEDA KHAN

Introduction

South Africa's history of competitive sport began with the establishment of various sports clubs in the mid-to-late nineteenth century, first among Whites and then spreading to Black communities in the urban centers of Cape Town, Kimberley, and the eastern Cape.[1] By this stage, the country's "traditional system" of social relations was founded on an acceptance of "white domination and black subordination" which had already given rise to formal and informal social segregation measures based on race and racially-based class distinctions.[2] Thus, while legislated racial segregation was in its infancy and custom dictated the racially-based hierarchical nature of colonial society, this provided the context for the development of the country's sports history. Inevitably, the racial politics of the era was reflected in the establishment of racially exclusive sports clubs and segregated public recreation and sporting facilities.

Black communities, which often unquestioningly accepted the stratification of society as the norm, proceeded to voluntarily implement segregation based on culture, ethnicity and religion, within their own communities. Thus Coloreds separated themselves from Black Africans; Colored Christians from Muslims; while Muslims separated themselves into those of Indian descent and 'Cape Malays,' i.e. those who regarded themselves as being exclusively of Indonesian descent. [3] In the sporting world, these societal divisions took the form of separate sports clubs at community level and (aided by the authorities' provision of ethnically separate residential areas and sports facilities during the twentieth century), the exclusion of those perceived as outsiders from the use of those facilities.

Given that the impress of racial politics cuts deep in South African history, it follows that there is an intimate connection between sport and politics in this country, and hence that the history and development of sport has been shaped and determined by its racial politics. This chapter will explore a relatively unknown aspect of its racial politics, viz. sectarianism, and its impact on the sphere of sport among Black communities in Cape Town.

Sport and Politics: The Late Colonial Era

The Political Context

South Africa as a political entity did not exist in the late nineteenth century. During that period, Blacks in the Cape Colony enjoyed a measure of political equality, with a non-racial franchise open to all males who qualified, as well as a certain level of social interaction across the color line among the working classes with many attending the same schools - however, among the exclusively White upper class, there was little such fluidity. [4] Outside the Cape however, Blacks were socially and politically discriminated against and treated as a subordinate laboring class.[5]

Increasingly, those few educated middle class Blacks who tried to use the same public and private facilities as the White elite (such as first class railway carriages and hotels), were often prevented from doing so by *de facto* segregation which, by the late nineteenth century, was giving way to *de jure* exclusion.[6] Among Whites, there was widespread acceptance of an unwritten 'Color Bar' in which Blacks were deemed inferior to Whites and therefore were excluded from the private organizations founded by the affluent, educated upper class, as well as from the institutions and facilities they frequented.[7] Hence, the members of private interest groups, such as the Mountain Club of South Africa (MCSA) founded in 1891, were drawn from the social, economic and political elite which, given the racial stratification of colonial society, meant that the membership of such organizations was exclusively White – as was the case with the MCSA which only accepted its first Black member in 1986.[8]

While there was a measure of political and legal equality between Black and White at the Cape, this situation came under increasing pressure from the late nineteenth century onwards, with franchise restrictions put in place.[9] This was accompanied by the extension, or more stringent enforcement of, racial segregation in government institutions such as hospitals and prisons, resulting in the entrenchment of the perception and treatment of Blacks as subordinate to Whites in the political, legal and social spheres. [10]

Sport in the Late Colonial Era

Given the increasing number of racial restrictions imposed in the political and social arenas during the late nineteenth century, it is unsurprising that these restrictions impacted upon the development of sport, and that "elitism and racism, were the norm."[11] Indeed, given the reality of colonial racial politics, it was inevitable that sport could not be "a medium of cross-racial contact", and except for rare mixing on Imperial holidays, by 1900 Blacks were mostly excluded from competitions in which Whites participated.[12] Thus the establishment of racially separate sporting competitions, sports clubs and national associations during the nineteenth century simply reflected the prevailing social and political realities. Hence, the exclusively White South African Cricket Association was established in 1890, followed by the South African Cyclists' Union, the South African Amateur Athletics Association in 1892; and the National Swimming Association in 1899.[13] The 'Krom Hendriks' episode in 1894, in which a talented Colored cricketer was prevented by the South African Cricket Association from being part of the first South African tour to England, shows how deep-rooted racial distinctions had become by this period.[14] Further, this discriminatory episode highlighted the racial prejudice and determination of the White sporting and political establishment to institutionalize racial segregation in sport, as most of them heartily approved of "separate, ethnic-based athletic clubs," just as they approved of residential and recreational segregation.[15]

Given their exclusion from the newly-formed sports clubs and associations, Blacks eager to participate in the newly-arrived forms of sport, had little option but to form their own organizations. At first, sporting participation was confined to mission schools, but by the late nineteenth century the first clubs were being established (such as the first African cricket club in Port Elizabeth in 1869) and by the 1890s, Black tennis and croquet clubs had been formed in several towns and soccer and rugby had taken root in the Eastern Cape; while national and regional associations were formed, such as the Griqualand West Colored Cricket Union in 1892 and the Colored Rugby Football Board in Kimberley in 1897.[16] Both these associations represented all Black clubs, since the term 'Colored' at the time was often used as an umbrella term for all Black people.

In 1903, the South African Colored Cricket Board (a national body which aimed to represent all cricketers regardless of race or religion), was established.[17] Furthermore, given that the racial and class stratification of colonial society was the norm, it is not surprising to find that the tendency among the Black community was to establish separate clubs on ethnic, cultural or religious grounds. Thus separate sport clubs for Africans, Indians, Muslims ('Malays') and Coloreds were routinely formed. However, it should be noted that, among the Black community, this separation was generally not hostile or rigid and that teams formed by a particular group could and did include members of other groups, such as a 'Malay' team, selected from various teams for a tournament in Kimberley, which also included five Coloreds and one African.[18]

However, in the midst of this spirit of co-operation, a strident note of ethnic separatism was beginning to creep in when Colored, Christian cricketers in Kimberley separated themselves from the 'Malays' and

Africans playing in the Griqualand West Colored Cricket Union, and three breakaway clubs then formed the Diamond Fields Colonial Cricket Union in 1892.[19] In Cape Town, the City and Suburban Rugby Union, a Colored Christian Club founded in 1898, went even further, by excluding Muslims from membership until the early 1960s.[20] Notwithstanding, mixed competitions among the Black community were routinely held, while sporting associations representing all Black clubs were not unusual, leading to such a cordial level of co-operation and camaraderie among Black sports clubs in centers such as Kimberley, that it seemed there was every reason to expect that "this co-operation should deepen in the future".[21]

Sport and Politics: The First Half of the 20th Century

The Political Context

The opening years of the twentieth century, showed in no uncertain terms that political inequality and an increasing level of racial segregation would be the fate of Blacks in the country in the future. Expectations of the extension of the non-racial Cape franchise were dashed after Great Britain defeated the Boer Republics in 1902 as Britain bowed to Afrikaner and British colonial sentiment and again when the country was unified in 1910.[22] The first steps towards the residential segregation of Africans at the Cape were taken with the establishment of *Uitvlugt* (later renamed *Ndabeni*) in 1901 and the enactment of the Native Reserve Location Act in 1902. [23] These moves showed, not only that it was the authorities' intention to view and govern Africans as outsiders in the Western Cape, but that there would be *no* support for the struggle of Blacks for political equality. Further, they foreshadowed additional attacks on the land and franchise rights of all Black South Africans and the relentless formalization of racial segregation, as was signaled by the dispossession and eviction of thousands under the Natives Land Act no.27 of 1913.[24]

A plethora of laws followed, instituting and regulating residential segregation, such as the Natives (Urban Areas) Act, 1923; as well as further restrictions (through the Representation of Natives Act, 1936), on their already limited franchise rights and freedom of movement through the implementation of 'influx control' measures in the Western Cape.[25] Indian South Africans, long subjected to restrictions on access to land, the franchise and freedom of movement, were further targeted through the Asiatic Tenure and Representation Act, 1946.[26] Colored people were dealt with through the establishment in 1943, of a Colored Affairs Department which would segregate the administration of Colored affairs from that dealing with the affairs of Whites – this was perceived by many, as a step on the road to the further political marginalization of Colored people.[27]

With regard to segregation in the social sphere, by the early twentieth century racial distinctions were becoming more marked through the segregation or exclusion of Blacks from public leisure facilities such as theatres, cinemas and hotels.[28] In the voluntary or private interest sector catering to the White elite, an acceptance of the political status quo and consequent acceptance of racially discriminatory practices was common. Hence, organizations such as the Veld Trust (a soil conservation body established in 1943) had a constitutional bar to Black membership.[29] However, the constitutions of many others, such as the Mountain Club of South Africa, The Botanical Society and the Wildlife Society made no mention of race, doubtless secure in the knowledge that, if any Black person were to ignore the unwritten social conventions of the day, their applications would be declined, as in the case of the MCSA or the entire issue of Black membership would be simply avoided, as in the case of the Wildlife Society.[30]

In 1948, the Nationalist Party campaigned and won the national election on an 'apartheid' ticket, i.e. complete segregation among the 'races' in every sphere of public life – this enabled them to complete a process of formal and informal segregation which had been under way during the colonial and post-1910 decades, and institutionalize it throughout the country.[31] Under apartheid, a body of law was passed which, by consolidating and extending existing racially discriminatory legislation, further subordinated and sought to permanently exclude Blacks from the mechanisms of political power. These laws were founded on the Population Registration Act No.30, 1950[32] which gave the force of law to the informal, often permeable racial groupings which historically had always been recognized in South Africa. The Group Areas Act no. 41, 1950 provided for the establishment of separate residential areas to which members of the various population groups were restricted; the Reservation of Separate Amenities Act No. 49, 1953 provided for public premises to be reserved for the members of a particular race, regardless of whether the facilities were substantially equal or not and in the main, they were greatly skewed in favor of Whites.[33] For the sporting sector, the consequences of apartheid legislation such as this would be to further disadvantage Black sportsmen and women and greatly retard sporting development.

The Political Context - Sectarianism among Black Communities

Black communities did not simply passively accept the relentless implementation of racial discrimination and the efforts to treat them as inferior or to reduce them to the position of laborer – hence a number of political organizations were active during the early twentieth century.[34] Nor did all Black communities simply accept the attempts to divide Black communities through discriminatory legislation which gave preferential treatment to some and ranked Africans (who had the fewest rights of all), at the bottom of the 'racial hierarchy of privilege.' Many politically astute politicians such as Dr Abdurahman of the Colored organization, the African Peoples' Organization, recognized the politically divisive tactics of the Government, after the betrayal of Black political aspirations by the South Africa Act in 1910 and argued for Black political unity and joint action.[35] Ultimately, however, Black political organizations remained ethnically separate during the first half of the twentieth century, each either mired in the protection of their few rights and privileges, or a refusal to accept the necessity for unity.

During the late 1930s/early 1940s, the rise of radical organizations in Cape Town, with a non-racial agenda (including the National Liberation League, the Non-European United Front, and the Non-European Unity Movement, did little to stem the separatist strategies of Black Colored political organizations as none ultimately succeeded in establishing a united Black struggle for full democratic rights.[36]

Given the oppressive political climate of the twentieth century and the inability of Black political organizations to form an effective united front to face the threat of segregation and disempowerment of all Blacks, it proved easy for the Government to exploit divisions through legislation and policies which perpetuated a racial, cultural and ethnic hierarchy. Fear of the loss of one's position in this 'hierarchy of privilege' often provided the motivation for the defense of the few rights each group had, instead of opting for Black political unity. In turn, the voluntary acceptance of separatism provided fertile ground for the growth of ethnic, cultural and religious prejudice among Black communities and allowed sectarianism to take firm root and flourish. Hence it was the response of Black communities to the 'racial hierarchy of privilege' which gave real impetus to the growth of sectarianism as many voluntarily implemented it within their own communities and policed it with vigor, as would be seen in the sporting sector.

The Political Context - Sectarianism in Cape Town

A strong contributing factor to the growth of sectarianism in Cape Town was the emergence of a specific Colored identity. While it is true that the roots of this identity may be traced back to colonial times, it also needs to be recognized that, in the nineteenth century, the term 'Colored' generally referred to "all non-European people" and that organizations with the term 'Colored' in their name, such as the 'Colored People's Association of South Africa' often did not exclude Africans. [37] The Colored identity which emerged in the early twentieth century however, was far more strident and would, over time, even develop into hostility towards other Black communities. Fueled by fears of further political marginalization by Whites, many Colored people, particularly from the emerging elite, chose to dissociate themselves from Africans for fear of being relegated to the same low social and political status. This fear was often expressed through the formation of Colored organizations, such as the African People's Organization (APO), which was established in 1902.[38] While the APO claimed to stand for the principle of equal rights for "all civilized men" and its President, Dr Abdurahman (from 1905 to

1940), was not averse to united Black action, he felt that the role of the APO was primarily to "deal with the rights and duties of the Colored people of South Africa as distinguished from the native races." [39]

The next decade would see an even more forceful Colored exclusivism being promoted. In 1919, the United Afrikaner League was established, supported by the anti-Muslim newspaper, *The Clarion*, which attacked Abdurahman's leadership on the basis that, as a Muslim, he had no right to represent "Christian, 'true' Colored South Africans." [40] In 1925, the Colored organization, the African National Bond was formed, with the objective of gaining the recognition of Coloreds and 'Malays' as distinct races, as well as protection from "unequal and inequitable competition on the part of the Native." [41] The ANB supported the Government's policy of racial segregation, but wanted a higher status than Africans since, they maintained, they were more 'civilized' than Africans. [42]

The virulent strain of Colored separatism espoused by the United Afrikaner League and the African National Bond, which regarded Africans as outsiders in the Western Cape, and Indian South Africans and Cape Muslims as exotic aliens and thus un-South African, was far more aggressive than the Colored separatism of the Teachers League of South Africa[43] and the 'Colored distinctiveness,' but broad 'Non-European' unity subscribed to by the APO. Together, however, the combined impact of these ideologies was to entrench the ethnic tensions and cultural divisions bequeathed by the late colonial era. It was inevitable that these tensions and divisions would spill over into the sporting sector.

Sport and Politics

The Growth and Entrenchment of Sectarianism in Sport among Black Communities[44]

At first, moves towards unity in sport among Blacks had a promising start in the wake of the country's unification in 1910, as indicated by the affiliation of the Durban and District Indian Cricket Union to the South African Colored Cricket Board in 1913, and their participation in a racially-inclusive tournament held in Kimberley in 1913.[45] Throughout the first half of the twentieth century, players from one cultural/racial group continued to play for clubs catering for other groups, such as two African soccer and rugby clubs in Cape Town which both had Colored members as well as a racially mixed rugby team in District Six.[46] Tellingly though, the Colored member of the rugby club did not attend any meetings, despite playing in all the matches.[47] During this period there were also attempts to start inclusive Black sporting associations in the various sporting sectors, such as the 1912 announcement by Dr Abdurahman who, in his capacity as president of the Western Province Colored Board, stated his intention of bringing all existing unions in Cape Town into one. In the sphere of sport, Abdurahman was a strong proponent of unity and co-operation.[48]

However, notwithstanding the fact that there have always been instances of multi-racialism throughout the history of organized sport in South Africa,[49] this has usually been the exception, rather than the rule. The racial hierarchy, which gave certain groups within the Black community a few more privileges than those below, while leaving Africans at the bottom, was extremely divisive. The increasingly segregationist policies of the State in the twentieth century reinforced and encouraged the fault lines of "cultural and religious particularism"[50] in sport throughout South Africa. This was vividly illustrated by the situation in the province of Natal where, not only was there "a clear race line between Indians and Colored [which] extended to all walks of life," but Africans, Indians, Coloreds and Whites all lived separate lives as regulated by Government and which was voluntarily supported by the social customs of those communities.[51] Thus sectarianism in sport became firmly entrenched in Natal, with each group discriminating against the other, as seen in the cricket sector, with Indian clubs discriminating against all "those who are not of Indian parentage"; Indian clubs barring Coloreds from membership; Indian and Colored clubs discriminating against 'Malays'; and Colored clubs discriminating against Africans, Indians and 'Malays.'[52] To a greater or lesser extent, this situation in Natal was reflected in the rest of the country.

As sectarianism in sport mirrored the highly stratified society South Africa had become during the first half of the century, the move away from it reflected the politics of the period as well. As moves towards united political action began to take root in response to the institutionalization of segregation in society, so the sporting sector responded. Thus it was that, during the late 1940s onwards, the first tentative moves away from sectarianism began to be taken and "inter-racial umbrella organizations" in cricket and soccer were established.[53] However, it would be some decades before sectarianism among Blacks in sport would be seriously dealt with.

Sport and Sectarianism in Cape Town

As in the rest of South Africa, divisions and tensions existed among the various Black communities in Cape Town and these formed the basis of ethnic, cultural and religious discrimination in sport, as was evident from the number of ethnically-based sports clubs established from 1903 to 1956.[54] However, in contrast to the clubs of the late nineteenth century, with their fairly fluid racial boundaries and generally co-operative spirit, the twentieth century clubs were far more rigid in terms of their membership and often hostile to outsiders.

Anti-Muslim sentiment among Colored sports clubs soon asserted itself in the form of a prohibition on Muslim membership – for example, the Western Province Football Association, a body for Coloreds only, excluded Muslims from the competitions it organized, triggering the establishment of the Western Province Moslem Soccer Union in 1912.[55]

Anti-Muslim sentiment on the part of Colored clubs became more pronounced as the century advanced, with clubs barring Muslims as well as Africans from joining their clubs – as in the case of the Maitland-Parow District Cricket Union, which excluded "Mohammedans" and "Natives" from membership.[56] Attempts to amend these restrictions were unsuccessfully made throughout the 1930s, while other clubs went further and also barred Muslims from using their sports facilities, as was the case when Muslim cricket and rugby clubs in Claremont were prohibited from using the Rosmead Sportsground.[57]

The football sector was especially stringent when it came to deciding who qualified to be members, instituting 'passing out parades,' in which elders and administrators decided upon the 'suitability' of potential recruits based on physical markers, with kinky hair and dark skin color used as obstacles to membership.[58] The application of this type of discrimination resulted in a hurtful personal experience for a young boy in 1949, who was suspended from the Cape and District Football Association (CDFA) when they found out he was Muslim, and even though his teacher interceded on his behalf and pleaded with the chairman of the Association, William Herbert, to allow him to remain, "he told me sorry, he cannot help it . . . I was heart-sore."[59] The case of Bluebells Football Club, which tried to gain entry to the CDFA, shows just how difficult it was to break down anti-Muslim prejudice, as Bluebells had to form the Wynberg Action Committee before the discriminatory clause was finally lifted.[60] These were some of the ways in which clubs such as those allied to the Western Province Football Board, the Alliance Football Association and the CDFA, kept out Africans and Muslims until these discriminatory clauses were finally abandoned in the late 1950s and 1960.[61]

Commenting on the 'passing out' (i.e. discriminatory) procedures of the past, one sportsman noted that,

if you've got a Moslem name or surname, you were not allowed to pass out . . . they had what they called the pencil test, they used to take a pencil and put it through your hair – and [if] your hair's curly, you're like an African and you were not allowed at CDFA . . . these were all things to justify or keep the Moslems and Africans from not participating.[62]

This type of discrimination led many keen Muslim sportsmen and women to pretend to be Christian by adopting Christian names in order to be able to join clubs and use their sports facilities, as in the experience of a young Muslim resident of Simon's Town in the 1940s who was forced to use the Christian name of 'George' in order to be accepted by a local badminton club.[63] A similar experience befell a young Muslim tennis player during the 1950s, who was eager to play badminton as well. As a Muslim, however, she was prohibited from joining the club, Collegians, so she adopted the name of 'Gay' in order to become a member.[64] The situation had not improved much by the late 1950s, as Abdurahman

Adams, a Muslim, had to go by the name of A. B. Adams in order to join the Temperance Rugby Club because it was a "Christian club."[65]

There was also tension between Cape Muslims and Indian Muslims. The Cape Muslims were known by the pejorative term 'Bushmen Muslims' by some Indian Muslims[66] who looked down on them, presumably because they were far less rigid about not marrying outside their community and married locals who converted to Islam. Indians were discriminated against in the sporting sector and were forced to form their own sporting bodies, such as the Western Province Indian Football Union in 1924, as they were not allowed to play in the White, Colored or 'Malay' unions.[67]

Prejudice on the part of Coloreds against Africans appeared to be the trigger for the exclusion of Africans from their clubs. This prejudice was on display in 1913, when a number of Colored cricketers in the South African Colored Cricket Board refused to participate in the inclusive tournament organized by the Board because they were opposed to the inclusion of Africans.[68] Many sporting associations had an explicit 'No Natives' clause in their constitutions, along with their 'No Muslims' rule, and even when pressure exerted on clubs succeeded in getting them to drop restrictions on Muslim membership, as in the case of the Maitland-Parow District Cricket Union in 1941, restrictions on Africans would remain firmly in place.[69]

Colored exclusivism was widespread throughout the sporting sector and included the new sport of mountaineering. Early in 1931, a group of Colored mountaineering enthusiasts in District Six, Cape Town, approached the Mountain Club for information "with a view to starting a Colored mountain club,"[70] the Cape Province Mountain Club (CPMC). However, since many of the documents (such as the original Constitution) relating to the early history of the CPMC have either been lost or are not available to non-members[71] it is not possible to state with certainty whether this Club was restricted to Colored members or not. It is, however, known that Cape Town Councillor, Dr Abdurahman (a Muslim), attended the opening of the CPMC's mountain hut on 16 December 1931, and while Club tradition holds that he was instrumental in securing the use of the hut for the Club, this claim cannot be verified in the relevant Cape Town Council documents.[72] However, notwithstanding whether this claim was true or not, it does not provide evidence of a non-sectarian approach on the part of the CPMC, as demonstrated by the example of a Colored cricket union in the mid-1930s. This union was happy to accept a donation from a Muslim businessman and make him their patron, while simultaneously refusing entry to 'Mohammedans.'[73] While in later years the CPMC has insisted that it has always been 'non-racial,' this claim is open to question given the lack of documentation; the political and sports context of the 1930s; as well as the recollection of anti-Muslim bias by some of its members.[74]

While prejudice was often a catalyst for separate clubs, it sometimes occurred as a result of a passive acceptance of the status quo i.e. an acceptance of existing ethnic and religious divides as a societal norm. This is the position taken by a member of the family which started the Salt River Tennis Club, who insists that there was no constitutional bar to Muslim membership, and that the separation of sports clubs on religious grounds, simply "grew out of a social thing, so groups would form around that – there was no conscious effort to be separate, it just happened."[75] A similar rationale was given by a Simon's Town resident, in trying to explain why there were separate sports clubs for Coloreds, Africans and Muslims, saying that, "Everybody played for separate teams in those days . . . I don't know why it was like that because it was before apartheid, but that's the way it was at the time."[76] In a similar vein, a fellow Simon's Town resident, while acknowledging the practice of Muslims adopting Christian names in order to be accepted by Colored clubs, rejects the notion that they were forced to do so because of the cultural and religious segregation practices of the period, maintaining that, "We lived together and respected one another's religions and cultures."[77] This was also the position of a former resident of the Claremont area, whose memories were of communities "so integrated there was never any problem between Muslim and Christian Coloreds . . . things could have been so different if it had not been for the government's interference."[78] However, a more realistic response from a former rugby and cricket player, was that, "By the 1960s when I started playing sport, things had already begun to change [but] people were very conservative in the early years despite the fact that many people lived in mixed communities such as Bo-Kaap and Claremont."[79]

Numerous former residents of socially and culturally mixed areas such as District Six, have been similarly insistent that differences in religion and culture were no bar to social interaction and they reminisce about the cordial manner in which Christians and Muslims celebrated and respected each other's holy days.[80] Such memories however, appear to be selective, as they do not address the reality of the cultural and religious discrimination which existed in these same communities, nor does it explain the fact that much of this discrimination was voluntary, and predated the apartheid era. Given the socio-political context of the time and the ethnic and religious bigotry which motivated the exclusion of some sectors of the Black community from their sports clubs and facilities, this insistence that these neighborhoods were a haven of cultural and religious harmony, appears to be motivated by a reluctance to confront the ugly realities of the past and a tendency to view the past through "the golden glow of nostalgia."[81] Another rationale put forward for this tendency, is that people who had been subjected to the trauma of apartheid-era forced removals, coped with this pain by developing a common positive narrative, also described as a "then and now" narrative.[82]

While Muslims formed their own clubs as they had done in the past, most did not exclude Christians either in their Constitutions or in practice – most were "predominantly but not exclusively Muslim."[83] Again, as in the past, such clubs were formed for reasons of religious and community unity[84] and were not manifested in a constitutional bar. However, there was one club which specifically excluded Christians, viz. the Vineyard Rugby Club in the up-country area of Paarl, which was established in 1944. Using as justification the abuse of alcohol during celebrations after winning matches, a 'Muslims only' clause was inserted into the Constitution, which was only removed some years later.[85] For the most part, however, Muslim sporting clubs were formed, less as an expression of sectarianism, and more as a manifestation of "Muslim insularity"[86] i.e. a desire to cocoon the Muslim community from external cultural and religious influences. Non-Muslim members wishing to join these clubs could then do so while respecting the cultural norms of the club.

To place this further into context, it should be borne in mind that Muslims in Cape Town were a small religious minority, living in culturally diverse communities and that, while social relations with other members of the community were usually very cordial, often social interactions and friendships between Muslims and non-Muslims only "went so far," stemming from the Muslim community's desire to remain "distinct as a cultural minority."[87] Thus the recreation activities pursued by the Muslim communities and the sports clubs they established were used as a kind of 'cultural glue,' to bind these communities together. Increasingly however, Muslim clubs began to be formed either in response to their exclusion from Colored clubs, or as an acceptance of a perceived social custom, as was the case with the establishment of the Wisteria Tennis Club. In 1934 three young Muslim teachers at Muir St Primary School in District Six decided to start a tennis club based in Salt River as a pleasant way to spend their leisure hours.[88] At the time, there was a Christian tennis club, the Salt River Tennis Club, which had been granted land by the local authorities to establish a tennis court in Salt River, but according to Galima Brown, one of the founders of Wisteria,

> it did not occur to us to join the Hanmer's club, as it was not the done thing at the time. Christians and Muslims did not join the same clubs at that time. Eventually the Council said that they would build a court for us next to the Hanmers and also develop a park. The Hanmers were nice people, but it never occurred to either party to develop a closer relationship – the two clubs remained separate . . . we also had non-Muslims joining us at some stage, although it did not seem to be the done thing for Christian clubs to accept Muslims. Still, there was no antagonism between the clubs or the members.[89]

The situation had not changed much by the mid-1940s, as a new young member[90] recalled,

> Wisteria Tennis Club . . . was essentially a Muslim club, as at that time, all the sports clubs were not only racially segregated, but also on an ethnic and religious basis. . . . Next door to us was another club that belonged to another union, a 'Christian' club – the Salt River Tennis Club – they seemed rather elitist to us

. . . at that stage these segregated clubs were the rule, we did not question it, but just fitted into the way things were. At least in our club there were always a few Christians, but this was not the case in other clubs. Some even had anti-Malay discrimination written into their Constitutions. Anyway, this was probably why we never mixed with the club next door.

These recollections were similar to those of a fellow young member who joined Wisteria at about the same time and who remembers that, "in those days, the clubs were run along separate lines for Christians and Muslims."[91] In the early 1950s a young Muslim member of a softball club was at a union meeting representing her club, Ohio Cubs, when various objections were raised to Muslims becoming members of the Union. As a representative of her club, she registered her strong objection, but the proposal must have been accepted, as she left her club in protest and joined Wisteria Tennis Club instead.[92]

Before the apartheid era began in 1948 therefore, the tradition of separate, often exclusive sports clubs on ethnic, cultural and religious grounds was well entrenched, not only in the racially separate African townships but also in culturally diverse communities such as District Six, Claremont and Simon's Town. These divisions were set to deepen in the apartheid era and would only be radically challenged as political changes began to take place in the future, and the sporting sector (as it has done throughout South Africa's history), would reflect those changes.[93] However, given the entrenched nature of intra-Black divisions, the fight to eradicate these divisions would be a long and arduous one.

Conclusion

Throughout the history of competitive sport in South Africa, sport and politics have been inextricably intertwined. Hence the political context prevailing in Cape Town during this period is of vital importance in analyzing the factors shaping and determining the nature and direction of sports development among Black communities. Clearly, political factors such as the relentless imposition of racial and ethnic segregation and its acceptance by most communities as a social norm, played a major role, as did the fact that discrimination was carried out on the basis of a 'hierarchy of privilege,' to the extent that non-Africans could feel superior to Africans. Fear of the loss of these privileges, in turn fueled the fear of further social and political marginalization. In Cape Town these factors, combined with the rise of an aggressive form of Colored identity, undoubtedly played a strong role in promoting and perpetuating sectarianism among Black communities. In this regard, the work of historians and sports historians has richly described the way in which the ambiguities, contradictions and discriminatory practices of the political authorities were imitated by the Black elite in the political, social and sporting spheres.[94]

The political factors highlighted above certainly play a major role in considering the reasons why culturally and religiously distinct (but fairly permeable) sporting bodies of the late nineteenth century, with their generally friendly sporting interactions, developed into the rigidly segregated, even overtly hostile relationships of the twentieth century. However, these political factors do not fully explain the stringent cultural and religious exclusivism which was practiced to the extent where discrimination on cultural and religious grounds was rigorously enforced and policed by a number of sports clubs during this period. A pointer to the more fundamental reason for this, is the explanation that the reason some Black sports administrators clung to their separate organizations, was that they used such organizations as a source of "potential political power," and hence "jealously guarded their . . . positions."[95] These ethnically separate organizations were thus regarded by Black sports administrators as a mechanism to compensate for their exclusion from political power and influence in society. From this, it may be further argued that, in a political context in which discrimination on various grounds had become the norm and in which Blacks had been stripped of all meaningful power, intra-Black discrimination was a way for the Black elite to exercise some power themselves, albeit in a negative, even destructive, manner. It was a way for the Black elite, rendered impotent in their daily lives, to attempt to give meaning to their lives by controlling and shaping the world within their own communities in a way which gave them the power and agency they otherwise lacked.

The consequences of ethnic, cultural and religious separation among Black communities in the sporting sector during the period under review, was to further stunt sports development, since clubs which were already handicapped by the small number of poor quality sporting facilities provided by local authorities, refused to compete across artificially-created boundaries and declined to share their expertise and facilities. Another consequence of sectarianism in sport was the further entrenchment of racism, religious bigotry and ethnic divisions to such a degree, that it would take decades and a determined effort on the part of the proponents of non-racial sport, to eradicate it from the sphere of sport during the second half of the twentieth century.[96] Since ethnic, cultural and religious sectarianism was the inevitable result of a society in which deep divisions based on race and class had become normalized, it would not be until Black communities started to reject sectarianism from the 1960s and particularly the 1970s, that fundamental changes could be made in the sporting sector and the struggle for non-racial sport could seriously begin.

Notes

[1] Odendaal et al., *Cricket and Conquest* 29, 32-33; Nauright 43, 65; Odendaal et al., *The Blue Book* 111; Odendaal, "South Africa's Black Victorians" 198-199; Odendaal, "The thing that is not round" 33-34.

[2] Bickford-Smith, "A 'special tradition of multi-racialism?'" 47.

[3] Coloreds are the descendants of the indigenous Khoisan people, White settlers and slaves brought from the East coast of Africa, India and the Indonesian archipelago from the earliest days of colonial settlement in the seventeenth century (Lewis 8). Cape residents of Indian descent are mainly the descendants of free immigrants from India, who arrived in the late nineteenth/early twentieth centuries, while those forcibly brought to the Cape during the earlier era of slavery, were largely integrated into the 'Cape Malay' community (Davids 174-175, 194-195). The term 'Cape Malay' seemed to be synonymous with the term 'Cape Muslim' and was erroneously given to the people of Muslim faith, who were thought to have been brought to the Cape from Malaysia and the Indonesian Archipelago: the descendants of slaves, prisoners and political exiles (Bickford-Smith, *Ethnic Pride and Racial Prejudice* 35). However, 'Cape Malay' ancestry is actually Afro-Asian and includes large numbers of people (mainly slaves) from Mozambique, Madagascar, India and Ceylon, in addition to the Indonesian Archipelago (Shell 42-45).

[4] Bickford-Smith *Ethnic Pride and Racial Prejudice* 29; Bickford-Smith, "'A special tradition of multi-racialism?'" 47.

[5] Tatz 2; Maylam 95-97.

[6] Bickford-Smith, *Ethnic Pride and Racial Prejudice* 121-122.

[7] Bickford-Smith, "The Background to Apartheid" 6.

[8] The Mountain Club of South Africa, "The Mountain Club, its origins and doings" 7; Burman 16; Child 5.

[9] Tatz 2-3.

[10] Bickford-Smith, "'A special tradition of multi-racialism?'" 48; Bickford-Smith, *Ethnic Pride and Racial Prejudice* 99-163.

[11] Nauright 25; Desai et al. 6.

[12] Desai et al. 5; Nauright 25, 45.

[13] Nauright 43.

[14] Odendaal et al., *The Blue Book* 2.

[15] Odendaal et al., *Cricket and Conquest* 244-251, 248-249, 265.

[16] Odendaal, "South Africa's Black Victorians" 196-199, 207.

[17] Odendaal et al., *The Blue Book* 19.

[18] Odendaal et al., *Cricket and Conquest* 235.

[19] Odendaal et al., *Cricket and Conquest* 307.

[20] Nauright 50.

[21] Nauright 65; Odendaal, *The Story of an African Game* 65; Odendaal, "South Africa's Black Victorians" 207;Odendaal et al., *Cricket and Conquest* 236.

[22] Thompson 144; Horrell 1.

[23] Goldin 24; Davenport and Saunders 645.

[24] Letsoalo 35.

[25] Horrell 1-3; Goldin 71.

[26] Horrell 2, 5-6.

[27] Goldin 56.

[28] Bickford-Smith, "A 'special tradition of multi-racialism?'" 50.

[29] National Veld Trust 50.

[30] Khan, "Towards Environmentalism" 55, 119; Mountain Club of South Africa, *Minutes* 10 February 1954 and 09 February 1955.

[31] Posel, *The Making of Apartheid* 1.

[32] Horrell 16.

[33] Horrell 71,113; Khan, "Towards Environmentalism" 113.

[34] Lewis 29; Worden, 90.

[35] Lewis 59.

[36] Goldin 55-59; Khan, "The Origins of the Non-European Unity Movement" 98-100, 133.

[37] Adhikari, *Not White Enough, Not Black Enough* 12; Goldin 26, 30.

[38] Lewis 20.

[39] Lewis 26; Goldin, 33, 38.

[40] Lewis 124-125.

[41] Lewis 128.

[42] Lewis 128.

[43] Adhikari, *Let us live for our Children* 17-18.

[44] It should be noted that sectarianism in sport was not confined to the Black community, as anti-Semitism among Whites was also a stumbling block to Jews wishing to join sports clubs – a matter raised during a meeting of the Mountain Club of South Africa in 1929. Hence, a member who "regretted that there seemed to be a tendency for Jews to be excluded from the club" was quickly slapped down for raising the issue at all (Mountain Club of South Africa, Annual General Meeting 13 December 1929).

[45] Desai et al. 8.

[46] Wilson and Mafeje 121; Booley 43.

[47] Wilson and Mafeje 121.

[48] Odendaal, *The Story of an African Game* 64.

[49] Desai et al., 201-205.

[50] Odendaal, "'The thing that is not round'" 30.

[51] Desai et al. 167.

[52] Desai et al., 48, 69-70, 166-167, 170-172.

[53] Alegi 107-108; Odendaal, "'The thing that is not round'" 51; Odendaal, *The Story of an African Game* 105-106.

[54] District Six Museum 151-153.

[55] Cleophas and van der Merwe 129.

[56] Pick 15.

[57] Pick 15-17; Taliep, "Belletjiesbos" 69.

[58] Parker 10; Rive 7; Cleophas and van der Merwe 136; District Six Museum 22-23.

[59] Parker 6, 11.

[60] Cloete 11.

[61] District Six Museum 44, 52, 58.

[62] Cloete 19-20.

[63] Odendaal, "'The thing that is not round'" 30; Davidson.

[64] Jardine.

[65] Abrahams.

[66] Desai et al., 165. Derogatory terms such as 'Bushman' and 'Hottentot' were often used to describe the indigenous Khoisan people. When used against other groups, they were also meant as an insult.

[67] District Six Museum 67.

[68] Desai et al., 44.

[69] District Six Museum 23; Pick 15, 18.

[70] Mountain Club of South Africa, *Minutes* 13 April 1931.

[71] Cape Province Mountain Club, "CPMC"; Bruyns.

[72] Mountain Club of South Africa, *Newspaper Clippings* 17 December 1931; Cape Province Mountain Club, "A brief history"; Cape Town Council, *Minutes*; Cape Town Council, *Minutes of Meetings of the Improvements and Parks Committee.*

[73] Pick 17.

[74] Odendaal, "Climbing to Greater Heights" 102; Knipe-Solomon; Brock.

[75] Hanmer.

[76] Roberts.

[77] Simpson.

[78] Liberty.

[79] Majiet.

[80] Adams 11.

[81] Taliep, "A Study in the History of Claremont" 15.

[82] Adhikari, *Burdened by Race* 55-56; Trotter, "Removals and Remembrance" 12-13; Schreuders 9.

[83] Odendaal, *The Story of an African Game* 61.

[84] Odendaal, "'The thing that is not round'" 28.

[85] Patel.

[86] Taliep, "Belletjiesbos" 69.

[87] Taliep, "Belletjiesbos" 68-69.

[88] Brown.

[89] Brown.

[90] Khan.

[91] Hendrickse.

[92] Jardine.

[93] Odendaal, "'The thing that is not round'" 53.

[94] Including Adhikari, *Not White Enough;* Cleophas and van der Merwe; Lewis; Desai, et al.

[95] Magubane viii; Nauright 72.

[96] The struggle for non-racialism in sport was given focus and direction by the formation of the South African Council on Sport in 1973 – a body which came to be recognized as the internal sports wing of the anti-apartheid movement (Archer and Bouillon 228-230; Booth 483).

Works Cited

Abrahams, Yusuf (Jowa). Personal interview. 12 October 2013.

Adams, Zuleiga. "Memory, Imagination and Removal: Remembering and Forgetting District Six." Masters mini-thesis, University of the Western Cape, 2002.

Adhikari, Mohammed. *"Let us live for our children": The Teachers' League of South Africa, 1913-1940.* Rondebosch: UCT Press; Cape Town: Buchu Books, 1993.

Adhikari, Mohammed. *Not White Enough, Not Black Enough: Racial Identity in the South African Coloured Community.* Athens: Ohio University Press; Cape Town: Double Storey Books, 2005.

Adhikari, Mohammed. *Burdened by Race: Coloured Identities in Southern Africa.* Cape Town: UCT Press, 2009.

Alegi, Peter. *Laduma! Soccer, Politics and Society in South Africa, from its Origins to 2010.* Scottsville: University of KwaZulu-Natal Press, 2010.

Archer, Robert and Antoine Bouillon. *The South African Game – Sport and Racism.* London: Zed Books, 1982.

Bickford-Smith, Vivian. "A 'special tradition of multi-racialism?' Segregation in Cape Town in the late nineteenth and early twentieth centuries." *The Angry Divide: Social and Economic History of the Western Cape.* Eds. Wilmot James and Mary Simons. Cape Town: David Philip, 1989. 47-62.

Bickford-Smith, Vivian. "The Background to Apartheid in Cape Town: The Growth of Racism and Segregation from the Mineral Revolution to the 1930s." Paper presented at the History Workshop, University of the Witwatersrand, 6-10 February 1990.

Bickford-Smith, Vivian. *Ethnic Pride and Racial Prejudice in Victorian Cape Town*. Johannesburg: Witwatersrand University Press, 1995.

Burman, Jose. *A Peak to Climb*. Kaapstad: C Struik, 1966.

Booley, Abdurahman. *Forgotten heroes: A History of Black Rugby, 1882-1992*. Cape Town: Manie Booley Publications, 1998.

Booth, Douglas. "Hitting Apartheid for Six? The Politics of the South African Boycott." *Journal of Contemporary History* 38: 3 (2003), 477-493.

Brock, Brian. Personal interview. 19 October 2015 and 15 May 2017.

Brown, Galiema. Personal interview. 24 August 2004.

Bruyns, Peter. Personal interview. 12 October 2017.

Cape Province Mountain Club. "A brief history of the CPMC." *http://capeprovince-mountainclub.co.za/index.php/about*

Cape Province Mountain Club. "Cape Province Mountain Club." *http://capeprovince-mountainclub.co.za/index.php/cpmc*

Cape Town Council. *Minutes of Council Meetings*. 3CT 1/1/85 – March – September 1931; 1/1/86 – September – 22 December 1931. Western Cape Archives and Record Service.

Cape Town Council. *Minutes of Meetings of the Improvements and Parks Committee*. CT 1/4/5/1/22 – January – December 1931. Western Cape Archives and Record Service.

Child, Greg. "Technicolour Darkness." *Outside Online*, June 2004. 1-10. http://outside.away.com/outside/destinations/200406/climbing_south_africa_1.html Accessed 05 November 2009.

Cloete, Rashied. Interview by Francois Cleophas. 07 April 2008. Sports Memory Project. District Six Museum Archives, Cape Town.

Cleophas, Francois. J. and Floris J.G. van der Merwe. "Contradictions and Responses concerning the South African Sport Color Bar with special reference to the Western Cape." *African Journal for Physical, Health Education Recreation and Dance* 17 (2011), 124-140.

Davids, Achmat. "Politics and the Muslims of Cape Town: A Historical Survey." *Studies in the History of Cape Town* 4 (1981), 174-220.

Davidson, Zainab (Patty). Personal interview. 05 September 2013.

Davenport, T.R.H. and Christopher Saunders. *South Africa: A Modern History*. London: Macmillan Press Ltd., 2000.

Desai, Ashwin, et al. *Blacks in Whites: A Century of Cricket Struggles in KwaZulu-Natal*. Pietermaritzburg: University of Natal Press, 2002.

District Six Museum. *Fields of Play: Football Memories and Forced Removals in Cape Town. A District Six Museum Exhibition Catalogue*. District Six and Basler Afrika Bibliographic Publication, 2010.

Goldin, Ian. *Making Race: The Politics and Economics of Coloured Identity in South Africa*. London: Longman, 1987.

Hanmer, Tom. Personal communication. 20 February 2010.

Hendrickse, Latiefa. Personal interview. 15 September 2010.

Horrell, Muriel. *Laws affecting Race Relations in South Africa, to the end of 1976*. South African Institute of Race Relations, 1978.

Jardine, Rugaya (Gay). Personal interview. 02 October 2010.

Khan, Achmat. Personal interview. 25 March 2004.

Khan, Farieda. "The Origins of the Non-European Unity Movement."
    BA History Honors research essay, University of Cape Town, 1976.
_____. "Towards Environmentalism: A socio-political evaluation of
    trends in South African Conservation History, 1910-1976, with a
    specific focus on the role of Black conservation organizations." PhD
    thesis, Department of Environmental and Geographical Science,
    University of Cape Town, 2001.
_____. "The Politics of Mountaineering in the Western Cape, South
    Africa – Race, Class and the Mountain Club of South Africa: The
    First Forty Years, 1891 – 1931." Paper presented at the 11th Sports
    Africa Conference, Sporting Subalternities and Social Justice,
    University of Free State, Bloemfontein, 10 - 13 April 2017.
Knipe-Solomon, Colleen. Personal interview. 22 June 2009.
Letsoalo, Essy, M. *Land Reform in South Africa: A Black Perspective.*
    Johannesburg: Skotaville, 1987.
Lewis, Gavin. *Between the Wire and the Wall: A History of South African
    'Colored' Politics.* Cape Town: David Philip, 1987.
Liberty, Irma. "Khan's 'playing field' article superb." *Weekend Argus* 27
    September 2014.
Magubane, Bernard. "Sport and Politics in an Urban African
    Community: A Case Study of African Voluntary Organizations."
    Master's Sociology thesis, University of Natal, 1963.
Majiet, Rushdie. Personal interview. 27 July 2013.
Maylam, Paul. *South Africa's Racial Past: The History and Historiography
    of Racism, Segregation and Apartheid.* Aldershot: Ashgate Publishing
    Limited, 2001.
The Mountain Club of South Africa. "The Mountain Club, its origins
    and doings during the first two years." *The Mountain Club Annual,*
    vol.1, 1894, p. 7-9.
Mountain Club of South Africa. *Minutes of Meetings.* B1.7, vol.VII,
    13/12/1926-11/06/1941. Special Collections, University of Cape
    Town. BC 1421 MCSA.
Mountain Club of South Africa. *Newspaper Clippings.* J4.7.2 Book 2,
    03/12/1928 – 23/07/1932. Special Collections, University of Cape
    Town. BC 1421 MCSA.
Mountain Club of South Africa. *Minutes of Meetings.* B1.9, vol IX,
    09/12/1949-09/03/1955. Special Collections, University of Cape
    Town. BC 1421 MCSA.
National Veld Trust. "Membership Form." *VeldTrust News* vol. 1 (1944),
    4.
Nauright, John. *Sport, Culture and Identities in South Africa.* Cape Town:
    David Philip, 1997.
Odendaal, Andre. "South Africa's Black Victorians: Sport and Society.
    In South Africa in the Nineteenth Century." *Pleasure, Profit and
    Proselytism: British Culture and Sport at Home and Abroad, 1800-1914.*
    Ed. J.A. Mangan. London: Frank Cass, 1988. 193-214.
_____. "'The thing that is not round' – The untold story of black
    rugby in South Africa." *Beyond the Tryline: Rugby and South African*

Society. Eds. Albert Grundlingh, Andre Odendaal and Burridge
Spies. Johannesburg: Ravan Press, 1995. 24-63.

_____. *The Story of an African Game: Black Cricketers and the unmasking
of one of Cricket's greatest Myths, South Africa, 1850-2003*. Cape Town:
David Philip, 2003.

Odendaal, Andre, et al. *Cricket and Conquest: The History of South African
Cricket Retold*, 1795-1910, vol.1. Cape Town: BestRed, 2016.

Odendaal, Andre, et al. *The Blue Book: A History of Western Province
Cricket, 1890-2011*. Auckland Park: Fanele, 2012.

Odendaal, Lize. "Climbing to Greater Heights, Together." *Tribute*,
November 1993, 100-102.

Parker, Ismail. Interview by Francois Cleophas. 14 February 2008. Sports
Memory Project. District Six Museum Archives, Cape Town.

Patel, Moosa. "History of the Paarl Muslim Community."
http://www.patelspoetry.com/hist-res-paarl-muslim-community.html

Pick, William. *One for the Chuck: Glimpses into the History of the Maitland-
Parow and Districts Cricket Union, 1912-1976*. Western Province
Cricket Association and Cricket South Africa, 2015.

Posel, Deborah. *The Making of Apartheid, 1948-1961*. Oxford: Clarendon
Press, 1991.

Rive, Richard. *Writing Black*. Cape Town: David Philip, 1981.

Roberts, Ronald (Rocky). Personal interview. 6 June 2013.

Shell, Robert. *Children of Bondage: A Social History of the Slave Society at
the Cape of Good Hope, 1652-1838*. Hanover, N.H.: Wesleyan Press,
1994.

Simpson, Derrick. "Light on 'no Muslims' rule." *Weekend Sunday Argus*
28 November 2014.

Tatz, C.M. *Shadow and Substance in South Africa: A Study in Land and
Franchise Policies Affecting Africans, 1910-1960*. Pietermaritzburg:
University of Natal Press, 1962.

Taliep, Wiesahl. "A Study in the History of Claremont and the Impact
of the Group Areas Act, c1950 – 1970." History Honors research
essay, University of Cape Town, 1992.

Taliep, Wiesahl. "Belletjiesbos, Draper Street and the Vlak: Colored
Neighborhoods of Claremont before the Group Areas Act." *African
Studies* 60: 1 (2001), 65-85.

Thompson, Leonard. *A History of South Africa: From the Earliest Known
Human Habitation to the Present*. Johannesburg: Jonathan Ball
Publishers, 2014.

Trotter, Henry. "Removals and Remembrance: Commemorating
Community in Colored Cape Town." Masters thesis, Yale
University, 2002.

Wilson, Monica and Archie Mafeje. *Langa: a Study of Social Groups in an
African Township*. Oxford: Oxford University Press, 1963.

Worden, Nigel. *The Making of Modern South Africa: Conquest, Apartheid,
Democracy*. Chichester: Blackwell, 2000.

Caster Semenya:
Running Against Gender and
'Dysconscious' Racial Discrimination

GIBSON NCUBE

Introduction

Neil Thompson defines discrimination as the "unfair or unequal treatment of individuals or groups; prejudiced behaviour acting against the interest of those who characteristically tend to belong to relatively powerless groups within the social structure."[1] In his definition of discrimination, Mark Butler develops that it refers to "differential treatment based on prejudices that are attached to a particular group."[2] These definitions highlight that discrimination centrally operates as a form of prejudicing and systematic exclusion and disadvantaging an individual or group of individuals.

South African athlete Caster Semenya has undoubtedly been treated unfavourably, both on the sporting arena as well as in the media. In an era where doping and performance enhancement are the main concerns facing contemporary athletes, focus on Semenya has been on her gender identity. Her gender has been challenged and various stakeholders have questioned whether she is feminine enough to compete with other women. Until 2009, when she competed at the world championships in Berlin, there had never been a sporting personality whose gender status had created as much media and even medical attention as Caster did. Ever since then, Semenya has undergone numerous medical gender-verification tests to ascertain and gauge her femininity.

Caster Semenya was born in 1991 in the village of Ga-Masehlong in the province of Limpopo, in the North of South Africa. Even though she has external female reproductive organs, Semenya was born without a womb and ovaries. As a result of chromosomal abnormality, she possesses internal testes. This led to her having a condition called hyperandrogenism which means that her body naturally produces high levels of testosterone. After winning the 800 metres event at the 2009 World Track and Field Championships in Berlin, she was barred from further competitions until her gender had been verified. She thereafter underwent numerous, often invasive, tests which sought to ascertain if she was indeed a woman and whether her hyperandrogenism gave her an unfair advantage on the track. The tests hinged primarily on analysing Semenya's testosterone levels and comparing them with those female athletes considered "normal." Such testing was in essence flawed in that it solely used results of testosterone checks as a measure of femininity. Testosterone tests, undoubtedly unreliable, have subsequently been used to grant or deny eligibility to race. Although the International Association of Athletics Federations eventually cleared her to race after eleven months of tests and deliberations, Caster's body and gender continue to be questioned in the media whenever she races.

Beyond the physical and genetic disposition that has been described above, Semenya is identified as intersex. Reis states that "intersex generally refers to a variation in genital anatomy, but not all intersex conditions involve ambiguous genitalia."[3] In Semenya's case, she is intersex because she has external female genitalia although internally she has male reproductive organs in the form of internal testes. The main challenges that have been faced, and continue to be faced, by intersex individuals are societal attempts to identify and fix a single and unitary sex and gender to such individuals. Grabham explains in this regard that: "depending on their socio-economic background, ethnicity and geographical location, some intersexual people choose to, or are able to, resist the normalising force of sex binaries, but some do not, or cannot."[4] Semenya has had to grapple with attempts to fix a specific sex and gender identity to her intersexuality.

In this chapter, I argue that Semenya has experienced two interrelated forms of discrimination. Firstly, she has experienced gender-based discrimination. Her gender identity has been questioned because it fails to fit neatly within the traditional dichotomy of masculine and feminine. Minh-Ha points out in this light that "despite our desperate, eternal attempt to separate, contain, and mend, categories always leak."[5] Semenya's gender refuses containment into fixed categories and rather floats in a liminal space imbued with agency. Davison and Frank concur that "the performativity of gender situates it as a dynamic and on-going social construction. This type of thinking resists the assumption that there is something 'natural,' or true or false, about any gender."[6] In the second instance, because she is neither the first nor the last female athlete in a continuum of female athletes of colour to be deemed unfeminine because of her muscular physique, some form of dysconscious racism (credulous practice of justifying inequality by accepting and perpetuating the status quo) can be said to discriminate against Caster Semenya. The overarching argument that I make in this chapter is that Caster Semenya's athletic career is unwittingly involved in a larger project of questioning socially imposed gender categorisations. She challenges in essence what it means to be a woman and the extent to which, in her case, she has been deemed unfeminine owing to her hormones and physical build. The discrimination that she faces attempts to protect, so to speak, women whose hormones and bodies deftly fit into the socially constructed and imposed gender categories.

Theorising the intersection of bodies, genders and race within sports

By its very nature, sport focuses on bodies and how they can be deployed to compete with other bodies. A discussion of sporting competitiveness would be almost impossible without examining the manner in which bodies are constructed and perceived. Duquin explains that "performance has been made the dependent variable, and the athletic self is characterised as performer/producer. Sport discourse represents the athletic body as a tool or machine whose purpose is successful performance."[7] This successful performance of sporting bodies has principally been embedded upon the separation of genders and sexes. Davison and Frank point out that the strict separation of genders and sexes in sports particularly haunts women in that the "goal for an individual woman to do well in sport is eclipsed by the stigma of having to continually defend or publicly discuss how one is gendered and/or sexually defined."[8] They conclude in this line of reasoning that:

When hegemonic (or the dominant view of) femininity is seemingly transgressed through sport, it is often assumed that heterosexuality is similarly in question. If someone is perceived as being 'unfeminine' they are also assumed to be lesbian. Such transgressions of hegemonic femininity tend to have negative social consequences. Of course, while women engaging in sport may contest an ideal femininity, this does not automatically imply that all women athletes are lesbian.[9]

Davison and Frank's statement infers that there exists a hegemonic femininity. Any other form of femininity which does not conform to the dictates of this hegemony is automatically considered unfeminine. This begs the question as to what constitutes hegemonic femininity as opposed to other non-conforming femininities. Pyke and Johnson explain that hegemonic femininity is founded mainly on whiteness. They affirm that "controlling images reaffirm whiteness as normal and privilege white women by casting them as superior."[10] They further state that, as a result, women of colour are objectified and framed as "overly aggressive, domineering and unfeminine."[11] Such imagery that casts non-white femininities as inferior to the hegemonic notions is part of a complex process and system that Baker calls "psychological dominance."[12] This dominance compels black bodies to internalise their supposed inferiority to the superior whiteness.

In order to fully appreciate what constitutes hegemonic femininity, there is need to understand how genders and sexes have been traditionally constructed and perceived. Judith Butler explains in her critical oeuvre that gender is a social construct. She elucidates that far from being "a stable identity," gender is in fact "an identity tenuously constructed in time – an identity instituted through a stylised repetition of acts."[13] She further develops that "gender is instituted through the stylisation of the body and, hence, must be understood as the mundane way in which bodily gestures, movements, and enactments of various kinds constitute the illusion of an abiding gendered self."[14] What Butler implies here is that, from birth, individuals are socialised in such a way that they repeat and perform bodily acts and comportments that are socially judged to conform to their biological sex. Butler further argues that performing gender is thus "to do, to dramatise, to reproduce" acts that supposedly adhere to social dictates of how biologically sexed bodies should be. In her explanation of what it thus means to be a woman, Butler highlights that:

> To be a woman is to become a woman, to compel the body to conform to an historical idea of 'woman,' to induce the body to become a cultural sign, to materialise oneself in obedience to an historically delimited possibility, and to do this as a sustained and repeated corporeal project.[15]

Butler's use of verbs such as "compel," "conform" and "induce" is fascinating in that it infers that there exists a socially pre-constructed femininity into which all females should strive to achieve. Krane expounds that sport is one such domain in which hegemonic femininity can be challenged. She begins by acknowledging the constraints female athletes face because "within women's sport environments, females continue policing themselves, emphasising the importance of balancing the perceptions of masculine athleticism with feminine appearance."[16] The insurmountable hurdle presents itself for female athletes like Caster Semenya when there is no sense of equilibrium between 'masculine' athleticism and feminine appearance. Krane illustrates that what is considered feminine involves "being emotional, passive, dependent, maternal, compassionate and gentle."[17] However, such characteristics cannot be readily applied to femininity within the sporting domain. This is because sport is essentially active, competitive and aggressive. Krane contends that "women in sport who adhere to hegemonic feminine ideals become privileged over females who are not perceived as fitting these standards."[18] Krane concludes that:

> Challenging hegemonic femininity frees women to develop their own definitions of acceptable body shape and appropriate sporting activities. The ultimate goal of challenging social norms surrounding femininity is to empower women to make their own choices about how to look and act and to define their own version of an ideal female body.[19]

Caster Semenya undoubtedly falls into this category of female athletes who contest hegemonic definitions of femininity. Budgeon posits that such contestation of hegemonic femininity reveals the emergence of diverse femininities, each with its autonomy within the continuum of feminine expressions:

> The multiple forms of femininity evidently being enacted in relation to new femininities are ordered hierarchically by applying a measure of individuation repeatedly constructed as a personal failure to overcome 'pathetic,' dependent traditional femininity and assert personal choice.[20]

This consideration of gender, particularly how it plays out on the sporting arena, has shown that gender is a complex sociocultural phenomenon. This phenomenon is further complicated by what Harrison terms the "alchemy of race."[21] In his analysis of the construction of gender in sport within British media, Vincent points out that the media function in such a way that there is an evident "rewarding [of] female athletes whose physical appearance conforms to a Eurocentric heterosexual femininity."[22] Comparing the media treatment of tennis players Anna Kournikova and the Williams sisters, Serena and Venus, Vincent contends that "Serena and Venus were frequently framed in 'strong Black women' and 'natural athletes' narratives"[23] whilst focus on Kournikova was on her grace, beauty and exquisite femininity. As for Semenya, although South African media has supported her in her fight to be recognised as a woman, there has been body and gender shaming of this athlete in other domains. For example, stand-up comedian Trevor Noah jokingly claimed about Semenya that "he is a woman." Although this might be viewed simply as comedy, it cannot be downplayed that there is more to jokes than just entertainment. Jokes and comedy also serve as a critique and policing of behaviours. In the case of Trevor Noah's joke, it undoubtedly reinforces heteropatriarchal stereotypes and discriminations against gender non-conforming individuals. This denigration of Caster Semenya's body also feeds into racist discriminations that frame black female bodies as unusually strong. Vincent contends that:

> These narratives are underpinned by the notion that African American women have inordinate strength and invincibility that enables them to overcome situations that White women could not withstand. This enduring stereotype is problematic because it perpetuates the dominant cultural view that African American women are not vulnerable to racism and sexism, which serves to marginalise their public support.[24]

What this implies is that black women's femininity is undermined particularly when it exudes great physical strength. Such concentration on the physical strength of the black woman reinforces colonial perceptions about black female bodies as grotesque and beastlike.[25] Leonard attests in his analysis of black female athletes in the United States of America that there is a "hyperfocus on which black women are rendered undesirable and therefore invisible within a sports media context."[26] He further illustrates that "black women have difficulty entering into the sporting world, as few sports of celebration and visibility are those seen as sexually desirable, a process defined through whiteness."[27] The beauty of sportswomen is often embedded on 'white' standards which denigrate and side-line blackness and black bodies. Leonard concludes in this regard that:

> The Williams sisters, as black women, are denied acceptance as female athletes. They are seen as black athletes who because of their blackness, physicality, and strength are imagined apart from their athletic sisters and therefore positioned in relationship to black male athletes.[28]

There is thus an evident racist slant in this form of discrimination of sportswomen of colour principally because they aesthetically do not fit the dictates of what whiteness defines as femininity and beauty.

The above discussion has shown that the sporting arena is a space in which gender can be rethought, contested and challenged. Importantly, the sporting arena allows for a questioning of traditional modes of perceiving genders. More than just being a space in and through which there is a replication of traditional gender roles, sports make it possible to understand that there exists a wide spectrum of gender expressions.

Be that as it may, discrimination continues to present itself against athletes, particularly black female athletes, whose genders are deemed at odds with the so-called normative forms of gender. In the following section, I set out to analyse the discrimination faced by Caster Semenya owing to her femininity being diametrically opposed to hegemonic feminine norms.

Too fast and muscular to be a woman and to race with women

One characteristic of sport, competitive sport especially, is the segregation of sexes. Cooky, Dycus and Dworkin rightly posit that "sport maintains the myth of absolute categorical sex/gender differences between men and women."[29] In their argument, "preventing women and men from competing with one another—a central role for sex testing—ostensibly ensures that sex-segregated sports are free from 'intruders' who are not 'real' (i.e., biological) women."[30] Caster Semenya has been viewed as an intruder because her body deviates in its non-conformity to Western definitions of femininity.

Unsuspectingly playing into the dichotomist vision of gender, the South African magazine *You/Huisgenoot* sought to dispel the notion that Semenya was not feminine enough to be a woman and to race with women. The magazine gave the athlete a makeover and made her the cover of their issue published in September 2009. The cover page, with Caster wearing a dress, her hair flowing back, nails painted and jewellery on her neck and hands had the caption "We turn SA's power girl into a glamour girl – and she loves it." This caption is telling of how this magazine constructs Semenya as needing some sort of aesthetic alteration and transformation so as make her the much desired "glamour girl" and not the "power girl" that she is. Behr and McKaiser explain that the "connections between language and prejudice really are critical"[31] and they further develop that:

It is amazing just how oblivious we all are – both as 'ordinary' folks, and as professionals, observing and writing about the world around us – to our uncritical acceptance of linguistic markers as normative. Instead of simply recognising that words are arbitrary and, to the extent that they are not arbitrary they are sociolinguistic inventions rather than natural phenomena.[32]

The above words are important in understanding why *You/ Huisgenoot* chose to add the adjective "power" to describe Semenya. It can be inferred from the caption that one cannot be a woman and have a powerful physique. Moreover, it is worth asking why the adjective "glamour" should be seen as more befitting in the project to "feminise" Semenya. It is important to read in the choice of words that "power girl" has double connotations. Initially it can imply that Caster has some sort of power that is derived from her fame within the athletic domain. This can also be read as referencing Semenya's strong and quasi masculinised body which is viewed to possess more strength than that of the "normal" woman. Moreover, the fact that the magazine sought to make Semenya a "glamour girl" has to be examined against the way in which Glamour magazine traditionally promotes hegemonic femininities, predominantly white and heteronormative. The choice of words points to a greater project in attempting to control and prescribe to Semenya a particular form of femininity which is reckoned to be more desirable than the one that she embodies.

Behr and McKaiser clarify that "one of the reasons why the media represent sex and gender identities clumsily, thoughtlessly, and with a lack of sensitivity to psychological and biological complexity, is because of the role that language plays in setting us up, from a young age, to naturalise that which was invented all along."[33] It is thus essential to challenge the way in which languages are deployed to buttress traditional conceptions of both sex and gender. Nyong'o also highlights that the *You/Huisgenoot* makeover of Semenya can be interpreted in this manner:

The headline can only mean: refer back from this image, which we presented to you as the true, real Caster, to the prior, excessive and disturbing image, and you will somehow have your perception of her gender stabilised.[34]

Nyong'o's argument centres on the fact that the magazine attempted to feminise Semenya. Although this might have been originally an attempt to defend her, it is hard not to read in this purported defence, a disguised effort to "fix" and assign to Semenya a gender identity that the magazine deemed correct and acceptable. Nyong'o asserts that "we should contest the essentialist conviction that bodies must have a stable sex that presents itself in appropriate dress, voice, attitude and performance."[35] It was as if by offering her a makeover, there was both a "visual enthymeme to reclaim her body"[36] and a camouflaged endeavour to deny the original Semenya, viewed as deviant in the way her gender was fluid instead of stable.

Caster Semenya's entrance into international sports has been a pivotal moment to rethink our understanding of sex and gender. Semenya, in the documentary "Too Fast To Be a Woman: The Story of Caster Semenya" questions what it means to be a woman: "The way you were born, is the way you were born. There is nothing to change that. I've a deep voice, so what." She questions critics who categorise her as unfeminine because she has a deep voice and a muscular body. Semenya clearly challenges in this instance the fixedness of gender. A deep voice is one of the "definitive" characteristics of masculinity, manhood and maleness. However, by barefacedly asking why it matters that she has a deep voice, she is in effect destabilising the features that classify one as male or female. In so doing, she claims the deep voice as a central feature of her femininity. As such, she offers various ranges of being a woman and feminine. The tone of the "so what," at the end of the phrase, is particularly telling of the manner in which she dismisses hegemonic definitions of gender and gender categorisations. By standing firm and resolute in her gender identity, Semenya contests the disciplinary apparatus that seeks to ensure that her gender identity aligns itself to the dictates of hegemonic femininity. Miller contends that "perhaps the preeminent strategy used to discipline female athletes who too directly challenge gender binaries has been to question or disparage their sexual orientation."[37] This is mostly relevant considering that Caster has been called a lesbian. The question though is not whether she is a lesbian or not. The question to ask is why and how sexual orientation should necessarily be an issue in competitive sport. Does this therefore suggest, for example, that a lesbian athlete has or will have an unfair advantage over a heterosexual athlete? The answer to this question undoubtedly reveals a form of gender-based discrimination against Semenya because sexual orientation cannot in any way give an athlete (with a non-normative sexual orientation) an advantage over other athletes whose sexual orientation is normative.

Nyong'o offers a fascinating analysis of the inordinate media focus that has surrounded the person, gender, sexuality and sexual orientation of Semenya. Nyong'o argues that the athlete has been framed as "a sexualised monstrosity," and such framing has been "especially shameful and traumatic" for the athlete. The disproportionate concentration on Semenya's gender identity has been founded on a discriminatory heteropatriarchal discourse whose thrust centres on the perpetuation of the traditional gender dichotomy of masculine and feminine.

Although Semenya's body and gender provide a pivotal locus of unthinking and rethinking perceptions on bodies and genders, it is worth pointing out as a conclusion to this section that she has largely remained a silent and passive object of discussion. In the mediatisation of her gender identity, she has continued to be what Foucault terms "an object of information, never a subject in communication."[38] Young concurs and affirms that Semenya "became both hyperpresent (i.e., her body scrutinised by the media) and absent (i.e., lack of voice, objectified as an 'unnatural' freak of nature)."[39] Her body and gender have been used and spoken about by the media and she herself has said very little. In a way, she has not participated in the mediatised narrative about her gender. Neither has she contested the discrimination that she has had to face, on and off the sports arena. However, as I will explore shortly, being silent is not always necessarily passivity. There is also agency that can be located in the silence that she decides to espouse. In effect, had she decided to actively defend her gender identity, she would have rendered herself an active participant in the whole debacle of questioning of her identity. She remains silent because she has nothing to defend, in her eyes she is a woman and there is nothing more or less to that finality.

Davison and Frank appropriately point out that whilst intersex and transgender "athletes potentially occupy an important position to sport and gender reform, the lived realities of being transgendered and competing in sport involve daily struggle, harassment, humiliation, and sometimes violence."[40] For Semenya, this struggle has been predominantly one of being quiet and letting the media discuss what it perceives as her gender insubordination. In spite of the fact that Caster Semenya is framed as a "docile" body which is "subjected, used, transformed, and improved,"[41] there is nonetheless some agency found in this seeming docility. Semenya embraces her femininity even though it is viewed as aberrant and deviant. This agency is found in the passive resistance proposed by Semenya's bodily deployment and gendered contestation. This agency is further amplified by the manner in which she is involved, albeit passively, in calling for a reform in the way sporting bodies are viewed vis-à-vis gender politics. Sloop contends that Semenya's silence should also be read as a form of fighting back to the dominant discourses that have spoken about her and on her behalf as well: "despite the oft-made claim of the short shrift silence is given, its meaning as a rhetorical gesture has been taken up in multiple ways."[42] In her silence and passivity, Semenya finds an "illocutionary force"[43] which creates an "emancipatory narrative [that] creates new forms of power [and] configures new ways to fight back against past and present injustices."[44] Semenya is able to fight back against the discrimination by not actively contesting the prevailing discourses about her gender identity. Rather, she silently fights by affirming her femininity and not attempting in any way to justify herself.

Dysconscious racism or misogynoir

As previously pointed out, Caster Semenya is in no way the first nor the only female athlete who has a muscular or masculine physique. Most competitive sportswomen are in effect muscular and far from fitting the dictates of hegemonic femininity. Sportswomen such as Martina Navratilova, Steffi Graf and Amélie Mauresmo undoubtedly had strong muscular builds. However, they did not receive the same questioning of the genders or the unreasonable body shaming that black sportswomen such as the Williams sisters and Caster Semenya have had to contend with. The question to ask then is if race has a role to play in the discrimination that these sportswomen of colour have had to perpetually deal with.

I attest that there is effectively at least some level of dysconscious racism and at worst misogynoir (misogyny directed towards black women), in the treatment of Caster Semenya. Bailey explains why there is an inordinate focus on Semenya: "the specter of the Black woman's body at the intersections of socially constructed and medically reinforced hierarchies of biological difference remains a trope in contemporary media and dates back to our earliest uses of mass communications."[45] Bailey further speaks against the "racist gender standards that created the controversy by highlighting the ways her Blackness played a role in her coming to the world's attention."[46] These assertions by Bailey highlight the fact that Semenya became a mediatised phenomenon mainly because of the colour of her skin. The question to ask is if the situation would have been different had Semenya been white, for example. The treatment of Semenya can however not be neatly separated from the racist trope stretching back to slavery which framed black women as inherently as strong as their male counterparts.

The femininity of black female athletes is often cast and framed against that of their white counterparts. Serena Williams's femininity was often compared to that of Anna Kournikova with the latter being the benchmark standard of femininity. At the 2016 Rio Olympics, the 800 metre race was won by three African women, with Caster Semenya winning the gold medal. Lynsey Sharp from the Great Britain, who came sixth in that race complained after the race that "everyone can see it's two separate races." Her insinuation was that Caster Semenya, Francine Niyonsaba and Margaret Wambui who had won the race did not necessarily fit into the women's category. Her statement that the race was split into two suggests that there were two distinct categories, one of authentic women and another of women whose femininity and womanhood was questionable. Did the three medal winners not fit into the category of authentic women athletes merely because of their physique or rather because of their race as well? Comments such as those made by Sharp reflect some dysconscious racism that discriminates against female athletes of colour. Sharp's assertions can be read as implying that the race was split in two: dainty white women on one hand and masculinised women on the other. Douglas highlights that statements such as those by Sharp should be understood as part of "new racism(s)" in which "racial antipathy is increasingly conveyed through expressions of subtle and understated racial discourses."[47] Douglas further states that this "new racism" needs to be appreciated against the wider sociohistorical background in which black athletic bodies are entering a predominantly white sorting culture and an equally white controlled mainstream media. Douglas affirms in this line of thought that this subtle and understated racial discrimination has operated mainly through the policing of sporting spaces as well as bodies and genders of sport practitioners. This policing of spaces ensures that black bodies and genders do not disrupt the spaces that were previously white dominated:

> Thus surveillance operates as part of the racial discourse of Whiteness insofar as it organizes and disseminates differential forms of social knowledge about Blacks and Blackness integral to sustaining racial inequality. Thus various discourses of

Whiteness are conveyed through the continuing observation, categorization, and imposition of norms that seek to *fix* in the public imaginary the myriad ways in which the sisters are deemed inferior according to the standards of White normativity.[48]

The racial discrimination of Semenya and other black female athletes is embedded upon "racist and sexist stereotypes"[49] whose objective are to perpetuate and reproduce gendered and racial hierarchies. McKay and Johnson argue that the denigration of black women's bodies underscores the fact that they "were constructed as 'sexually grotesque' and compels a discussion about the ongoing role of racism in creating an aesthetic that depicts black bodies as diseased, animalistic, deviant and hypersexual."[50] The bodies of black female athletes, particularly intersex athletes, are synecdochically fashioned as deviant and disruptive of normative discourses of gender and sporting bodies. McKay and Johnson rightly conclude that "since sport both reinforces and reproduces the persistent, resurgent and veiled forms of white power that permeate society," there is need for a "systematic targeting and outing of racist and sexist narratives in sport."[51] Such an approach will make it possible for black "women and men to envision and achieve equality within a broader framework of social justice."[52]

Conclusion

This analysis of the gendered and racial discrimination that has been faced by Caster Semenya has shown that Semenya is one of many intersex women whose bodies and gender identities are located at the precarious fault line of what societies deem to be correct and what science describes as existing. Semenya's entrance into the world of sport has provided an important moment to rethink the intersection of race and gender particularly against the background of the discrimination of black intersex athletes.

Indeed the sociocultural space of sport is predominantly well positioned to allow for a systematic examination of the possible ways in which race, sexuality and gender interconnect and overlap. This chapter has examined the manner in which Semenya, as a symbol of discriminated sporting bodies, has challenged and contested the categorisation and definition of genders, bodies and sexualities. Gender and sexuality has often been considered and constructed against the dichotomy of masculine and feminine. Semenya has however shown that the time has come to see beyond this dichotomy and envision the multifarious possibilities of gendered expression and experiences.

Endnotes

[1] Thompson, Neil. *Anti-Discriminatory Practice*. Basingstoke, Palgrave Macmillan, 2001, p. 33.

[2] Butler, Mark. *Equality and Anti-Discrimination Law*. London, Spiramus Press, 2016, p. 25.

[3] Reis, Elizabeth. *Bodies in Doubt: An American History of Intersex*. Baltimore, The Johns Hopkins University Press, 2009, p. x.

[4] Grabham, Emily. "Citizen Bodies, Intersex Citizenship." *Sexualities*, vol. 10, no. 1, 2007, p. 41.

[5] Minh-Ha, Trinh. *Women, Native, Other: Writing Postcoloniality and Feminism*. Bloomington, Indiana University Press, 1989, p. 94.

[6] Davison, Kevin G, and Blye W. Frank. "Sexualities, Gender and Bodies in Sport: Changing Practices of Inequity." *Sport and Gender in Canada*, edited by Philip Young and Kevin Young, Toronto, Oxford University Press, 2007, p. 179.

[7] Duquin, Mary E. "The Body Snatchers and Dr. Frankenstein Revisited: Social Construction and Deconstruction of Bodies and Sport." *Theory and Practice*, vol. 18, 1994, p. *269*.

[8] Davison and Frank, p. 180.

[9] Davison and Frank, p. 181.

[10] Pyke, Karen D., and Denise L. Johnson. "Asian-American Women and Racialised Femininities: 'Doing' Gender Across Cultural Worlds." *The Kaleidoscope of Gender: Prisms, Patterns and Possibilities*, edited by Joan Z. Spade and Catherine G. Valentine, California, Sage Publications, 2008, p. 81.

[11] Pyke and Johnson, p. 78.

[12] Baker, Donald G. Race. *Ethnicity and Power*. Boston, Routledge Kegan Paul, 1983, p. 37.

[13] Butler, Judith. "Performative Acts and Gender Constitution: an Essay in Phenomenology and Feminist Theory." *Theatre Journal*, vol. 40, no. 4, 1988, p. 519.

[14] Butler, p. 519.

[15] Butler, p. 522.

[16] Krane, Vikki. "We Can Be Athletic and Feminine, But Do We Want To? Challenging Hegemonic Femininity in Women's Sport." *Quest*, vol. 53, no. 1, 2001, p. 116.

[17] Krane, p. 117.

[18] Krane, p. 118.

[19] Krane, p. 123.

[20] Budgeon, Shelley. "The Dynamics of Gender Hegemony: Femininities, Masculinities and Social Change." *Sociology*, vol. 48, no. 2, 2014, p. 326.

[21] Harrison, Anthony Kwame. "Black Skiing, Everyday Racism, and the Racial Spatiality of Whiteness." *Journal of Sport and Social Issues*, vol. 37, no. 4, 2013, p. 318.

[22] Vincent, John. "Game, Sex and Match: The Construction of Gender in British Newspaper Coverage of the 2000 Wimbledon Championships." *Sociology of Sport Journal*, vol. 24, 2004, p. 437.

[23] Vincent, p. 445.

[24] Vincent, p. 445.

[25] Ahuja, Neel. "Postcolonial Critique in a Multispecies World." *PMLA*, vol. 124, no. 2, 2009, p. 557.

[26] Leonard, David J. "Dilemmas and Contradictions: Black Female Athletes." *Out of Bounds: Racism and the Black Athlete*, edited by Lori Latrice Martin, Denver, Praeger, 2014, p. 210.

[27] Leonard, p. 210.

[28] Leonard, p. 218.

[29] Cooky, Cheryl. et al. "What Makes a Woman a Woman? Versus 'Our First Lady of Sport': A Comparative Analysis of the United States and the South African Media Coverage of Caster Semenya." *Journal of Sport and Social Issues*, vol. 37, no. 1, 2012, p. 34.
[30] Cooky, Cheryl. et al., p. 35.
[31] Behr, Mark, and Eusebius McKaiser. "A Girl Is Not a Boy Is Not a Girl Is Not a Boy: A Dialogue on Media's Feminisation of the Athlete Caster Semenya." *Communicatio: South African Journal for Communication Theory and Research*, vol. 39, no. 2, 2013, p. 172.
[32] Behr and McKaiser, p. 172.
[33] Behr and McKaiser, p. 175.
[34] Nyong'o, Tavis. "The Unforgivable Transgression of Being Caster Semenya." *Women & Performance: A Journal of Feminist Theory*, vol. 20, no. 1, 2010, p. 96.
[35] Nyong'o, p. 98.
[36] Young, Stephanie L. "Running Like a Man, Sitting Like a Girl: Visual Enthymeme and the Case of Caster Semenya." *Women's Studies in Communication*, vol. 38, 2015, p. 333.
[37] Miller, Shane Aaron. "'Just Look at her!': Sporting Bodies as Athletic Resistance and the Limits of Sport Norms in the Case of Caster Semenya." *Men and Masculinities*, vol. 18, no. 3, 2015, p. 297.
[38] Foucault, Michel. *Discipline and Punishment: The Birth of the Prison*. New York, Vintage Books, 1977, p. 200.
[39] Young, p. 336.
[40] Davison and Frank, p. 187.
[41] Foucault, p. 200.
[42] Sloop, John M. "'This is Not Natural': Caster Semenya's Gender Threats." *Critical Studies in Media Communication*, vol. 29, no. 2, 2012, p. 90.
[43] Lara, Maria Pia. *Moral Textures: Feminist Narratives in the Public Sphere*. Oxford, Blackwell Publishers, 1998, p. 5.
[44] Lara, p. 5.
[45] Bailey, Moya. "Misogynoir in Medical Media: On Caster Semenya and R. Kelly." *Catalyst: Feminism, Theory, Technoscience*, vol. 2, no. 2, 2016, p. 4.
[46] Bailey, p. 11.
[47] Douglas, Delia D. "Venus, Serena, and the Inconspicuous Consumption of Blackness: A Commentary on Surveillance, Race Talk, and New Racism(s)." *Journal of Black Studies*, vol. 43, no. 2, 2012, p. 130.
[48] Douglas, p. 135.
[49] McKay, James, and Helen Johnson (2008) "Pornographic Eroticism and Sexual Grotesquerie in Representations of African American Sportswomen." *Social Identities*, vol. 14, no. 4, 2008, p. 491.
[50] McKay and Johnson, p. 493.
[51] McKay and Johnson, p. 500.
[52] McKay and Johnson, p. 500.

Bibliography

Ahuja, Neel. "Postcolonial Critique in a Multispecies World." *PMLA* 124: 2 (2009), 556-563.
Bailey, Moya. "Misogynoir in Medical Media: On Caster Semenya and R. Kelly." *Catalyst: Feminism, Theory, Technoscience* 2: 2 (2016), 1-31.

Baker, Donald G. *Race, Ethnicity and Power.* Boston: Routledge Kegan Paul, 1983.

Behr, Mark, and Eusebius McKaiser. "A Girl Is Not a Boy Is Not a Girl Is Not a Boy: A Dialogue on Media's Feminisation of the Athlete Caster Semenya." *Communicatio: South African Journal for Communication Theory and Research* 39: 2 (2013), 169-181.

Budgeon, Shelley. "The Dynamics of Gender Hegemony: Femininities, Masculinities and Social Change." *Sociology* 48: 2 (2014), 317-334.

Butler, Judith. "Performative Acts and Gender Constitution: an Essay in Phenomenology and Feminist Theory." *Theatre Journal* 40: 4 (1988), 519-531.

Butler, Mark. *Equality and Anti-Discrimination Law.* London: Spiramus Press, 2016.

Cooky, Cheryl., et al. "What Makes a Woman a Woman? Versus 'Our First Lady of Sport': A Comparatve Analysis of the United States and the South African Media Coverage of Caster Semenya." *Journal of Sport and Social Issues* 37: 1 (2012), 31-56.

Davison, Kevin G, and Blye W. Frank. "Sexualities, Gender and Bodies in Sport: Changing Practices of Inequity." *Sport and Gender in Canada.* Eds. Philip Young and Kevin Young. Toronto: Oxford University Press, 2007. 178-193.

Douglas, Delia D. "Venus, Serena, and the Inconspicuous Consumption of Blackness: A Commentary on Surveillance, Race Talk, and New Racism(s)." *Journal of Black Studies* 43: 2 (2012), 127–145.

Duquin, Mary E. "The Body Snatchers and Dr. Frankenstein Revisted: Social Construction and Deconstruction of Bodies and Sport." *Theory and Practice* 18 (1994), 268-281.

Foucault, Michel. *Discipline and Punishment: The Birth of the Prison.* New York: Vintage Books, 1977.

Grabham, Emily. "Citizen Bodies, Intersex Citizenship." *Sexualities* 10: 1 (2007), 29-48.

Harrison, Anthony Kwame. "Black Skiing, Everyday Racism, and the Racial Spatiality of Whiteness." *Journal of Sport and Social Issues* 37: 4 (2013), 315-339.

Krane, Vikki. "We Can Be Athletic and Feminine, But Do We Want To? Challenging Hegemonic Femininity in Women's Sport." *Quest* 53: 1 (2001), 115-133.

Lara, Maria Pia. *Moral Textures: Feminist Narratives in the Public Sphere.* Oxford: Blackwell Publishers, 1998.

Leonard, David J. "Dilemmas and Contradictions: Black Female Athletes." *Out of Bounds: Racism and the Black Athlete.* Ed. Lori Latrice Martin. Denver: Praeger, 2014. 209-230.

McKay, James, and Helen Johnson. "Pornographic Eroticism and Sexual Grotesquerie in Representations of African American Sportswomen." *Social Identities* 14: 4 (2008), 491-504.

Miller, Shane Aaron. "'Just Look at her!': Sporting Bodies as Athletic Resistance and the Limits of Sport Norms in the Case of Caster Semenya." *Men and Masculinities* 18: 3 (2015), 293-317.

Minh-Ha, Trinh. *Women, Native, Other: Writing Postcoloniality and Feminism*. Bloomington: Indiana University Press, 1989.

Nyong'o, Tavis. "The Unforgivable Transgression of Being Caster Semenya." *Women & Performance: A Journal of Feminist Theory* 20: 1 (2010), 95-100.

Pyke, Karen D., and Denise L. Johnson. "Asian-American Women and Racialised Femininities: 'Doing' Gender Across Cultural Worlds." *The Kaleidoscope of Gender: Prisms, Patterns and Possibilities*. Eds. Joan Z. Spade and Catherine G. Valentine. Los Angeles: Sage Publications, 2008. 76-88.

Reis, Elizabeth. *Bodies in Doubt: An American History of Intersex*. Baltimore: The Johns Hopkins University Press, 2009.

Sloop, John M. "'This is Not Natural': Caster Semenya's Gender Threats." *Critical Studies in Media Communication* 29: 2 (2012), 81-96.

Thompson, Neil. *Anti-Discriminatory Practice*. Basingstoke: Palgrave Macmillan, 2001.

Vincent, John. "Game, Sex and Match: The Construction of Gender in British Newspaper Coverage of the 2000 Wimbledon Championships." *Sociology of Sport Journal* 24 (2004), 435-456.

Young, Stephanie L. "Running Like a Man, Sitting Like a Girl: Visual Enthymeme and the Case of Caster Semenya." *Women's Studies in Communication* 38 (2015), 331-350.

Notes on Contributors

Eileen M. Angelini

Recipient of a 2010-2011 Canada-U.S. Fulbright award as a Fulbright Visiting Research Chair in Globalization and Cultural Studies at McMaster University (Hamilton, ON) and named Chevalier dans l'Ordre des Palmes Académiques in August 2011, Eileen M. Angelini received her B.A. in French from Middlebury College (Middlebury, VT) and her M.A. and Ph.D. in French Studies from Brown University (Providence, RI). Dr. Angelini, named to the 2013-2017 Fulbright Specialist Roster, was the Grantee for a Fulbright Specialist Project, "Francophone Culture: Literature, Pedagogy and Additional Language Acquisition" at the University of Manitoba (Winnipeg, Manitoba). Expanding upon her 2010-2011 Canada-U.S. Fulbright award, her Fulbright Specialist award allowed her to focus on the francophone populations of North America in the context of human rights research, indigenous culture, and social justice. Three of her main projects are on the little-known history of the KKK attacks against Franco-Americans in New England in the first half of the 20th century, the Acadian Deportation, and the Montreal Riots of 1955. Simultaneously with her Fulbright Specialist Project, she was a Researcher and Teacher for the Bureau of Jewish Education in Getzville, NY where she drew upon her background in researching Jewish-Christian relations and documentary filmmaking (www.francedivided. com; https://vimeo.com/ 223916415). In this position, she taught the Holocaust from an interdisciplinary approach to help students understand that the Holocaust is not simply a Jewish question, but rather one that involves us all, regardless of religion, ethnicity, gender, or nationality. Dr. Angelini was appointed as the David Julian and Virginia Suther Whichard Distinguished Visiting Professor in the Humanities in the Thomas Harriot College of Arts and Sciences at East Carolina University for the 2018-2019 academic year.

Jayson Baker

Jayson Baker thinks, writes, and teaches across culture studies with special attention to different eras of internationalization, and themes of community, citizenship, and identity. He challenges students to closely read narrative form and develop a concern for representations of race, ethnicity, class, gender, and sexuality recognizing complicity with and resistance to social hierarchies worldwide. Dr. Baker believes this is a central goal of the best liberal arts education. His work appears in *Studies in the Humanities* (Indiana University of PA Press), *Adaptation* (Oxford UP), and *Widescreen* (University of Leeds- Subaltern Media) among others. Dr. Baker has been a faculty participant at The Futures of American Studies Institute at Dartmouth College, presenter at the British Film Institute, and frequent conference presenter.

Travis D. Boyce

Travis D. Boyce is an Associate Professor of Africana Studies at the University of Northern Colorado. His research interests are in contemporary African American history and popular culture --- the intersection of race, fashion, and social media in the sporting world. His work can be found in various peer-reviewed journals and edited book volumes. He is the co-editor of *Historicizing Fear* (in press with the University Press of Colorado) and a guest co-editor for the *Fashion, Style & Popular Culture* journal that will focus on "Fashion, Style, Aesthetics, & 'BlackLivesMatter.'"

Stephanie M. Burchett

Stephanie Burchett is a professional photographer and third-year Master of Fine Arts candidate at the University of Arizona. Her current photographic and lens based work interrogates the continued legacy of inequality and polarization in America with specific interest in how the archive, traditional photographs and new technologies serve as a barometer of this crisis. She participated in her inaugural museum show at the Museum of Contemporary Art in Tucson, Arizona in 2017. Additionally, her work has been shown in, Colorado, New York, China and Mexico.

Michael J. Durfee

Michael J. Durfee earned his Ph.D. in history from the State University of New York at Buffalo with a focus on the postwar urban crisis, race, and the history of alcohol and drugs. Dr. Durfee's dissertation entitled, *Crack Era Reform: A Brief History of Crack and the Rise of the Carceral State* is the first history of both local and national responses to crack cocaine. His research interests include drug policy, mass incarceration, and police/resident relations. Dr. Durfee is currently an Assistant Professor of History and Director of Africana/Black Studies at Niagara University while also serving as a contributing editor to *Points: The Blog of the Alcohol and Drugs History Society*.

Raúl Fernández-Calienes

The Reverend Professor Raúl Fernández-Calienes, Ph.D., teaches at St. Thomas University. He earned his doctorate at the University of Sydney, and he has three master's degrees including one from Princeton Theological Seminary. He is a Senior Fellow at the St. Thomas University Human Rights Institute. A sought-after researcher and editor, he is co-editor of several monographs, including *Women Moving Forward* (three volumes) and *Reaching for Life* (two volumes). For several years, he has served as Managing Editor of the *Journal of Multidisciplinary Research*, a peer-reviewed academic publication. In addition, he is a Team USA dragon boat racer, a dragon boat racing coach, and a U.S. National and International Race Official.

Gibson Ncube

Gibson Ncube holds a Ph.D. in French and Francophone literatures from Stellenbosch University, where he is currently a Postdoctoral Fellow in the Department of Modern Foreign Languages. His research interests are in comparative literature, queer, gender and cultural studies. His latest work has been published in such journals as the *Journal of Literary Studies*, *South African Review of Sociology*, *Journal of Commonwealth Literature*, and *Social Dynamics: A Journal of African Studies* as well as has book chapters published in *Virgin Envy: The Cultural (In)significance of the Hymen* and *Beyond the Arab Spring in North Africa*. Ncube is presently working on a monograph on the literary representations and constructions of queer identities in North African cultural imaginations.

Farieda Kahn

Farieda Khan is an Independent Researcher based in Cape Town, South Africa. Her 2001 Ph.D. thesis examined twentieth-century South African conservation history, with a particular focus on the role of Black conservation organizations. Her research areas are: South African Environmental History, Cape Town Social History and South African Sports History. She is currently working on the history of mountaineering in Cape Town, both as a leisure pursuit and as a sport. In particular, she is conducting research into the socio-political history of mountaineering clubs in Cape Town, focusing specifically on the hidden history of Black mountaineering clubs. She has also published "Anyone for Tennis? Conversations with Black Women involved in Tennis during the Apartheid Era" in *Agenda*, 85 (2010) and "From Conservation to Environmental Justice – Trends in the Development of Environmental Civil Society Organizations in South Africa" forthcoming in *The Great Convergence – An Environmental History of the BRICS Countries* edited by S Ravi Rajan and Lise Sedrez, Oxford University Press India, Delhi.

Richard Pioreck

Richard Pioreck's plays include *Say It Ain't So; Joe, Nicolette and Aucassin* (book and lyrics); *This Is It!; How I Came to Be; Grocery Encounters; Ups* (co-written with Reed Farrel Coleman); *Seat of Power; GosAPP; An Unexpected Turn of Events; In Some Ways You're Better Off; and #1 With a Bullet;. Winesburg* (book and lyrics) – based on Sherwood Anderson›s *Winesburg, Ohio*, has been developed in workshops. He has also written the screenplay for *Green*, based on *The Merry Wives of Windsor*. Moreover, he has written for *Memories & Dreams* (Baseball Hall of Fame) and *MLB Insider*. He teaches creative writing and literature at Hofstra University, where he has created and taught the course, "The Simpsons Save America Literature" for the last ten years.

Tatiana Prorokova

Tatiana Prorokova is a postdoctoral researcher in the Department of English and American Studies at the University of Vienna, Austria.

Her current project examines representations of the environment and climate change in fiction since the Industrial Revolution. She holds a Ph.D. in American Studies from the University of Marburg, Germany, a European Joint Master's Degree in English and American Studies from the University of Bamberg, Germany, and a Teaching Degree in English and German from Ryazan State University, Russia. She was an Ebeling Fellow at the American Antiquarian Society (2018) and a Visiting Scholar at the University of South Alabama (2016). Her research interests include war studies, ecocriticism, gender studies, and race studies, and are reflected in her publications in academic journals and edited collections. She is a co-editor of *Cultures of War in Graphic Novels: Violence, Trauma, and Memory* (Rutgers University Press, 2018).

Lightning Source UK Ltd.
Milton Keynes UK
UKHW012039150123
415285UK00006B/51